The *W*eight of the Weather

ALSO BY MARK SANDERS

First Hunt
Gone Fishing
The Suicide
Before We Lost Our Ways
A Dissimulation of Birds: Stories
Here in the Big Empty
Conditions of Grace: New and Selected Poems
Landscapes, with Horses
Riddled with Light: Metaphor in the Poetry of W. B. Yeats

EDITED WORKS

The Sandhills & Other Geographies: An Anthology of Nebraska Poetry
The Sandhills II: Poets of the Great Plains
Jumping Pond: Poems and Stories from the Ozarks (with Michael Burns)
On Common Ground: The Poetry of William Kloefkorn, Ted Kooser,
Greg Kuzma, and Don Welch (with J. V. Brummels)
The Plains Poetry Series, vols. 1-8
The Main-Travelled Roads Chapbook Series, vols. 1-22
The PlainSense of Things, vols. 1-3
Three Generations of Nebraska Poets (with Stephen Meats)
A Sandhills Reader: Thirty Years of Great Writing from the Great Plains
The Red Book: The Selected Poems of Kathleene West
Verdigris Creek Bridge: A Literary Reunion

The *W*eight of the Weather:

Regarding the poetry
of Ted Kooser

EDITED

BY

MARK SANDERS

STEPHEN F. AUSTIN STATE UNIVERSITY PRESS

NACOGDOCHES ✳ 2017

A NOTE ON THE TEXT

Most of the pieces included in *The Weight of the Weather* appear as they were first published; where any substantive revision has occurred, as made by the authors, the latest version is used here. Editorial interference has been kept purposefully to a minimum: typographical errors, misquotations, and misspellings have been corrected, book titles have been uniformly italicized, poem titles placed inside quotation marks, and standards of American style of punctuation have been utilized. Similarly, particularly in the interviews, a standardized format has been adopted to enhance readability. Oddities in documentation, as made by the authors, are intact as first published because research styles have changed considerably since the earliest writings included in the book. Representative reviews are excerpts from omnibus reviews, and this may result in abrupt transitions or ambiguous comparative remarks. Inasmuch as it was possible, the interviews, memoirs, and commentaries retain their original content and spirit. Citations of Ted Kooser's poetry appear as they were published in the original articles and as they were acknowledged at the time of such publication.

For more information:
Stephen F. Austin State University Press
P.O. Box 13007 SFA Station
Nacogdoches, Texas 75962
sfapress@sfasu.edu
www.sfasu.edu/sfapress
936-468-1078

Book Design: Kimberly Verhines

This book is for Kimberly, who shares the same creative vision

And

for three of my earliest encouragers:
Don Welch (1932-2016), William Kloefkorn (1932-2011),
and Ted Kooser

"there in the twilight,
the road past our house
a long door asking us in."
—Don Welch, "Indian Summer"

"At certain moments
an element swells the lungs with something akin to faith."
—William Kloefkorn, "Not Such a Bad Place to Be"

"There is nothing to harm us here."
—Ted Kooser, "An Empty Place"

ACKNOWLEDGMENTS:

Grateful acknowledgment is made for permission to reprint the following:

David Baker. "Ted's Box" was published in *The Midwest Quarterly*, 46.4 (2005). Reprinted by permission of the author. "On Restraint" originally appeared in *Poetry* 168.1 (1996) and was collected in Baker's *Heresy and the Ideal: On Contemporary Poetry* (U of Arkansas Press, 2000). Reprinted by permission of the author.

David Baker and Tim Hofmeister. "Something Just Happens: A Conversation with Ted Kooser" was published in *Talk Poetry: Poems and Interviews with Nine American Poets* (U of Arkansas Press, 2012), edited by David Baker. Reprinted by permission of the editor.

William Barillas. "The First Order of Wonder: An Interview with Ted Kooser" appeared in *The Bloomsbury Review* (Jan./Febr. 2008). Reprinted by permission of the interviewer. "From 'Further Views'" is excerpted from Chapter 7 of William Barillas' *The Midwestern Pastoral: Place and Landscape in Literature of the American Heartland* (Ohio UP, 2006). Reprinted by permission of the author.

JV Brummels. "To Ted, from Two Cow" was published in *The Midwest Quarterly*, 46.4 (2005). Reprinted by permission of the author.

Victor Contoski. "Words and Raincoats: Verbal and Nonverbal Communication" appeared in *On Common Ground: The Poetry of William Kloefkorn, Ted Kooser, Greg Kuzma, and Don Welch* (Sandhills Press, 1983), edited by Mark Sanders and J. V. Brummels. Reprinted by permission of the publisher.

Chapman Hood Frazier. "A Conversation with Ted Kooser" first appeared in *Shenandoah* (2012). Reprinted by permission of the interviewer.

Dana Gioia. "Poetry Chronicle" appeared in *The Hudson Review* 33.4 (1980-81). Reprinted by permission of the author. "The Anonymity of the Regional Poet" originally appeared under the title, "Explaining Ted Kooser" in *On Common Ground: The Poetry of William Kloefkorn, Ted Kooser, Greg Kuzma, and Don Welch* (Sandhills Press, 1983), edited by Mark Sanders and J. V. Brummels; it was subsequently reprinted in Gioia's *Can Poetry Matter: Essays on Poetry and American Culture* (Graywolf, 1992). Reprinted by permission of the author.

George von Glahn. "Ted Kooser: Searching for Signs" appeared in *Late Harvest: Plains and Prairie Poets* (BkMk Press, 1977), edited by Robert Killoren. Reprinted by permission of Maureen Powers, the author's daughter, on behalf of the author's estate.

Twyla Hansen. "Tuesdays with Ted" was published in *The Midwest Quarterly*, 46.4 (2005). Reprinted by permission of the author.

Arnold Hatcher. "An Interview with Ted Kooser" was originally published in *Voyages to the Inland Sea VI: Essays and Poems by Harley Elliott and Ted Kooser* (Center for Contemporary Poetry, 1976). Reprinted by permission of the Series Editor, John Judson.

Jonathan Holden. "Ted Kooser: The Chekhov of American Poetry" appeared in *The Old Formalism: Character in Contemporary American Poetry* (U of Arkansas Press, 1999). Reprinted by permission of the author.

Michael A. Istvan, Jr. "A Small Aid for Kooser Research" appeared in *Midwestern Miscellany* 40 (2012). Reprinted by permission of the author.

William Kloefkorn. "Inhalations" was published in *The Midwest Quarterly*, 46.4 (2005). Reprinted by permission of the author.

Greg Kuzma. "A Review of *Official Entry Blank*" appeared as part of an omnibus review in *Pebble* 5 (1971). Reprinted by permission of the author.

Shawn Leary. "Ted Kooser" appeared in *Omaha* (March 1979). Reprinted by permission of the author.

Glenna Luschei. "A Sunday Afternoon with Ted Kooser and the Gaffneys." Published here, for the first time, by permission of the author.

David Mason. "Introducing Ted Kooser" appeared in *The Dark Horse* (Summer 2005). Reprinted by permission of the author.

Paul McCallum. "Teasing Out the Lies, Stitching in the Life: Ted Kooser's Writing Seminar, University of Nebraska-Lincoln, Spring 1988" was published in *The Midwest Quarterly*, 46.4 (2005). Reprinted by permission of the author.

Stephen Meats. "An Interview with Ted Kooser" was published in *The Midwest Quarterly*, 46.4 (2005). Reprinted by permission of the interviewer.

Lex Runciman. "Excerpt from an Omnibus Review . . ." was originally published under the full title of "On Ted Kooser, Kim Robert, and William Stafford" in *Cutbank* 1.7 (1976). Reprinted by permission of the author.

Mark Sanders. "The Sense of Measured Compatibility in Contemporary Nebraska Poetry" first appeared in *Northeast* (1980); it was subsequently revised and shortened for publication in *Concerning Poetry* 13.2 (1980). The version printed here is the earlier version from *Northeast*. Reprinted by permission of the author. "Excerpt from an Omnibus Review . . ." appeared, as a full review, under the title, "Mark Sanders Reviews Barnes, Carlile, Elliott, Kooser, Smith, and Waters" in *Nebraska Review* 2 (1982). Reprinted by permission of the author. "An Interview with Ted Kooser" was originally published in *On Common Ground: The Poetry of William Kloefkorn, Ted Kooser, Greg Kuzma, and Don Welch* (Sandhills Press, 1983), edited by Mark Sanders and J. V. Brummels. Reprinted by permission of the publisher. "Portraits of Kooser" was published in a slightly different version in *The Midwest Quarterly*, 46.4 (2005). Reprinted by permission of the author.

Steven P. Schneider. "Ted Kooser" was first published in *American Writers: A Collection of Literary Biographies, Supplement 19* (Scribner's, 2009), edited by Jay Parini. Reprinted by permission of the author.

Karl Shapiro. "Untitled Introduction to *A Local Habitation & A Name*" appeared as the foreword to Ted Kooser's second full-length book, published by Solo Press, 1974. Reprinted by permission of the publisher, Glenna Luschei.

Mary K. Stillwell. "The 'In Between' Landscapes of Transformation in Ted Kooser's *Weather Central*" was published originally in *Great Plains Quarterly* 19.2 (1999). Reprinted by permission of the Center for Great Plains Studies, publisher.

Don Welch. "The Love of the Well-Made" was published in *The Midwest Quarterly*, 46.4 (2005). Reprinted by permission of the author.

Appreciation is due editorial assistants at SFASU: Kirstie Linstrom, Christina Kramer, and Taylor Stevens. Thanks especially to Kimberly Verhines at SFA Press for her enthusiatic belief in this project.

CONTENTS

COMMENTARY AND CRITICISM

INTRODUCTION

The Weight of the Weather: Regarding the Poetry of Ted Kooser had its genesis circa 1985, toward the end of my term as an English instructor at Southwest Missouri State University. A few years before, J. V. Brummels and I had coedited *On Common Ground: The Poetry of William Kloefkorn, Ted Kooser, Greg Kuzma, and Don Welch.* Inspired by its success (the book sold out its 1000 copy pressrun in fewer than four months), I believed continued scholarship on Kooser and other writers marginalized by region would secure my academic niche. My department chairman, Dr. Gleason, had been pestering me with advice: "Had you started your doctorate, we could have kept you. Had you had more books, we could have."

Thus, I plotted. I wrote a proposal to the National Endowment for the Humanities Fellowship program for a book-length study on Kooser's poetry. The volume would explore Kooser's poetics, his connectivity to the American literary canon, and risk new territory: the vernacular of Plains poetry and the post-Modern functionality of Regionalism or—as it was called in those days—Sense of Place writing. The Kooser study would be the first in a series devoted to critical overviews of poets undervalued because of their place outside established literary circles. I hoped to bring writers, off the radar, on the fringe, into larger critical discourse. Yeats's claim we should always find the new thing to do seemed right-minded for this project. Unfortunately, NEH didn't agree. The proposal was rejected. Reviewer response was sharp: there was no real interest in regional studies, especially in poetry; the topic's insularity did not adequately address a broader social and cultural context; and, the suggested poet was not someone who had enough *earned* history. Indeed, little commentary on Kooser's poetry had yet been written, save for a few longer pieces—notably von Glahn's and Gioia's—and a few dozen book reviews, most of them about *Sure Signs. Too little* was all the point. The research would have brought new material to the conversation.

For the next fifteen years, I set aside my idea for the Kooser book, as well as other authors I had planned to research. I taught full-time, attended graduate school and received my doctorate; I concentrated on a different regionalist—W. B. Yeats, and I thrust the bulk of my creative energies into writing poems and creative prose and in publishing my Sandhills Press imprint. I began two series—the Plains Poetry Series and the Main-Traveled Road Chapbook Series—and published about 40 books, most by poets from the Great Plains. Meanwhile, the Kooser project collected academic dust until I came across Dana Gioia and William Logan's *Certain Solitudes: Essays on the Poetry of Donald Justice* (published in 1998). I began revising my prospectus and sent it out for three or four years to university press editors. One remarked, "Ted Kooser is not an important enough poet. He is not known outside Nebraska." Another editor claimed such a book would only sell about 100 copies to Midwestern libraries.

Many of the Plains people I know—and this is complimentary—own a stubborn earnestness and tenacity for things they believe in. I was raised in a family of such people, among them farmers who bartered with drought and hail and unfair market prices, teachers who taught the unteachable, and laborers who built while they demolished their own health. Failure was giving up, and, undaunted by the naysayers, I retained my commitment to the "Kooser" book. More than thirty years later, the book has evolved into *The Weight of the Weather*. Despite its long time coming, the work is stronger for the wait. The selections collected here provide Kooser's readers and critics a foundation for future scholarship; furthermore, the book makes available isolated and rare commentaries that might otherwise have been overlooked.

The title of this collection comes from an early interview I had with Kooser in 1977, when he mentions a poem by that name (originally published in 1969 in the long defunct *University of Nebraska Review*). I describe this encounter in my memoir, "Portraits of Kooser," and recall well his discussion of the concept. Kooser said the weather's weight, metaphorically, will eventually flatten everything on the Plains. The pressure weather lays on locale is not malevolent but an ambivalent fact of environment. The human impulse—the artist's and poet's impulse—is to stand firm in such weather and observe it, to catch the moment that falls to us, as a leaf might, or snow, or how a gate shuts, or how someone old kneels at a grave, not to mourn, but to watch a spider. The moment caught in evocative particularity is an immeasurable gift that Kooser, poem after poem, shares with us. If Robert Frost in his generation desired to have at least one unlodgeable poem in the American canon (and he had more than several), Kooser of his generation has given us permanent poems that will stand the weather's weight equally well.

The Weight of the Weather is organized into four sections: interviews, memoirs, critical comment, and a proposal for further research. Interviews and criticism are arranged chronologically, while memoirs are ordered alphabetically according to authorship—primarily because most of the memoirs were published in 2005. In the first section, "Interviews," Arnold Hatcher's is perhaps the first published interview with the poet. Included originally in *Voyages to the Inland Sea VI* (1976), series editor John Judson had the critical vision to find in Kooser's poetry the value of regional letters. That book, it should be mentioned, also includes an early checklist of Kooser's publications and reviews of his early books through 1976. This checklist sparked

Danny Gillane's bibliographic work on Kooser several decades later, as well as Michael Istvan's. Hatcher's interview is followed by the one I did for *On Common Ground* in 1983. The 1977 interview is not included as it is buried among volumes of my archival material in Grand Island, Nebraska. That interview lasted a little more than an hour and was taped on a cassette recorder. The *On Common Ground* interview, unlike my first, was a much cleaner, less clumsy operation, conducted through the mail as I wintered out heavy snow in the Ozarks in early 1983.

By Kooser's count, he has done more than 100 interviews. Much *is* repetitive, and some interviewers are woefully uninformed about Kooser's work. In 2005 or so, when renewed work on this book was well underway, I suggested to Ted that he might have a new interview with me. He remarked in his responding letter he had already done so many it might be best to use what was already available. Thus, the selections in *The Weight of the Weather* stand as representative of his numerous conversations. Stephen Meats's interview was included in his 2005 tribute to Kooser in *The Midwest Quarterly*. Meats, the long-time poetry editor of the journal, gathered numerous memoirs written by Kooser's friends, students, and fellow poets. Meats's interview provides unique insight as he asks questions not posed by other interviewers. Baker and Hofmeister's interview is particularly lively: Baker, an astute critic and brilliant poet himself, asks thought-provoking questions relative to the literary canon and delves into Kooser's metaphorical genius. William Barillas's interview continues his discourse on Kooser begun in *The Midwestern Pastoral*, a volume devoted to the study of important Heartland writers. In his book, Barillas defines Midwestern pastoralism as a significant form of American letters—not unlike what I had proposed to the NEH in 1985. Barillas's discussion affirms Kooser's place in the company of his literary forebears and friends. His interview with Kooser addresses specifically how the poet's immersion in locale informed his role as poet laureate, and he, too, asks questions others did not think to ask (a point that Kooser has apparently appreciated in his response to Barillas's work). The most recent of the interviews is Chapman Hood Frazier's, who leads Kooser into discussions about poems he had not talked about previously.

The book's second section, "Memoirs," includes offerings from fellow Nebraska poets, specifically J. V. Brummels, Twyla Hansen, William Kloefkorn, Don Welch, and myself. Glenna Luschei was also once a Nebraskan and, like Kooser, had studied with Karl Shapiro. Her memoir recounts her first meeting with Ted at a friend's house; she went on to publish Ted's second full-length collection, *A Local Habitation & A Name*. Brummels' memoir looks back to the late 1970's when Kooser was the publisher of Windflower Press. Twyla Hansen, despite her knowing Ted for many years, describes him as a poetry teacher at UNL, as does Paul McCallum who took Ted's seminar in 1989 (I was a classmate of Paul's in that seminar). Both Kloefkorn and Welch consented to the use of their memoirs prior to their deaths—Kloefkorn passed away in 2011 and Welch in 2016. They were among Kooser's contemporaries in Nebraska, part of an impressive list of distinguished writers. Kloefkorn's "Inhalations" discusses his appreciation of Kooser's metaphor. Welch—who also studied with Shapiro—focuses on the concept of the "well made" poem. Rounding out the selection, David Baker's "Ted's Box" recalls how the young poet discovered Kooser's poetry in the mid-1970's while still a student at Central Missouri State University. With the exception of Glenna Luschei's contribution, the memoirs were included in the tribute issue of *The Midwest Quarterly*. My "Portraits of Kooser" was amended in 2017 to update the portraiture.

In the third section, "Commentary and Criticism," the reader will find excerpts from early book reviews of Kooser's poetry, particularly Kuzma's and Runciman's. Few reviews were written about Kooser's first several books; he was not widely acknowledged until the 1980 publication of *Sure Signs*. Those first notices sometimes grasped for a critical framework (a case in point is my fumbling review of *Sure Signs*, the first book review I ever wrote) because reviewers were hard pressed to get past the regional. Also included is Karl Shapiro's introduction to *A Local Habitation & A Name*. Shapiro was largely responsible for the publication of Kooser's first book, but he was also the one who introduced Kooser to Luschei, the publisher of *Local Habitation*. Shawn Leary's article was written for the long-defunct *Omaha* magazine in 1979; it serves as a first introduction to the poet. Leary's article included a photograph of Kooser sitting at his writing desk in his home, a cat on his lap; this is the same cat that introduced himself to me during my 1977 visit to Kooser's home.

The very first long published essay devoted to Kooser's work is George von Glahn's, published in 1977 in Robert Killoren's *Late Harvest* anthology of Midwestern poets. Von Glahn had a prophetic view of Kooser's poetry far ahead of virtually everyone else. This is perhaps why Kooser dedicated his poem, "Sure Signs," to him. *The Weight of the Weather*'s delay is due in part to my desire to use von Glahn's essay; I worked hard to locate the author but discovered he had died suddenly in 2002 from a heart attack. Ongoing search to reach family members through Spring 2017 took me to his nephew Christian Glahn, who expeditiously put me in touch with his cousin Maureen Powers, who gave me permission to publish her father's work. This book would have been incomplete without the essay.

My "Measured Compatibility in Contemporary Nebraska Poetry" began as a seminar paper in 1977 and is the second long essay devoted to Kooser's work, though it also includes commentary on Kloefkorn and Welch's poetry. The essay was accepted for publication in 1978 but did not appear until 1980. I presented the essay at the Western Literature Association in Fall 1980 at St. Louis. In my audience were Richard Etulain, author of *The American West*, and Cather scholar Susan Rosowski. Etulain asked me during the Q&A which of the poets in my study would become the most regarded; when I responded it would be Kooser, I explained that Kooser most transcended the provincialism of sense of place writing. Sue Rosowski would later tell me I would be the proselytizer of Plains poetry, a weight I am certain I have failed to carry adequately.

Following the publication of Kooser's *Sure Signs*, critical attention to Kooser's work increased. One of the first reviewers to take notice was Dana Gioia, a businessman who was also a poet and critic. He regularly contributed reviews of new work as a "Poetry Chronicle" for *The Hudson Review*. The piece here notes his surprise about and admiration for Kooser's selected work. Gioia became an ardent supporter of Kooser's work for years thereafter.

During my undergraduate years at Kearney State College, I found a copy of *Heartland II*, an anthology edited by Lucien Stryk, and, somewhat later, the *Late Harvest* collection. These books put into my mind the desire to publish a combined selected poems and critical anthology devoted to Nebraska poets. The end result was *On Common Ground*, and, in addition to my interview with Kooser, the book brought forth two substantial essays on Kooser's work. Victor Contoski contributed "Words and Raincoats," and Dana Gioia found occasion to hone his promotion of Kooser's poetry. "Explaining Ted Kooser" was later revised for Gioia's *Can Poetry Matter* under the title, "The Anonymity of the Regional Poet."

David Baker's "On Restraint" from 1996 compares the concept of poetic restraint in books by several contemporary poets, including Kooser. While Baker focuses specifically on *Weather Central*, the overall discussion speaks to the discipline that keeps poets from moralizing and reaching for platitudes that detract from observation and music. Jonathan Holden's "The Chekhov of American Poetry" examines Kooser's particularity, his power of observation and detailing, which Holden calls "a humanitarian vision." In both essays, the beauty of restraint is that universality is achieved but not at the expense of creating agendas or resorting to sentimentalism. As Holden points out, Kooser creates a "great art" possessed of a beauty that creates "memorability, enticing surfaces." Indeed, Kooser's work is evocative because it draws upon the emotions of the reader and not upon the self-indulgences of the poet. Mary K. Stillwell, Kooser's biographer (*The Life and Poetry of Ted Kooser* was published in 2013), drives the point further in her substantial work when she identifies, among Kooser's poetic devices, "direct, plain-spoken language; use of interior and exterior landscapes; and explicit metaphor that particularizes" experience.

David Mason's "Introducing Ted Kooser," originally published in *The Dark Horse*, a very fine journal from Scotland, seeks to make the poet known to an overseas audience, where even Americans abroad were clueless of Kooser's poetic achievement. Mason also connects Kooser to a literary community, inclusive of Dickinson, Whitman, Stevens, and Williams, and sets the stage for Kooser to be understood and valued contextually—that his work is not some anomaly, but that it is both part and directive of American poetics. In the excerpt from William Barillas's *The Midwestern Pastoral*, the critic examines the pastoral tradition found in Kooser's work and how the poet embraces locale and its people to set a "social history" of the country. The final selection in the third section of *The Weight of the Weather* is Steven P. Schneider's comprehensive overview. As it examines the body of Kooser's accomplishment rather than one or two titles or some singular, common theme, Schneider's essay fills gaps in Kooser studies. Kooser has suggested this is the best study of his work to date.

The final chapter proposes recommendations for continued scholarship on Kooser's writing. Michael Istvan, who does a tremendous job as a Kooser bibliographer (and has expansive, unpublished work on the matter), makes suggestions, based upon his findings, about where Kooser research might proceed. The suggestions are not exhaustive, but as a poet to be highly regarded, a national poet of excellence comparable to Frost, Stevens, Williams, Whitman, Robinson, Swenson, and others, there is a veritable vein of gold to mine in Kooser's writing. Ultimately, it is Istvan's hope that his research will compel further long studies. Indeed, Kooser studies continue. Linda Ray Pratt has a chapter devoted to Kooser in her forthcoming book on Plains literature; furthermore, Daniel Simon interviewed Kooser during the summer of 2017 for a publication he edits at the University of Oklahoma.

My hope, too, is that *The Weight of the Weather: Regarding the Poetry of Ted Kooser*, will rouse the critics and wake them to an imperative: to explore the gifts and mastery of Kooser's poetics, unparalleled among his contemporaries.

—Mark Sanders, Nacogdoches, Texas, July 2017

Interviews

An Interview with Ted Kooser

Arnold Hatcher

Arnold Hatcher: Don't be offended, Ted, but there are undoubtedly some people who will be reading this interview who've never heard of you. Would you mind saying some things about yourself by way of an introduction?

Ted Kooser: Well, let's see . . . . I'm 36 years old, divorced, have one son, Jeff, age eight. I make my living as an underwriter, which is sort of a lay medical clerk in an insurance company. When you apply for health insurance, and the agents ask you all of those "have you ever had this, have you ever had that?" questions, I'm the one who gets to read the answers, and who decides if you get the policy. I've been doing this work since I dropped out of graduate school in 1964. And I also write, and paint, and edit Windflower Press, and once in a while I teach a night course in poetry writing for the University of Nebraska.

Arnold Hatcher: What happened with you and graduate school?

Ted Kooser: When I came to Lincoln, in the fall of 1963, I had a "readership," which is a sort of scholarship that you are awarded but that you actually earn by grading papers for someone in the department. It paid a little, and my wife was teaching school near here, so we had enough money to live. I fully intended to pursue graduate studies all the way through the Ph.D. at the time. But what happened was this: Karl Shapiro was teaching here then, and I took several courses from him, six hours of creative writing and three more in a seminar he taught in William Carlos Williams. These courses were spread over two semesters of that year. When I got to the end of the second semester, my advisor told me that he wasn't going to recommend me for any more money because I hadn't been playing the academic game. He thought that I should've taken Bibliography, Old English, and so on and not Karl's classes! You see, Karl was someone that the department respected but who they really didn't trust with their graduate students. At least my advisor felt that way.

So I threw up my hands and dropped out.

I didn't have any idea what I was going to do with my life after this happened. I thought that maybe I could make my own way through school, living on Diana's salary and whatever I could pick up working part time painting signs and so on. I spent about half of the summer just sitting in a daze, wondering what I would do, and then I decided that I had to start making a little money. I saw an ad for a job as a "Management Trainee" at one of the local insurance companies, and I thought I'd see if I could stand it for a couple of months until school started. In short, I got the job, and I began to like it, and I never went back to graduate school, except to take enough night classes to finish my M.A.

Arnold Hatcher: Would you say that you are happy the way things worked out?

Ted Kooser: Oh, yes. It took me a long time to get over my need to identify with the teaching profession, though. I somehow felt that doing what I was doing was not respectable. I really wanted to teach, you see, but my opportunity had been spoiled for me by my own interest in taking classes from Karl and by the rigidity of the system. The chairman of the department, one of the finest men I know, felt sorry for me I think, and he let me teach one section of creative writing each semester, at night. It helped me a great deal to be regarded by him as a fit instructor. He was succeeded by another chairman who had also been extremely kind to me. I have not taught for the past couple of years, for various reasons, and I think I've outgrown the need to be thought of as a teacher.

I guess all this sounds as if the teaching was for *me*, and not for my students; actually, I think I did a good job at it!

Arnold Hatcher: So now you're following in Wallace Stevens' footsteps, working for an insurance company… what's it like there?

Ted Kooser: I'm hardly following Stevens. He was an executive, you know. Vice-President. I'm more or less a clerk, like Bartleby. What's it like?... Well, it's an 8-to-5, actually 4:30, job, five days a week. When I go home at 4:30, I leave it behind me. I don't have to correct papers into the wee hours or try to work up a paper for the PMLA. I like to work, and I enjoy the people that I work with, for the most part.

Arnold Hatcher: I'm sure that your job has had some effects on your poetry hasn't it?

Ted Kooser: Definitely. I think that the biggest effect is in the level of language I use. You see, all day long I have to talk to and communicate with people who for the most part don't know anything about literature. There's no lofty discourse on the arts over coffee in an insurance company! What I think has happened is that my level of discourse in my poetry has been brought down to a more basic level by working with these people. Those poets who are working within the academy often write poetry which complements their academic life, poems full of literary sensibility, in-jokes, and so on. I have come to the point where I am trying to communicate with people who aren't knowledgeable about poetry or who may never have read any poetry at all. I show my poems to the people who I work with from time to time, just to see if I'm getting through to them, and I'm delighted when I am!

I had a wonderful compliment from Denise Levertov in *The American Poetry Review* recently. She was discussing a poem of mine, "Old Soldiers' Home," and she said that a person wouldn't have needed to graduate from high school to understand it. I don't think I've ever heard anyone say anything about my work that pleased me more than that.

You know, Karl Shapiro told me once long ago that if I wanted to be a good poet I ought to get out of school. I can see now what he was saying. You write poems toward your community; it's only natural that you would. If you write poems toward your community as a teacher, you are likely to limit your communication to teachers. They will support and sustain you, and perhaps that's all you really want. If so, fine. But I, personally, would rather write poems that people on the street can understand and enjoy. Not poems, of course, that don't cause them to stretch *a little* to understand them. Not McKuen poems. Poems that present new things to them in ways that they can appreciate and understand. Poems *about* things, and other people . . . poems with good stories behind them. Too much of the poetry today is about nothing, or next to nothing. I call it The Poetry of the Ingrown Toenail. Poems about little whiny problems. It's no wonder so many people are turned off by contemporary poetry. So much of it is about minor complaints.

Arnold Hatcher: You are identified with Regionalism and Sense of Place. Do you have any feelings one way or the other about this?

Ted Kooser: That identification bothers me only when I suspect that someone is saying that I am posing as a Regionalist to capitalize on the current interest in Regionalism. Bret Harte, as you'll recall, went west to capitalize on the available folklore of the Old West, writing stories and, for that matter, twisting stories around just for the money in it. Twain hated him for his phoniness. Well, I'd hate to be thought of as a sort of Bret Harte of poetry.

I think it's important to remember that I've lived in Iowa and Nebraska all of my life. I have nowhere else to write about. I certainly have not set out to be a Midwestern poet, but I am one, by geography alone.

Lately, we've seen in the little magazine and literary quarterlies more and more talk about Midwestern Poetry, Sense of Place, Regionalism, and so on. It is interesting to note that the magazines involved in this are all being published in the Midwest; you won't find *Paris Review* or *Partisan Review* or *Hudson Review* discussing these things. You see, many writers and editors in the Midwest are defensive about their lives out here. They are constantly confronted by the truth that the big money in writing and publishing goes east. The biggest grants go to magazines in the east, like *Paris Review*, and from what I've read, these magazines really have other ways to get money, patrons about them and so on. The magazines out here have to struggle along with little money and little support. All this leads to a resentment of what is called The Eastern Literary Establishment.

So, over a period of time, editors, critics, and writers of all kinds who live on the plains have tried to publish the idea that we too have an important culture, worthy of attention. I agree with that; we *do* have such a culture, a rich one, but I'm not sure that the argument doesn't go unheard everywhere but out here. We are all sympathizing with each other but nobody outside is listening.

The whole argument is a little pathetic. We will never succeed in getting a poet living in Kansas onto the front page of the *New York Review of Books*. Nothing we can say in our articles and interviews and editorials will do that. *If*, however, he is a *very* good poet, he may get there on his own. It will be infinitely harder for him to get their attention than it would if he were living in Manhattan, but it can be done.

In defense of the eastern literary community, I'd have to say that, after all, they are inundated by their own art. They really don't have a lot of time to be noticing what's going on out here.

The poet who will make it on the front page of the *New York Review* will also make it into all of the literary magazines in the Midwest and West. He will be a poet who is writing well and beautifully and truthfully. It won't be a poet who is trying to climb the literary ladder, at least I hope not. We desperately need a poetry that is true to the heart, not a poetry that is true to this or that school or this or that fashion. The minute you start to think about what you *ought* to be writing, you begin to write illustrations of theory, not poems. I wish that everyone would just try to write as well as they know how, and to write truthfully. The little magazines are absolutely *full* of poetry of second intensity, third intensity. A lot of it has to do with the fact that poets feel obliged to publish lots of poems in lots of magazines; after all, teaching jobs are often based on the number of publications, and teaching is about the only thing that can support a poet. It's a real mess, I think. The minute poets get the idea that poetry can be a vocation, I think they lose their perspective. The arts have always been a secondary activity. The work of society goes first. Oh, it may be that there have been societies which had full-time artists and respected them, but they were always artists who were making art that had utility to those societies . . . potters, silversmiths, painters on commission, doing celebratory portraiture, and the like.

Modern poetry has no utility to society. Oh, I guess it has a *little* utility, but for the most part, all of the poets in the country could suddenly disappear and no one but their spouses and children would notice. And their students, of course. It would take their students at least a week to get over it.

No, I think that poets and writers must realize that they cannot be true to their art if they are making it for money. The poet must accept his lot; he will always be alone within our society, and unless he is independently wealthy he will always have to work for a living, doing something that *has* utility for the society, digging ditches, roofing buildings, selling aluminum siding, teaching school...

Arnold Hatcher: ...working for an insurance company...

Ted Kooser: Ah, yes, even that!

I'd like to back up a minute. I think that I've left the impression somehow that to appear on the front page of the *New York Review of Books* is to make it. It *is*, under present standards. We still look to New York for our judgments. I wonder if this is altogether necessary. Why can't we declare our independence of New York? Or, to avoid the *we*, which implies a group position, why can't an artist living in the Midwest or in the Southwest or in the Northwest simply declare himself free? Artists in the hinterlands have proven that it is possible to subsist there without a lot of money, and it's money that keeps us looking East. Who needs New York? Who wants to be Updike or Roth or Bellow? And, I think that to want to be rich is to be willing to be corrupted.

I'm sorry that I'm rambling about like this. I hope that I'm getting across. To summarize this hodgepodge, let me say that I believe that what is wrong with American writing today is that writers are being true to things other than their hearts. So rarely do we see a poem in one of the little magazines that is honest that we want to tear it out and make a thousand copies of it and strew them from a plane.

Arnold Hatcher: Do you think your own work fulfills your personal standards?

Ted Kooser: Yes, sometimes. I write a lot of poems that are undoubtedly influenced by what is in fashion. It's very difficult to avoid this. But, over the past few years I've read less and less that interested me, and so I've stopped reading most of the magazines. You can't be influenced by what you don't see, and, after all, my struggle with language is between my brain and its articulation, not between my articulation and Literature. I can carry on my own struggle to write well and honestly without help from the outside.

Arnold Hatcher: Surely, though, you continue to read poetry!

Ted Kooser: Yes, but looking for it in the magazines seems to be an awful waste of time. I prefer to read the collections of poets who have already shown me their honesty, like Dick Hugo. And I read poems of dead poets whose work I love . . . Ransom, Jarrell . . . I think a great deal of Denise Levertov's poetry, Gwendolyn Brooks', Linda Pastan's, Nancy Willard's. These are all women whose work transcends the polemics of writing Women's Poetry.

Women, who have certainly been oppressed, and other oppressed groups, minorities, often write poetry filled with social outrage—poems of political intent. What I think they overlook is that poetry is a terrible means of political expression. Look who reads it! How many registered voters read poetry magazines? And the people who read poetry magazines are already converts. Most of them already believe in equality for women, for blacks, for chicanos. They don't need convincing. These groups need to get to the voter, and they're not going to do it with poems.

Arnold Hatcher: But don't you think that there is a place in poetry for poems of social protest?

Ted Kooser: Oh, yes, but let me put it this way: I object to the use of a poem or may I say something that is shaped like a poem as a vehicle for public address. These pieces are speeches, not poems. They just don't hold up on the page.

To completely avoid the state of society is also unhealthy, of course. I am asking for a poetry which knows its place. There are, for example, women who can write poems which clearly reflect the oppression of women without puffing them out with polemics. These women are writing truthfully of their own experience, are writing with an "I" and not a "we." Marge Piercy is such a poet; so is Louise Glück; so is Adrienne Rich.

Arnold Hatcher: There seems to be a great interest in surrealism again. I guess it would be called *neo*-surrealism this time around. How do you feel about this sort of writing?

Ted Kooser: I think that many young poets, sensing the popular resurgence of surrealism, have begun to fabricate dreams and fantasies as source material for their poems because their lives and the dreams which they actually have do not provide them with enough genuine experiences to fulfill their desire to write hundreds and hundreds of poems. A life, waking or dreaming, does not ordinarily provide a poet with an experience worth writing about everyday, or at least I think that is true of most people. But since many of our younger poets want to publish a great deal, in order to fill out their *curriculum vitae*, they use surrealism as an excuse to write about nothing, lots of poems about nothing. Another way to do this, to have lots of production, is to write lots of poems about writing poems, about language, everything turning in upon itself. Most of these poems will serve their purpose, filling out the lists of publications, and then vanish. There are poets writing today who will not have a single poem in print in twenty years, poets who are relying on surrealism as their primary emphasis now. I guess I should say that I mean none of their poems written *now* will be in print in twenty years. They may be able to write more durable poetry after they become a little more secure.

Arnold Hatcher: Another subject now . . . you seldom read your poems in public. Why is that?

Ted Kooser: Nor do I usually enjoy watching other poets read *their* poems in public. I am nearly always embarrassed for the poetry, which takes a terrible beating at the hands if its own maker, often being compromised and twisted by the delivery. It is of some interest to see how a poet reads his work, I'll have to admit, but I really believe that a poem belongs on a page and not in an auditorium.

I am not only embarrassed for the poem but for the poet as well. He too is compromised by the theatre of the reading. A poetry reading is a means of using a poet for something other than a maker of poems; it is a means of making him an entertainer. If the audience of poetry readings had their way, there would be no more books of poems; instead, there would be poets on every corner, wearing interesting costumes and enter-taining people, like organ grinders, or for that matter, the *monkeys* of the organ grinders. Whenever *I* read to a group, I feel like Jack Benny.

I've thought lately of getting a ventriloquist's dummy and taking it with me to my readings. I could then have the dummy say my poems. The audience would surely *love* that!

But seriously, Arnold, I believe that most poets compose as I do, in solitude, committing the language to the manuscript in silence and with reverence for the gifts of association that the solitude delivers to them. Somehow I feel that if the communication is to be complete, the reader should share in the solitude. I would like to think of my readers as being alone with my poems. I would not think of entering a room and distracting them with a poor reading voice and a bright necktie.

I might be criticized for neglecting to honor the tradition of Oral Poetry, in which the poet, or the story-teller, recites to a group of illiterate people by the fire. It presents a pleasant picture. But those things happened long ago, and under different circumstances. There were no books; there were few people who could have read them anyway. If a person wanted to hear a story like this, he had to walk miles cross-country under all sorts of terrible conditions to hear it, and, for that reason, few could attend. Printing was devised out of the need for more accessible stories, particularly religious stories, and although printing cost society the intimacy and drama of the fireside reading, it did widen the audience of literature.

Our present society exhibits a nostalgia for simpler times, and I suspect that the poetry reading may be part of this Now, though, a person doesn't have to walk ten miles across a frozen moor to get to the fireside; he can park right out front!

I will say, though, in conclusion, that the arguments I have against readings may have been invented in self-defense. I am quite uncomfortable in front of groups, and get terribly nervous when I have to give a reading. Part of the anxiety probably comes from shyness, and part from the idea that my poetry has somehow turned against me, making me do something that I don't want to do.

For the poet who needs money, the poetry reading is a good thing too. Teaching and readings are two means of support that many poets engage in... also Poetry-in-the-Schools.

Arnold Hatcher: Now, about your writing habits . . . people are usually interested in writing habits...

Ted Kooser: I write a poem that I think is good enough to keep about every week or ten days. I write when I feel like it and I seldom try to write when I don't feel right about it. Although every writer is different, I find that I write best when I wait for the right moment. I can usually feel it coming on, and I then must sit down by myself and let it work itself out.

I used to try to write every day, but I feel as if there is only so much emotional weight available to me at a particular time, and that if I write daily, the poems are diluted. If I wait between poems, I am much more likely to have something of importance to bring to them.

But, as I said, every writer works differently. It has taken me a long time to figure out what was best for me, and everyone must do this for themselves.

I guess what I've said, it sounds as if I should be able to put together forty or fifty poems that I like each year. Actually that isn't so. After a few weeks, many of the poems that I thought were worthwhile have lost their interest. At the end of the year I may have fifteen or twenty poems that I'd like to carry forward toward a book.

Arnold Hatcher: Do you submit most of your poems to magazines as you write them?

Ted Kooser: I usually wait for a week or two. If the poem still looks good to me, I'll send it out to an editor whose judgment I respect, like, say, E. V. Griffith of *Poetry NOW*, or Jerry Costanzo of *Three Rivers Poetry Journal*, Hilda Gregory and Bernice Slote here in Lincoln at *Prairie Schooner*. I consider very carefully rejections from these people, and I question the advisability of sending out a poem any more after a couple of good editors have turned it down. Fortunately for me, all of the poems that I've written during the past couple of years, or all but a few of them, have been accepted for publication, which surely must say something for my method of writing, waiting for the poem rather than trying to force it out.

I should say that I don't believe that it should be the editor's sole responsibility to decide the value of a poet's work. The poet should be doing it too—should be editing his *own* work. All poets should be able to tell the difference between their best work and their third-rate work. They may not be able to tell their best from the second-best, but they can tell their best from third-rate and fourth-rate stuff. Some poets send out everything. It's extremely risky, I think.

Take this, for example: let's say that a poet sends out a batch of poems which includes first-rate work as well as fourth-rate work, and the submission goes to an editor who is either incompetent or malicious. That editor might well accept ten of the worst poems and publish them as a representative selection. It could do a great deal of damage to that poet.

All in all, I think that a poet must choose his magazines carefully, and choose his work carefully. As is evident to me, there isn't enough care of this sort given in many instances. Without naming her, I know of one young woman who sends out everything she does, or it looks like it. When I was editing *The New Salt Creek Reader*, I'd get fifty poems in a batch from her that I was supposed to sort through. Sometimes there would be half a dozen versions of the same poem! It occurred to me that these poems were being offered to me without restraint; I could print any of them that I wanted to. What if I'd printed five different versions of the same poem? I could have called the section of the magazine *A Selection of Poems by So-and-So!*

Arnold Hatcher: But you didn't do it . . . .

Ted Kooser: No, I couldn't. But someday, someone will. All of this is more of the same stuff . . . the emphasis on publication, getting lots of stuff in print. Perhaps if someone respected in the academic community would make a stand for quality in publication and not quantity it might help. If they could suggest to the people in charge of hiring writers to teach in universities that it's the quality of the writing that matters, not the number of publications, perhaps things would get better. Unfortunately, I don't know if too many hiring committees want to try to judge quality. They don't have the time.

You see, *everybody* can get published somewhere if they persist in sending out work. Some ignorant editor at *Sweep Up Quarterly* or *Last Ditch Review* is going to accept it. When this poet gets enough of these publications, he can approach the hiring chairman and say, "Well, I've been published in a *number* of little magazines, including *Sweep Up Quarterly* or *Last Ditch Review,*" and unless the hiring chairman does his homework, he'll never look at these magazines to learn how really awful the work may be. I'm not sure that these people doing the hiring realize that there are quite a few *Sweep Up Quarterlies* in this country, all of them desirous of filling up fifty pages every quarter. It's literary pollution.

Arnold Hatcher: But if these magazines are so terrible, how do they survive?

Ted Kooser: Most of them don't, fortunately. They may last for a couple of issues, but they still have provided space in those two issues for a hundred poems, a hundred additions to the *curriculum vitae*. Offset printing is not awfully expensive, and it isn't too hard to get out a couple of issues of a magazine. It's easy to get plenty of poems to publish. You just mention that you're looking for work and the poems come flying from everywhere, many of them on English Department stationery, by the way; poems from people who are tired of teaching Freshman English and who want to work toward a cushy six-hour job teaching creative writing. When I was editing, I don't think I was ever pleasantly surprised by poems that came in a department envelope. Another disastrous mistake that you can make in starting a magazine, by the way, is to get listed in *The Writer* or *Writer's Digest* ! Jesus! You can't imagine the stuff that comes in! The presence of these writers' magazines on the stands encourages a lot of miserable people to write and submit and then to be heartbroken by rejection. It's sad. I have seen submissions by people who were so neurotic that they wrote me threatening letters when I turned their work down. But they all want to be rich, rich writers so that they can get on the Johnny Carson Show and gossip with Truman Capote and Burt Reynolds. The writer's dream.

Arnold Hatcher: Perhaps we should close now. Do you have anything that you'd like to say in conclusion?

Ted Kooser: Let me put it this way; here's an original thought I had the other night; see how you like it: *Money is the root of all evil.* Has a nice ring, doesn't it?

An Interview with Ted Kooser

Mark Sanders

Mark Sanders: You wrote an essay entitled "The Two Poets" for the Spring 1983 issue of *The Nebraska Humanist*. In the essay, you make a distinction between two types of poets: the public poet, and the poet who writes poetry. Your advice to beginning poets was they should write and not try to be a poet. That's a pretty sound suggestion. But how much should this advice pertain to poets who have become successful?

Ted Kooser: I believe wholeheartedly that poets, and artists in general, should avoid becoming embraced by the popular culture. Artists need detachment, and it's hard gaining that detachment and protecting it when you're participating in the popular culture by sitting between two pretty starlets on the *Tonight Show*. It's probably better that poets be kept under the front porch with the dogs.

Mark Sanders: You are one of the more successful poets residing in Nebraska. If success affects art negatively, how do you keep from producing poor poetry or, as Judson Jerome calls it, "proetry"?

Ted Kooser: I'm not comfortable with the word "success" when it's applied to me. I was brought up by people who equated success with money, and I don't think that they were unusual in that thinking. It could be said that I am a moderately successful businessman—I make a good salary at my job at the insurance company—but I am not a successful poet. In twenty-five years of writing and publishing poetry, I'd guess that I've received less than two thousand dollars for the sale of poems. I've made additional money doing readings, but that's not being a successful poet, that's being a successful performer of poetry. I don't know any poets who are successes as poets, nor do I care to. When money gets mixed into art, the art begins to decay. Once an artist discovers that he or she can make money by creating a certain kind of work, his or her work rarely progresses beyond that point. If every poet in this country were to be given a million dollars, it would mean the end of poetry. Not that poets and artists should suffer. I don't believe that anyone should have to suffer, but I mean that the arts should be kept apart as much as possible from financial considerations. Money stinks. A friend of mine is a nationally-recognized landscape painter. Several years ago he began attracting large sums of money for his paintings—two, three thousand dollars apiece. He began painting more and more of these successful paintings, and he's made a lot of money, but his painting is arrested. He's doing the same thing over and over. I've felt the temptation myself. Several months ago, I sold a poem to *The New Yorker*. It was the first time I'd been paid for a poem in years, and I got a little over a hundred dollars for it. Gosh, I caught myself saying, if I could write like that more often, I could make a lot of money! But what I was really saying was, if I could write the kind of poems that Howard Moss likes, I could make a lot of money. But who wants to spend his life writing poems for the poetry editor of *The New Yorker*? No, I want to write poems for *me*. There's another kind of success, I guess, and that's in getting published, even though there's not much money involved. Surely you know poets who have perfected a particular kind of poem that is easy for them to get published. It would be unfair of me to point a finger at a particular poet as an example, when there are thousands, but you know what I mean. Those poets are going to keep on writing the same damned poem over and over again all their lives, just because it's been successful for them. That's why I think highly of a poet like Greg Kuzma, who keeps experimenting, keeps exploring. Artists who undertake such explorations make mistakes. It isn't always safe. But they also open new territory. Art is all about this sort of pushing the frontiers out, pushing the horizons out. Faulkner once said, "To try something you can't do,…then try it again. That to me is success." Of the four poets presented in your book, Greg is probably the most serious artist in this sense. He is tireless in his trying of new things. Don Welch is probably next in line. I see his work changing, expanding its range. Bill and I are a little safer, I think. We are more likely to write the Kloefkorn poem, the Ted Kooser poem, though both of us seem to be worried about it, and if you look at the overall range of what we've done over the years, you can see both of us changing to some degree.

Mark Sanders: In the last few years, there has been a big hoopla over writers in Nebraska. A search for a new poet laureate was started, and finally, after many writers dropped out of the running, including yourself, Bill Kloefkorn was awarded the honorary title of Nebraska State Poet. What was your attitude toward all the proceedings? Where did good come from it, and where was the bad in it?

Ted Kooser: The controversy over the appointment of an official state poet is all in the past now, and there's not much to be gained raking over the coals. Those of us who opposed it had good reasons to do so, and we all had our reasons. For me, I was sure that naming a state poet would bring a lot of attention to one particular poet and no attention to other poets, many of whom could use some recognition. In a sense, my suspicions have been borne out. Bill Kloefkorn has been asked to do poetry readings from one end of the state to the other, and the sales of his books, at least from my own press, have increased tenfold. But I guess we need to keep it in mind that before all of this happened, *nobody* was getting much attention. The question remains: is it best for nobody to get any attention or for one person to get a lot of it? I do want to say that Bill was as good a choice as could have been made. He likes people, likes reading to them, and is a terrific performer of his own work. Lots of people go to poetry readings to be entertained, and Bill is a great entertainer. He's also a poet who knows poetry, and some of that sensibility and love of poetry is bound to run off on his audiences, which is good. All in all, I wish that this state poet business had never come up. It led to a lot of hard feelings among the writers and toward The Nebraska Committee for the Humanities, a worthwhile organization whose misfortune it was to get involved in such a sensitive issue. They really waded in blindly, and got in high water before they knew what happened. I was one of the ones, if not the ringleader of those, who stood on the bank and tried to raise the water level by pissing in it.

Mark Sanders: In the interview printed in *Voyages to the Inland Sea*, you told Arnold Hatcher that modern poetry had little utility to society. When Bill was given his distinction, John Ciardi remarked in his address, borrowing from Auden, that poetry made nothing happen. Did you mean the same thing, and do you agree with that philosophy?

Ted Kooser: I was there, but I can't remember what Ciardi said. And that *Voyages* interview goes back a long time. But I do believe that poetry has little practical value. We all know that, don't we? You can't carry water in it. You can't drive it to the grocery. One of the wonderful things about art is that it's worthless.

Mark Sanders: How do you compare yourself to your contemporaries in this state? Do you all serve the same function as "poet," or do you see your work as exclusive yet complementary to theirs?

Ted Kooser: There are a lot of poets in Nebraska, and most of them have matured to the point that they are doing their own work, in their own manner, and are not under the influence of anyone else. Naturally, some of the younger poets have imitated the work of older poets, but they'll get over that. I can see Don Welch's influence on his former students, Bill's influence on his former students, and so on. But the really mature poets are doing their own thing. You'd have a hard time finding much common between the poems of Don and Bill and Greg and me and Roy Scheele and the other poets who are getting their work out and establishing national reputations. I wonder if any of us are really reading each other very carefully. I doubt it. I mean, studying each other. I may be alone in this, but I'm really not very interested in anyone's work but my own.

Mark Sanders: When you consider that such writers as John G. Neihardt, Weldon Kees, Willa Cather, Mari Sandoz, and Wright Morris, have shaped Nebraska's literary culture, do you find what is being done currently to have the same importance as their contributions?

Ted Kooser: I'd rather not get into comparisons, Mark. We're really talking apples and oranges here. Cather and Sandoz and Morris are prose writers, and Neihardt was really a 19th century poet. Kees's work is more like what Don and Bill and Greg and I are doing, but that's mainly because he was a 20th century poet writing in his tradition, and so are we. I have faith that some of the poets living and working in Nebraska today have written, and will write, strong and enduring poems, and that these may become a part of the literary culture you're talking about. But those same poets will also write a lot of bad poems, a lot of failures, just as did Neihardt and Kees. Ninety-nine percent of all poems are failures. Winfield Townly Scott said that, and he's right. It's a good thing to keep in mind.

Mark Sanders: If you could do something to influence the contemporary literary climate of the state, or even the Midwest, what course would you suggest other than what is currently happening?

Ted Kooser: I don't really want to influence the contemporary literary climate. I think it ought to be left alone.

Mark Sanders: You once told me you thought "regionalism" was getting more attention than it deserves. Can you explain that feeling, and what would you rather have attention given to?

Ted Kooser: Most of the talk about regionalism and sense of place is little more than boosterism. The people doing all the talking are trying to defend their own writing and that of their friends. The defense is usually a lot better than the writing. There's nothing new about any of this. Writers have always been their own best cheerleaders. It seems to me like a tremendous waste of time. If writers spent more of their time writing, and less time patting themselves on the back, we'd all be better off.

The idea behind most of the sense-of-place talk is that there is some magical unifying theme pervading the writing of certain writers. This is complete nonsense as far as I can see. What writers on the Great Plains share is the Great Plains. They live there, and they share the same summers and winters. Some of this commonality of experience is bound to get into the poetry, and it does. People have known for years that the best way to involve a reader in what he's reading is to introduce concrete imagery, and when you live in a place you draw your imagery from what's around you. You can't draw from experiences you haven't had. Bill Kloefkorn and Don Welch and I have all lived nearly all of our lives in Nebraska, Kansas, and Iowa, so when we go to our experiences we have nothing else to draw from. Greg Kuzma has lived here, but he's also lived in the East, and he draws from both regions. He has a book called *Adirondacks,* for example.

What's important to me is whether the poetry that gets written is any good. Where it got written doesn't make much difference. Oh, I like to see the work of Great Plains poets getting published in national magazines, getting good reviews, but that's because I know and like these people, not because we're in the same Kiwanis Club, or better, the same fraternity, with a secret handshake.

Mark Sanders: You've been writing for nearly twenty years—writing and publishing. Out of all that time, out of everything you have done as a poet, what is your greatest success, what has been most gratifying?

Ted Kooser: Twenty-five years, actually . . . . A number of things have happened which have pleased me—the publication of my first poem, the publication of my first book, my first appearance in an anthology, my first critical notice in a national magazine. All of the firsts were very happy occasions. I've also greatly enjoyed meeting and corresponding with writers whose work I admire. Today, I am particularly happy to receive letters from distant strangers who have come across my poems and liked them. I especially like letters from school children. Several of my poems have been included in textbooks, and that's made me happy. I've always wanted to reach an audience of people who are not poets or poetry followers, and those textbook publications seem to confirm my ability to reach a broad audience with my work.

Mark Sanders: You are now a Second Vice President for an insurance company. Has this been beneficial to your poetry? Do you ever feel any desire to get back to the classroom? What has working at the company done for your sense of audience awareness?

Ted Kooser: I don't think that my job has been particularly helpful, but it has not interfered either. Teaching might have interfered. Teachers have to give of themselves more than I am willing to. When I taught night classes I found myself giving away good ideas, and particularly good metaphors, which are hard to come by. I'm not interested in letting students take my metaphors and misuse them.

Sometimes I think it would be fun to teach again, and I may some-day, but there are other considerations, including money. I'd have to take a fifty percent cut in income to go back to teaching. As to the last question, I think that the fact that I work all day long with people who are not literary has helped to keep the language of my poems from becoming literary. I often try out my poems on my co-workers, some of who would never read a poem without my imposition, and I watch carefully to see if they understand what I've written. It's a good test.

Mark Sanders: You were an editor for a number of years. First, it was

The New Salt Creek Reader and then *The Blue Hotel.* Both of these were pretty little magazines. What was your motivation for starting these, and what happened to them?

Ted Kooser: I started my *Salt Creek Reader* because I wanted to be in on what was going on in the literary world. I wanted the community of correspondence and publication. Eventually, after I'd begun to publish my own work in magazines and had struck up correspondences with other poets, like my friend Steven Osterlund, I felt that I could keep my place in the literary community without all the work and expense of publishing a magazine. So I discontinued my magazine. Later, I started up another, *The Blue Hotel,* thinking that I missed the activity, but I soon discovered that I wasn't all that interested in it. I got out one very good issue on the poetry of Brewster Ghiselin, and a double issue which is an anthology of contemporary Danish poetry and then I let it go. The money was always a problem, too. It's expensive, as you know, Mark, to publish magazines and books. There are government programs which give out grants of support, but frankly—and this is odd, since I'm on the state Arts Council—I'm not sure that the government should be backing literary magazines. I've given up asking for grants for my Windflower Press because I think that it, like any other little mom and pop grocery, ought to be able to survive on its own merit, *if* I'm putting out a product that has any utility for people. Too much of what the government has supported in its literary programs has been a complete waste of money, because the product that was produced was of no value to anybody. I don't feel the same way about direct fellowships to artists, though. That seems to make more sense to me. But every artist and publisher who goes to the government for money must ask himself or herself, does my acceptance of support from this government stand as an endorsement of what this government is doing in the world? In some sense, the artist is going in business with the government to produce art, and should we be going in business with a government that behaves as it does in its support of repressive countries like South Africa? You can go to jail for refusing to pay your income taxes, but you can't go to jail for refusing to accept government support.

Mark Sanders: Since you have been an editor, and since you are a critical reader, what do you find wrong with contemporary poetry?

Ted Kooser: We probably ought to avoid distinctions like *right* and *wrong*. Poetry, like all art, is by its nature right. It's an affirmation . . . . But I'm taking advantage of your question. As a reader, I can only attest to what I like and what I don't like. There is a lot of poetry being written and receiving high praise that I don't like at all. But somebody must like it. Louise Glück, whose poems I admire, recently selected Michael Ryan's *In Winter* for the National Poetry Series. Ryan's book is dreadful, I think, but it's obvious that my opinion is in the minority. Here's what I like to see in poetry: First, I like poems that move me. I am moved by poems in which strong feelings are present, but are held or controlled by language which is slightly detached and restrained. I detest poems of self-pity, though, and poems of self-absorption. I love poems which celebrate things—telephones, pigs, rocks, you name it. I also like poems that are well made. I find myself moved by those skills, too. I can't stand sloppiness. To go back to your question, I'd have to say that if I were to pass judgment on my contemporaries, and it looks as if I'm about to, I'd venture that the *me*-ism of the Sixties, the focus of attention upon the individual and not the community, has been too amply reflected in our poetry. I said that I didn't want to get into right or wrong, but I do think that it is morally wrong for people, all people, including poets, to spend so much time and energy in self-absorption. On a bigger scale, this is what nationalism is all about, and it's nationalism, I think, that places the whole world in great danger. But poets can't do much about that, I don't think. Artists merely reflect the world that they live in. It's the world that we live in that I'm unhappy with, I suppose, and the poets are more to blame for the state of the world than are the rest of the people.

Mark Sanders: You occasionally write book reviews. Does this help you to keep focus on your own writing?

Ted Kooser: I do enjoy writing book reviews, but I find myself saying the same things in all of them, and perhaps I should stop. I have a few axes to grind, a few statements about poetry that I like to make, and I've said these things again and again. The publication of these ideas is getting redundant.

Mark Sanders: *Hatcher* and—from what I understand, because I haven't seen it yet—*Blizzard Voices* are departures from your poetic voice. Why the departure? Did it allow you to examine other voices, such as Bly in his translations?

Ted Kooser: I did *Hatcher* for fun, and while *Blizzard Voices* is a little flatter than most of my lyrics, it's still mine. A poetic voice is a hard thing to define, although I can recognize the poetic voice of other poets. I like to think of myself as a writer, not just a poet, and I believe that writers should write all sorts of things—plays, novels, essays, poems, book reviews, etc. I don't want to confine myself to poetry. I want to keep trying new things.

Mark Sanders: When *Sure Signs* first came out, I read a review of it in an east coast magazine that wasn't exactly kind. How did you view that, and how did you come to terms with the review?

Ted Kooser: *Sure Signs* got a nasty review in *The New York Times Book Review.* The reviewer, somebody named Molesworth, took on six or seven new books, mine among them. The whole review was sneering in nature. He was as hard on Charles Simic and Louise Glück and the others as he was on me, so I was getting kicked in good company. The more your work gets around, the more likely it is that it will find its way to somebody who hates it. It hurts to get a bad review, but I've had lots of good ones, too, and they've more than offset this one bad one. Some reviewers are helpful. Mary Kinzie wrote about *Sure Signs* in *The American Poetry Review,* and I learned some things about my work from what she said. Dana Gioia, whom I understand is writing something for this book, is my most devoted critic, and he's taught me a lot. A lot of writers won't read their reviews, but I do.

Mark Sanders: A couple more questions: what do you think about the concept of this book, despite its slow progress? Where, do you think, should I go from here?

Ted Kooser: I wouldn't object to any book that paid attention to me and my work. I like the attention. I don't know what you intend to say in your introduction, Mark, but I hope that you won't try to define a "school" of Nebraska poetry, or to insist upon a commonality between the four of us, because I don't think it's there. Besides, we all are independent and should be viewed as individuals. I'm very pleased that you've gone to all of this work on our behalf, and I thank you for including me. I don't know what you should think of doing next. If I were you, I'd hole up and devote my energies to my own poems for a good long while.

Mark Sanders: What's next for you?

Ted Kooser: I don't have any definite plans, but I would like to spend more time on my short fiction. Short stories are very challenging, and I'd give anything to be good at writing them. I'll keep writing poems, too, of course.

An Interview with Ted Kooser

Stephen Meats

Stephen Meats: How would you say your parents influenced your becoming a poet?

Ted Kooser: My father was a storekeeper, loved the public, and was a marvelous storyteller. I remember a woman once said to me that she'd rather hear my dad describe a person than see the person herself. He had an interest in the theater, too, and he and Mother belonged to a group that got together to read plays. Sitting in our living room listening to those plays was, I think, my first experience of literature as fun. We also had a few books, a collected Balzac, a collected plays of Ibsen, the novels of John Fox, Jr., the works of Dumas pere. I read them all.

Stephen Meats: Same question about the landscape and the people of the Great Plains, particularly your region of Nebraska-Iowa. What role have they played in your becoming a poet and in your work?

Ted Kooser: I have never lived anywhere else, and I've always written about what I've experienced. I might have written about different landscapes if I'd lived somewhere else, but I think the poems might have been much the same. My interest is in writing about the ordinary, and the ordinary is everywhere.

Stephen Meats: What poems by other writers have served as touchstones for your own writing?

Ted Kooser: I have been thinking lately how much I may have been influenced by May Swenson's poems. I think *To Mix with Time* was one of the first books I read and reread. Several years ago someone brought out a posthumous book of her nature poems and when I read it I recalled how much I'd been inspired by her. I also remember being very interested in the poems of John Crowe Ransom. Also E. A. Robinson and Frost. I read anything and everything when I was young, and I couldn't possibly list all the poets who've had some influence on me. Today I look to Nancy

Willard and Linda Pastan and other Americans, and Thomas Tranströmer and Rolf Jacobsen, the two last in Bly's translations.

Stephen Meats: You mention that your father was a marvelous storyteller. I've heard from some of your close friends that you love to tell stories and to hear stories, as well. What role does narrative play in your work?

Ted Kooser: I have written very few poems in which narrative seemed to be leading. There's a poem in *Delights & Shadows*, "The Beaded Purse," that is indeed a narrative, but it seems quite unlike most of my work, which works with single moments rather than sequences of moments. Poets have tried to write narratives in verse and some of them are quite effective, at least to me as a literary person, but I have always wondered how they might be received by everyday readers. Novels are much less intimidating than poems, and if I were to choose between reading a good story in verse and one in prose I think I'd go for the prose. Literary people have interest in narrative poetry, but it's my guess that most narrative poems wouldn't compete very well in paperback on an airport book rack. David Mason has a new poem about the Ludlow Mine disaster that is very well done, and a part of it has been in *Hudson Review*.

Stephen Meats: Still dealing with influences, but in a different vein. Was religion a significant part of your life growing up? Has religious belief been important to your poetry?

Ted Kooser: We were Methodists but only went to church a few times a year, on holidays usually. I am not a traditional believer by any means, but I do believe in a universal order. But it doesn't have a personality. I don't think I have been much influenced by anything in any way churchly.

Stephen Meats: Your work has sometimes been described as "accessible." What is your view of such labels? I ask this because I find your work accessible, but not at all simplistic, yet I believe that some readers, and even some critics, have trouble separating the two.

Ted Kooser: I don't object to my poems being called accessible, and I work hard during the process of revision to make them clear. I revise away from difficulty and toward clarity and simplicity. It doesn't matter to me what critics say about it. There's no way to control what people want to say about your work. It's best not to pay any attention, and I don't read reviews of my work.

Stephen Meats: It has also been said that you write for the "common reader." Do you write with an "ideal reader" in mind? And could this reader in any sense be termed "common"?

Ted Kooser: I talk about imaginary readers in my *Poetry Home Repair Manual* and the idea is to have an imaginary reader for each poem we write. My imaginary reader is usually someone who has read a little poetry, has a couple of years of college or more, but is not a literary sophisticate. I don't think there is a common reader, if that means one imaginary reader for all work. If I've used the term *common* I have meant it in the sense of *ordinary*.

Stephen Meats: How did you get started writing, and at what point did you realize writing poetry would be a life-long calling? [In response to this question, Mr. Ted Kooser referred me to his recently published *The Poetry Home Repair Manual*, where he suggested I would "find some ready-made-sentences."—editorial note by Stephen Meats].

Ted Kooser: "I don't remember the specific date when I decided to be a poet, but it was during one of my many desperately lonely hours as a teenager, as I set about establishing myself as a poet with adolescent single-mindedness. I began to dress the part. I took to walking around in rubber shower sandals and white beachcomber pants that tied with a piece of clothesline rope. I let my hair grow longer and tried to grow a beard. I carried big fat books wherever I went—like Adolph Harnack's *Outlines of the History of Dogma* and Kierkegaard's *Fear and Trembling*. I couldn't have understood a word of those books if I tried, but they looked really good clenched under my arm and, as a bonus, helped me look as if I had big biceps. There were, it seemed to me, many benefits accruing to a career as a poet. There were fame and immortality . . . . There was also the delicious irresponsibility of the bohemian lifestyle . . . . But best of all was the adoration of women . . . . It didn't occur to me for a long time that in order to earn the title of Poet, I ought to have written at least one poem . . . . I was an artificial poet, a phony, when, by rubbing shoulders with poetry, I gradually became interested in writing it. I'd begun to carry books less cumbersome than Harnack and Kierkegaard, and one day I picked up the New Directions paperback edition of William Carlos Williams's *Selected Poems*. It weighed no more than a few ounces and fit in my pocket. I began to read Williams and soon discovered other poets whose work I liked: May Swenson, Randall Jarrell, John Crowe Ransom, to name a few. I began to read poetry when I had a moment free from pretending to be a poet, and soon I started to write a few poems of my own. The two sides of being a poet—the poet as celebrity and the poet as writer—began to fall into balance. I read poems, I wrote poems, and at times, sometimes for hours on end, I was able to forget about trying to attract women." [Excerpt from Ted Kooser, *The Poetry Home Repair Manual* (University of Nebraska Press, 2005), pp. 3-5; reprinted with the permission of the author.]

Stephen Meats: Your first collection (*Official Entry Blank*, 1969) was published by a university press and came out when you were a very young poet. How did that collection come to be published?

Ted Kooser: My friend, mentor, and teacher, Karl Shapiro took the manuscript to the University of Nebraska Press, which then had an ongoing poetry series. His influence must have been helpful.

Stephen Meats: How else did Shapiro influence your direction as a writer?

Ted Kooser: He taught me, by his example, that is was possible to write interesting poems about inanimate things.

Stephen Meats: How did you go about putting a book together?

Ted Kooser: Most of my books are little more than collections of poems that have appeared in journals over a period of years, sometimes arranged by theme or point of view. It takes between seven and ten years for me to get around 60 poems that have been published and/or that still please me enough to include. *Winter Morning Walks*, written over just one winter, was a different kind of project, and this was also true of *The Blizzard Voices*, which I wrote as a book, rather than as a compilation of single poems. *Braided Creek*, with Jim Harrison, is a compilation of about fifteen years' worth of little poems he and I sent back and forth with no intent to make a book. The idea for a book came about quite suddenly, when we realized how many poems there were. We had about 400 to choose from. But all three of my books from Pitt, and *Delights & Shadows* from Copper Canyon, were put together as I've described, as compilations of published work.

Stephen Meats: Besides creating poems, I know you also make paintings. When did painting become an active part of your creative life?

Ted Kooser: I was interested in drawing and painting as a child, long before I got interested in poetry. I still love to paint. I consider myself a dedicated amateur. I don't show my work or sell it, but I sometimes spontaneously give it away. It's nice to have something like that, something that I can be naïve about.

Stephen Meats: Near the beginning of your essay, "Riding with Colonel Carter," you mention briefly in passing that your poems resemble Disney animated films. Could you explain what you meant?

Ted Kooser: I don't have a copy of what I said, but what I meant to suggest is that my use of metaphor is something like those Disney films in which the forests have personalities, the trees have faces, etc.

Stephen Meats: Do you feel that your work as an insurance executive helped you or hindered you as a poet (I'm thinking of your short poem, "They Had Torn off My Face at the Office")? Maybe a different way of asking the same question is, how did you balance those different parts of your life—businessman and poet—that may seem to an observer as unrelated, or even incompatible?

Ted Kooser: That poem arose out of resentment for office work, but I managed to put that resentment behind me quite early. Later poems, like "Four Secretaries" in *Weather Central,* are better indicators of how I felt about the workplace. Lots of people have asked me about how I was able to do that kind of work and write poems and my answer is that I did both. I wrote every morning from 4:30 or 5:00 till I had to get my necktie on, and then I went to work. The two occupations never seemed incompatible to me.

Stephen Meats: You're not a teacher by profession, but I know that you have often taught poetry writing classes. What led you to want to teach, while you were pursuing a successful business career, and what—as a writer—have you learned from teaching?

Ted Kooser: I have always liked to teach, and probably would have stayed in the profession if I'd been a better scholar, but all I cared about was writing poems, and when I was in graduate school, creative writing as an academic pursuit hadn't arrived in Nebraska or most places other than Iowa and a few other schools. Now I teach tutorially. I take a dozen graduate student poets and see each of them for an hour each week, privately, in my office. It's a fine way to teach and I've had a lot of success with it. *The Poetry Home Repair Manual* owes a lot to what I've learned from teaching.

Stephen Meats: How did making the transition from being a poet working for an insurance company to being a poet working in an academic setting affect your writing?

Ted Kooser: I don't think it has affected it at all.

Stephen Meats: Many people have lamented the fact that poetry writing in America has become institutionalized in creative writing programs and the infamous workshop. As someone who has observed this phenomenon from both outside and inside the academy, what is your view of its effects on the development of American poetry?

Ted Kooser: We owe many good contemporary poems to the workshops, and many bad ones. I think if we were able to look back at this period from a hundred years from now we'd mostly notice that there were lots more poems being written than during the period before creative writing took hold on campuses. Nothing wrong with lots of poems being written. I say in the *Manual* that I wouldn't see anything wrong with a world in which everybody were writing poetry. It's a good thing for us to do with our time, and while we're doing it we're not causing anybody any trouble.

Stephen Meats: Teaching isn't the only way you have offered a helping hand to poets and to poetry. I'm thinking of your journal—back in the

'70s, wasn't it—*The Salt Creek Reader?* Could you give a brief history of the journal and your reasons for starting it?

Ted Kooser: I began my little publishing business in the '60s with poems on single sheets of paper that I sold for a penny. I stole the idea from Jon Bracker, as I recall, who had done a similar thing. I then founded *The Salt Creek Reader*, a more typical journal, and kept it going for a while. Then I let it lapse for a few years and picked it up again as *The New Salt Creek Reader*. After I got tired of that, I published a couple of issues of a new magazine, *The Blue Hotel*, and then tired of that.

Stephen Meats: You also conducted Windflower Press for a time. Could you give a brief history of your press and your reasons for starting it?

Ted Kooser: Windflower Press went hand in hand with the magazines. I started by publishing a couple of books by Bill Kloefkorn, one by Don Welch, one by Steven Osterlund. Later I did an anthology called *The Windflower Home Almanac of Poetry* which I really liked and have thought of reprinting. Then a pretty successful one called *As Far as I Can See: Contemporary Writers of the Great Plains*. Windflower was never a very serious publishing enterprise. I didn't want to throw that much time or money into it. I do think it performed a small service for a time. I was able to keep Bill Kloefkorn's *Alvin Turner as Farmer* and *Uncertain the Final Run to Winter* in print, for example.

Stephen Meats: Now, besides your teaching and publishing, you have another very rare opportunity, as Poet Laureate of the United States, to do something of benefit to poetry and poets. What do you hope to accomplish in this job?

Ted Kooser: I'd like to try to expand the audience for poetry, if even just a little, by showing people that poems need not be intimidatingly difficult. My major project is a weekly newspaper column, to be issued at no cost to the papers, in which I'll present a poem by an American poet with a few lines of introduction and the proper acknowledgments language. The poems will be examples of the kinds of works I am talking about: understandable yet having something unique to offer. By the time your issue comes out this ought to be up and running.

Stephen Meats: From the viewpoint of where you are now, what does the future of poetry look like in this country? For example, a friend of mine recently told me about seeing fabulous television programs on poetry in London. Do you think it's possible that we might see poetry programs on TV in this country?

Ted Kooser: We make a mistake, I think, in talking about American poetry as if it were one big thing. In fact it is Balkanized, with clearly separated communities that thrive in their own fashion. There is the rap poetry community, the slam poetry community, the cowboy poetry community, the literary poetry community. None of these has much to do with, or interest in, the others, and each is healthy in its own way. The literary poets are never going to persuade, say, the cowboy poets to write literary poems, and the cowboy poets aren't going to start writing literary poems because someone tells them that the literary poems are better. Because the success of TV programs has to do with advertisers, I am not optimistic about TV poetry programs having any kind of endurance. There was quite a good series back maybe 15 years ago, on public TV, called "Anyone for Tennyson," and it seemed to have an audience. But of course it didn't last more than one series of maybe eight programs. And I'd guess there have been others.

Stephen Meats: In your view, what are the biggest threats today to the expansion of poetry's audience?

Ted Kooser: Intentional obscurity and difficulty.

Stephen Meats: I take it from your answer that you place the primary responsibility on the shoulders of poets. Does anyone else share the responsibility with them, even if it's to a lesser degree?

Ted Kooser: Readers are consumers, and I suppose one might say that they need to become more sophisticated, but if we were talking about sushi would we tell people who don't like sushi that they ought to become more sophisticated?

Stephen Meats: What's your view of federal support for individual poets, poetry programs, and poetry publishing? Has it been helpful, harmful? Should there be more, less?

Ted Kooser: I am for funding for all the arts, at a level Congress will support. I don't think there's been any harm done by past funding.

Stephen Meats: Do you think your service as Poet Laureate is having, or will have, any effect on your writing?

Ted Kooser: I have been too busy to write poems and I doubt if I'll have time for it until I've completed my term and can get back into my usual routines. But I am not upset about this. I've written lots of poems and nobody's holding their breath waiting for one or two more.

Stephen Meats: Many of your poems deal with the subjects of old age and death. Has this always been true of your work?

Ted Kooser: Yes, I think it has. I have been thinking about the lives of the old all my life.

Stephen Meats: I know that you value the well-conceived and well-honed metaphor. Do you go looking for the striking figure, or do you depend on chance and coincidence?

Ted Kooser: I have never consciously designed a comparison to fit a situation. I am lucky to have the kind of mind that seems to come up with metaphors quite spontaneously.

Stephen Meats: How important is it, in your opinion, for a poet to indulge experimentation?

Ted Kooser: Artists of all kinds receive support for something they've done and then, because they enjoy success, the tendency is to repeat what they've done. I think we need to be aware of the dangers of receiving praise so that it doesn't begin to shape our artistic lives.

Stephen Meats: Do you find it necessary to write under any special conditions?

Ted Kooser: I just need to have peace and quiet. Part of the advantage of writing early in the morning is that everybody else is still in bed.

Stephen Meats: Do supersititions or rituals play any role in your writing, the way, say, a baseball pitcher wears the same cap all season or takes care not to step on the baseline?

Ted Kooser: No superstitions.

Stephen Meats: How did your recent battle with cancer affect your writing?

Ted Kooser: Actually, I guess we have to quit thinking of it as a recent history, because I have six years going on seven of good health. But of course something like that does change you forever. For one thing, I had spent my share of time worrying about something terrible happening to me, and then it did and I had to ask myself, OK, now what? Now how do you intend to live your life? In my case, the nearness of death made me very aware of everything in the world around me. There's a poem in *Delights & Shadows* called "Surviving" that is about this awareness.

Stephen Meats: What role did writing poetry play in your beating the disease and in your recovery?

Ted Kooser: I don't know that it actually helped with beating the cancer, but it did help me cope with it in that I was able to create a few little packets of order out of a chaotic time.

Stephen Meats: Is there such a thing as a "Ted Kooser poem"? If you had to choose a single poem to represent you (as the editor of an anthology might, for example), which poem would you choose?

Ted Kooser: I think "Etude" in *Weather Central* is a representative Ted Kooser poem.

Stephen Meats: You've just published an entire book of advice for aspiring poets, so this may be asking the impossible, but if you were only able to offer them a sentence or two of guidance, what would you say?

Ted Kooser: The best advice I could give is READ.

Stephen Meats: My final question may seem a little "off the wall" but if you were suddenly to recognize your first car, parked on some side street and evidently back in circulation again, how would you feel?

Ted Kooser: I had a strange experience about twenty years ago. My first car was a '49 Ford coupe, and I lowered the front end, put in an Oldsmobile grill, and pinstriped it. I did a lot of pinstriping for hotrodders when I was a teenager. I was driving on I-80 across Iowa and came up on the back of a coupe just like the one I'd had, and the pinstriping looked like mine. The license plate on the back said ANTIQUE.

Something Just Happens:
A Conversation with Ted Kooser

David Baker

Tim Hofmeister

David Baker: Ted, thanks so much for the chance to talk about your five new poems and about your work as a poet and Poet Laureate of the United States. Tim and I will step in and out with questions for you. I'd like to start with "Success," since it suggests issues relating to the public service of the laureate. Is it true that these five poems are the first you wrote and published since the laureateship?

Ted Kooser: Yes, that's right. While I was poet laureate I had very little time for writing, and these five poems are among a few that I felt worth publishing.

David Baker: Let's look at the poem here. This is "Success."

> I can feel the thick yellow fat of applause
> building up in my arteries, friends,
> yet I go on, a fool for adoration. Do I care
> that when it sloughs off it is likely to go
> straight to the brain? I am already showing
> the first signs of poetic aphasia,
> the words coming hard, the synapses
> of metaphor no longer connecting.
> But look at me, down on my knees
> next to the podium, lapping the last drops,
> then rolling in the stain like a dog,
> getting the smell in my good tweed sport coat,
> the grease on my suede elbow patches,
> and for what? Well, for the women I walk past
> the next morning, the ones in the terminal,
> wheeling their luggage, looking so beautifully
> earnest. All for the hope that they will
> suddenly dilate their nostrils, squeeze

the hard carry-on handles, and rise to
the ripening odor of praise with which I have
basted myself, stinking to heaven.

This is one of my favorite new poems of yours. I like it in part because
of the features that I admire in all your best poems—intensity of observa-
tion matched with a casual idiom, self-effacement alongside your obvious
delight in making, and maybe most, your genius for image and metaphor,
metaphor sustained like a metaphysical poet achieving that high trope of
conceit. Here, the conceit is self-basting, celebrity is high cholesterol.

Ted Kooser: I wrote it in fun, to answer all my friends, who kept
asking what it was like to be thrust into celebrity. They knew I am an
introvert, and that it would be difficult for me to be a public figure.

David Baker: For all the obvious good of the laureateship—both
for us and for yourself—we can't ignore the complaint in "Success." I
think about your larger body of poetry, where the typical Kooser hero
or persona is alone, that single soul out in the vast universe of nature
and of others. There's a lone student carrying his heavy backpack
through the hard wind, there's a man in awe of a stormy landscape, on
and on. The pressure on the protagonist of this poem is, of course,
public service. He is ironic and reluctant. But he is also delighted by the
"ripening odor of praise," even though he knows it will be, so to speak,
the death of him.

How did you manage such public life, so many appearances? You
have spent a lifetime in a kind of quiet anonymity in Nebraska. Was this
a shock to your system? Or did the honor override the shock?

Ted Kooser: I guess you might say that the honor overrode the shock.
I was at first terrified, but I decided that if the Librarian of Congress
was willing to take a chance on a poet from the Great Plains, I'd better
do the best job I could. So I threw myself into it and pressed forward.
In the twenty months while I was in the post, I made around two
hundred appearances and did one hundred interviews. I talked to little
groups and big ones, local book clubs and Rotary and Kiwanis groups,
and, of course, to lots of schools, both secondary and college. That
activity continues, and I've made another fifty appearances, I'd guess.

Tim Hofmeister: The laureateship gave you a unique opportunity to look at poetry across the country. I know we want to talk more about this in a minute. But first I want to ask a little more about your work as laureate. In fact, what is the nature of the laureateship? Are there official responsibilities and obligations?

Ted Kooser: The actual obligations are few. The laureate is asked to give a public reading at the opening of each term, in October, and a lecture at the close of the season, in May. In between the laureate has the privilege of giving away two Witter Bynner Fellowships of $10,000 to promising poets. It's optional, but you can also bring poets to read at the Library of Congress, where they're recorded for posterity. Again, I took on a whole lot in addition to these basics. One of the most pleasurable things I did was invite the singer-songwriter John Prine to the Library to talk about writing songs. I interviewed him on stage in the Coolidge Auditorium and he was the first folksinger who had been there since Woody Guthrie in the 1930s. You can see that interview on the Library's Web site, www.loc.gov.

By the way, the laureateship is in no way connected with the presidency, the executive branch, or even with Congress. Congress appropriates no money for it. It is a privately endowed program at the Library of Congress. I suppose that if the laureate were summoned to the White House and asked to write a poem for the president, somebody might want to do that. Not this guy. I did have one similar opportunity. I had an e-mail one day from a group of Cheney supporters saying if I would be willing to write a poem for Dick Cheney's birthday. And I responded that I would not be available on that occasion. And then after I hit the send button, I realized that there was no date in the invitation at all.

Tim Hofmeister: Did you realize you could've had some fun forwarding that e-mail?

Ted Kooser: I guess it didn't occur to me to do that. I wanted it out of the house as quickly as possible. But the thing is, actually, even if it had happened to be a politician I respected a great deal, I couldn't write a poem like that. Occasional poems simply do not work, and I don't like writing poems on request. I had written a few things for people's weddings and they're okay for that *one* moment, but as works of art, they just don't hold up.

David Baker: But that is one of the features of the British poet laureate, isn't it? They are obliged to do poems on command and for occasions. That may be—I looked this up—why we no longer remember the work of Laurence Eusden, Colley Cibber, Henry James Pyre, and some of the other less famous laureates from Britain.

Ted Kooser: And they do it for, I think, a small keg or butt of sherry. Yes, well, we'd all agree that the laureates in America have it a lot better.

Tim Hofmeister: I'd like to ask what you felt you've learned from being poet laureate about the state of poetry in the United States.

Ted Kooser: I became convinced fairly early that there is an enormous audience available to use as writers if we want to approach them, to bring them back. There are people who had poetry ruined for them in the public school by teachers who said, "The following poem has a meaning that I want you to dig out. I have it written down in the back of my Teacher's Guide." And so we fell upon poems as if they were walnuts we had to crack—rather than seeing poems as pleasurable experiences that we can take into our lives and use however we wish. A poem does not have to have *a meaning*!

I don't want to disparage all English teachers because lots of them do wonderful jobs with this kind of thing and really should be sainted. Everywhere I went when I gave a reading—and my work, for those of you who don't know it, is that I really work hard to make it available to kind of a broad, general audience—anyways, everywhere I went, someone would come up after the reading, some guy in the back, with his thumbs in his belt, and say, "My wife dragged me to this thing and you couldn't have gotten me to go to a poetry reading for anything, but I want you to know I had a good time and I'm going to give this po- etry stuff a chance." Modernism, the poetry of the twentieth century, beginning at about World War I, did its best to exclude a lot of readers by its difficulty, its elitism.

Tim Hofmeister: I know you've said there are different kinds of poetry in the United States. Don't you think that's a healthy thing in the United States?

Ted Kooser: Absolutely. I was saying somewhat facetiously that people will, from time to time, ask a question about the "state of American poetry." You can't really talk about it that way because you have these various groups doing things. You have the cowboy poets who are perfectly happy doing what they are doing. They have this big meeting in Nevada every year and they have a wonderful time. You have the rap poets who have a big following; you have the hip-hop. You know, all these various groups. All of them are thriving within their groups and they really don't have too much interest in each other.

Shortly after I was named poet laureate, I thought, "I'm going to go to the National Cowboy Poetry thing in Elko, Nevada. That ought to be fun." So I called up the Western Folklife Association that runs it and said I was just appointed Poet Laureate of the United States and I'd like to come to the Elko thing. And the response was, "So what!" They don't care about the Poet Laureate of the United States; they've got their own thing going. All those groups are there, and they are *thriving*. The only group that thinks everyone should be writing like them is us, the literary poets.

David Baker: Let me ask you something related to that. We're talking about school. We're all working in schools. And now you're talking about what happens to poetry in schools. Here are two passages I want to read for your response. This is from Jerry Thompson in the *Yale Review*: "Nabokov wrote that 'Art consists of specific details and not the general ideas Americans are taught from High School to look for in works of art.' He's unquestionably right; the difference between art and commonplace expression is in the last five percent of rigor." And this is Paul Kane: "Since virtually all literary themes can be reduced to commonplaces, there is clearly something other than cognitive content that attracts us."

I'm interested in what that other thing *is*. We get good at asking our students to find the theme of this or that poem. We take a beautiful poem and reduce it to its theme. You know: Nature is awful, nature is beautiful, we are all silly people doomed by fate or culture . . . . So what is it that we're missing in the treatment of poetry in school? What is that "thing" that makes the poem more than its testable content?

Ted Kooser: I think we respond to poems the same way we respond to works in a gallery. We walk through a gallery; we may not be crazy about abstract expressionism, but we turn the corner in a gallery and there is an abstract expressionist painting, and there's something that just happens to us, and this is an individual, a private response. There are poems that will immediately move us, emotionally move us. And we don't need to know exactly why that happens. I mean we can, upon analysis, figure it out: what is it about that painting that makes it so thrilling, but we have to use language to do that, and our response to a painting is not in languages but in the viscera, in the heart.

Allen Grossman has a beautiful poem called "Two Waters." It's one of my favorites. On this farm he's talking about, there are two kinds of water: the water that drained into the cistern from melting snow and falling rain and then the well water, which is of a different character. I think the reason that I love the poem so much is because that's the way it was at my grandparents' home. They had a cistern and a well. It's beautifully written but it also seems to be written for me. I bring my own experience to the poem. I don't know whether that's a decent answer.

David Baker: It's a fine answer. Your illustration about understanding poetry uses the example of an art gallery. Does your own work as a painter affect your poetry? Are your paintings miniatures, too, like the poems?

Ted Kooser: I do often paint very small paintings, five inches by seven, say, even smaller. I think a big part of making art of any kind is an attempt to secure order, and there can be a lot of pleasure in making something small and orderly.

Tim Hofmeister: I'd like to get back to the issue of audience again, as well. I guess my question would be, "How do we get more people to come out to the poetry readings?"

Ted Kooser: Well, people will read and enjoy poetry and go to poetry readings as long as those experiences are pleasurable. We have to remember that pleasure is an important thing to human beings. We all want to have a pleasurable experience, but to go to a reading where you're sitting in the audience for sixty minutes and someone is reading and not saying anything that you understand in any way is an altogether unpleasant experience. That has happened to a lot of people because of the difficulty and obscurity that evolved in the twentieth century.

In building a readership for poetry we have to think of having fun with little children. I really do believe children will be lifelong readers of poetry if we will spend time showing them that it is fun when they are small. A lot of teachers are very good at that, and poets like Shel Silverstein and Dr. Suess can provide material. Their work shows that poetry can be fun.

But all too often what happens is that Ms. Smith in the eighth grade says that the meaning of this poem is not what you said it is; in fact you get a D today because you didn't get the meaning right. So everybody gets out of school and they see a poem in the *New Yorker* and they go, "Ahh, I don't have to do that anymore, I got a D in that."

David Baker: I want to ask you more about this, the issue of availability. I am thinking about your own style and clarity, the simplicity of style in your poetry. I wonder whether you might agree with this little sentence of Edmund Burke. Burke says that "a clear idea is another name for a little idea."

Ted Kooser: No, I would not agree. It's great fun not to agree with Edmund Burke.

David Baker: I thought that is what you might say. Let me trace the tendency toward simplicity back a little farther. Your own style is a plain style or colloquial style, where the lyric poem is stripped down, image driven, and narrative based. So, I'm thinking of the American appeal to simplicity that runs all the way back to William Bradford, the first governor of Plymouth. In referring to the need for simplicity in his own language, he says "as by the scriptures we are plainly told." He extols the virtue of simplicity or plainness. This is embedded in our national character, even our politics and religion, and of course in one strain of our poetry.

Ted Kooser: That Shaker song, "T'is a Gift to Be Simple," might make a good thing to tack up over a writing desk. One of the most influential books for me as a writer is the Strunk and White *Elements of Style*. That book puts a lot of emphasis on the virtues of clarity and simplicity.

David Baker: Let me ask you to respond to one last quotation. This is Helen Vendler. And the question again is about style, your own. Vendler says that "a writer's true vision lies in the implications of his or her style." Now, as you think about what your style is or what you hope it is, do you see a connection between style and something larger, like vision?

Ted Kooser: That's very interesting. I'm not sure what Miss Vendler means, but I do think that style is an extension of personality. I am comfortable, as a person, with the style of my poems, if that makes any sense at all. I am saying poems out of my heart, and this feels harmonious with the person who I am. I tend to be someone who writes with a great deal of sentiment. I'm willing to take that risk at a time when people are suspicious of sentimental poetry. But I think that is what I need to do as a poet.

David Baker: Do you think your vision, then, is a social one? Or at least, do you think your style is crafted to be more available and public, rather than exclusive and academic?

Ted Kooser: Yes, absolutely. Let me turn back to this problem we have with excluding audience. I'd like to be on record as saying that anybody can write a poem that nobody can understand. That's really easy. On the other hand, it might be really hard to write a poem that everyone in a room found meaning in. I would fail at that, even though I would like to reach out to everyone in this room.

Tim Hofmeister: I have a question that relates to these issues—of the poet's ability to reach a broad audience, to speak or write in ways that are inclusive versus exclusive. "Availability" doesn't necessarily equate to "ease." Some of your poems that seem accessible are also challenging. I'm thinking of poems like "Praying Hands." You write a lot about hands, but here the hands are a made object. They are akin to particular objects in other poems—broken-down rural churches, off roadside shrines—with some religious connotation. I wonder why these objects keep coming back into the poetry. My first guess is that they have something to do with what David calls the Midwestern social text; these objects are a part of the community and they need to be represented.

Ted Kooser: I'm not a traditional believer in any manner of speaking, but I do go to church, I go to different churches. I like sitting with a group of people for about an hour who I imagine are thinking in the right direction. The denomination means nothing to me; it's the idea of being in a community. People who are actually spending some time thinking about their spiritual life.

When I was younger I was extremely intolerant of people who were devout believers. I have come to believe that nearly everyone is trying to live a good life, and this may be tremendously Pollyanna-ish of me to think this. There are a few evil people in the world and they cause a lot of trouble, but nearly everyone is trying to live a good life despite ignorance and poverty and the worst kind of circumstances.

Several years ago, I went to a wedding where the brother of the bride was a jailor in Texas, at the county facility that processes all the prisoners going to their executions in Huntsville. Now as you know—I hope you know—Texas executes maybe a hundred and fifty people a year, and Huntsville is where that happens. So these prisoners are coming to this county facility to be processed before they are sent on to death row. I said, "How many of these people are genuinely evil?" He said, "Ted, maybe one or two out of one hundred." He said the rest of them have just made stupid choices.

We might make fun of someone with a *Praying Hands* plaque on his wall. But I'm for kindness and tolerance toward all of these things; they're part of what we have and who we are. The world is too short of kindness.

Tim Hofmeister: You write quite a few poems about nature and seem to imply there is an order of things in nature. By contrast, in "The Red Wing Church," there's a sort of comedy going on. The church is all busted up, it's disintegrating and you find the pews on everybody's porches around town, and the cross is God knows where. On the other hand, in a passage from *Local Wonders* you carefully depict the Mennonite women, whose community is intact, and you invest them with a lot of respect. You begin by saying, "A person needn't be fearful of sixty-five-year-old Mennonite women in white lace caps." This implies, correctly, I think, that there is a lot of fear on the part of many people of other people who are like the Mennonite women.

Ted Kooser: I know nothing about the Mennonite religion really. All I have to draw on is that when I go into the store and those women are behind the counter, I like the way they count out the change. They're so careful not to cheat me of a penny. We really have a wonderful country full of lots of fascinating, beautiful people. I think we have a lot of stupidity in our leaders, but most of the people, I think, are pretty good people, doing as best they can.

Tim Hofmeister: A certain kind of poetic approach can challenge a reader with a vision of inclusion, and at a time when the country is divided in so many ways—Nascar Nation, *New Yorker* Nation, and so on. It's as if we've reached a point where people want to say, thanks to social stratification or the legal system or whatever, we are finally immune from one another. A sad view, really, which I find your poems often subvert.

David Baker: These issues—of clarity, inclusion, public utility—must be related to your work with "American Life in Poetry." Would you say something about that? How did your project get started? What have been your goals? And what do you see for the future of the project?

Ted Kooser: My wife is in the newspaper business, and for years she and I had been talking about how one might get poetry back into the papers. There was a time when lots of newspapers printed poetry. It was her idea to let papers use the column for free. She didn't think that, on the lean budgets which newspapers now operate, many could pay even five dollars a week. We wanted it to be free. After I was made poet laureate I approached the Poetry Foundation. Without them it couldn't have happened. They were behind the creation of the Web site and they continue to maintain it. And they have given me enough money to pay for a halftime assistant editor and a graduate assistant. I get no money from them, but that's fine. I am a volunteer. The column has been very successful, and at the time of this interview we have about four million readers. We have been published in around three hundred papers. I plan to keep the column going as long as I can, and, of course, as long as the Poetry Foundation continues to support it. What the column accomplishes is to show American newspaper readers that poetry is not something they need to fear, that there are poems that can be understood and appreciated.

David Baker: Let's backtrack now—to before the laureateship and the Pulitzer. Once upon a time, you were an insurance man back home in Lincoln. How did your work in business affect the poetry?

Ted Kooser: I believe that writers write for perceived communities, and that if you are a lifelong professor of English, it's quite likely that you will write poems that your colleagues would like, that is, poems that will engage that community. I worked every day with people who didn't read poetry, who hadn't read it since they were in high school, and I wanted to write for them. I am not looking for an audience of literary professionals, though it's nice when some of them like what I'm doing.

David Baker: And you retired, I think, around 2000?

Ted Kooser: In mid-1998 I was diagnosed with a squamous cell tongue carcinoma that had spread into my neck. I never returned to work after that. I was able to retire at age sixty about six months later, after an extensive sick leave. I'm delighted to say that I am cured now, I'm well, but it was a bad thing to go through. And it was the end of my insurance career, but I have never missed it for a minute.

As I began to come out of that illness, the University of Nebraska asked me to do some more teaching. I had, from time to time, taught as an adjunct. So they brought me in as a visiting professor. Later I was made Presidential Professor and given a renewable contract. Anyway, the insurance career was over in 1999. I had been just doing what I do, writing poems and painting pictures and doing a little bit of teaching. Then this poet laureate thing came out of the blue and I decided it was an opportunity to make some statements about poetry. I took this on and I worked pretty much seven days a week for two years. It was very important for me to show that someone from Nebraska could do that kind of work.

Tim Hofmeister: That's a pretty amazing commitment of time and energy. Are you still working so hard?

Ted Kooser: Now that I am out of office, I feel a bit more able to say "no" to things even though I am always honored when I am asked to come to some civic group or something or other like that. I still do a lot of that. But I'm trying to say "no" a little more because I need to get back to doing some writing and quiet down a little. I keep my calendar on a word processing document; and at the height of my activity, I had five pages of things to do, single spaced. It's down to about two and a half now. Over the next year or so, I hope to get back to where I can spend more time at home where I write best, and I can do some painting. I'm still teaching. I teach once a year in the fall semester, just one class, and I'll keep doing that. And then my newspaper column is something that doesn't take up a great deal of time, but I do have to put regular time on that during the week.

David Baker: So now, what is a normal day like for you, what is your habit and what do you expect out of yourself?

Ted Kooser: Well, all those years when I was at the insurance company, I learned that if I was going to do any writing at all, I had to do it early in the morning. And I got up at 4:30 A.M. every day, and I would write until maybe 7:00. Then I would get in and out of the shower and get my suit and tie on and go off to the insurance company. And I have continued that all these years. You know, once you get used to getting up at 4:30 in the morning, that's when you get up. My dogs are used to getting up at that time and if I don't get up, they're usually bothering me to get up. So I get up every morning and sit in the same chair every morning, with my coffee pot at hand and write in a notebook.

And I am a dismal failure as a writer twenty-eight days out of thirty. It's just junk when I'm done, after my two or three hours at it. But I've learned that unless I'm sitting there with my notebooks, on the day when the good one comes, I'm never going to get it at all. So I have to show up for work, which is one of the important things about doing this kind of work, or doing really any work.

Here is a little anecdote. This happened just before Thansgiving one year. I had broken an overhead door in one of the outbuildings on my farm and I went to the lumberyard to find a part for it. Here was this older guy who knows where things are, and he's sorting through all these boxes, and we started to talk about Thanksgiving coming. He said it was going to be a warm Thanksgiving and so he was going to pitch horseshoes after Thanksgiving dinner. I said something about horseshoe pitching and about the fact that I had an uncle with cerebral palsy who could barely walk but who could pitch horseshoes. He said, "Yeah, my uncle Ed was Tri-State Horseshoe Pitching Champion three years running, and I said to my uncle, 'Uncle Ed, how did you get so good?' And he said, 'Son, you gotta pitch a hundred shoes a day.'"

That's what it takes to get good at anything. You've got to be in there pitching horseshoes every day. If at the end of the year I've written ten poems that I think are really effective, then it's been a really good year for me—six to ten.

David Baker: How do you *know* your good poems? How do they assert themselves or stand out from the other ones? In horseshoes, it's clear. The thrower hears the ping and sees the shoe around the peg.

Ted Kooser: Sometimes I don't know. I have a sense of the quality of the work when it's finished. Maybe it's a ping. I want every part to snap into place at some point and become a whole. That poem "Success" is a good example. Or a poem David has written about, "Etude," which is as strong a poem as I've ever written. From the minute I wrote it I was delighted with it, with finishing it. I remember thinking, "Did I just write this thing?" I was astounded at the way it came together. So you have the feeling every once in a while when it all comes together and it feels like more than itself somehow.

David Baker: On those two poems, can you say what it is that came together, or why a particular poem may seem like your best one?

Ted Kooser: I think what happens is in that extended metaphor. The power is in having its parts, its vehicle and tenor, greatly separated and then moved into a relationship. In "Etude," we have a bird, a blue heron, and we have a guy sitting in a blue suit at a desk. It's a big stretch to make. And if you try a stretch like that with a metaphor, and you can't hold it up, it will just sag and fall away. It happens that in that poem I was somehow able to make it work. I do believe that a lot of this material or connection comes forth by dictation; something deep in me, something that I'm not really in control of. If I knew how to write a poem like that, I would do it every day. But I can't. What happens in my favorite ones is that, toward the end of the poem, the metaphor makes a circle, it goes way out here, way at this guy at the desk, and it comes back at the point where I say, "this pencil poised the air like the beak of a bird." Back we'll go to the heron and then it's all over. The figure is complete.

I have no idea how I wrote that, but I had to be sitting there for a long time to do it just so.

David Baker: We have talked a lot about plainness. But in some way, your best poems move beyond conventional definitions of the plain. I am thinking of what you have described just now, that sustained and pushed metaphor. Isn't that a very fanciful figurative metaphysical conceit, where you take an image and push it into a metaphor and take the metaphor and push it into a pattern, and push the pattern as far as it will possibly go until it nearly breaks? That's the way you were talking about the heron poem and that's what I see in "Success" and, really, the other four poems here. "Success" is not an imagist poem so much as a poem of conceit. "Two Men on an Errand" works that way, too. It develops an image—the men waiting at an auto repair shop—but pushes the whole image into metaphor and the metaphor into sustained conceit. There's a "foam rubber sandal," which seems like a car tire, and the older man "steering with his cane." And much more. This extends far beyond the simplicity of an isolated image. It seems to me, in some way, not plain at all. Is that a fair thing to say, or is that an insult?

Ted Kooser: No, it isn't plain in the common sense, and I thank you for describing it so clearly. I think one thing about working with metaphor this way is that you want both sides to work perfectly well together. It's a matter of paring away things that won't work in the comparison and being sure that the only things in the comparison are ones that play on both sides. Often, most of my work goes into fine tuning the central metaphor.

David Baker: You pare away? So perhaps you achieve the kind of plainness or economy even in the way you construct patterns of metaphor. No waste, even in elaboration.

Tim Hofmeister: It almost seems as though the breaking point between plain style and another kind of style is metaphor. But maybe you're saying it's more the way you manage the metaphor?

Ted Kooser: I don't know, Tim. I guess plain style is there in that I'm going for simplicity and plainness and clarity.

David Baker: The rhetoric is plain, the idiom. That's the virtue of the plain style in your poems. But the application of the metaphor, the pushing of the metaphor into extended conceit, that's the thing I like, that sort of irony, that pull of those two polarities. What we think of as usually different kinds of rhetoric. It shoves the image beyond its economical spare use.

Tim Hofmeister: I'm thinking of a passage in *Local Wonders* where you're talking to your postman. Your postman has seen one of your poems and also some mention of your poetry and he reluctantly says, "They say you have a gift for metaphor." What exactly does that mean? What I like about that passage is you work through with him what metaphor is and what metaphor does. And that contributes to a step in his understanding of what you're about.

Ted Kooser: I can't remember exactly how that passage goes, but the mailman had stopped me by the side of the road and said he read on the back of a book that I was a "master of metaphor" and he said, "What does that mean?" I said, "Well, you know, a metaphor is a kind of comparison of things." He said, "You mean when I say such and such and was like, it was like… well, you know what I mean." I said, "Yeah, that's right."

Tim Hofmeister: Do we have a natural gift for metaphor and to what extent, do you think?

Ted Kooser: No, all of us don't have a natural gift for metaphor. I happened to be blessed with an imagination that leans in that direction. I've worked with a lot of students who have learned to write poems that exclude metaphors because they are just no good at it. You cannot deliberately construct a metaphor. It arises in the process of writing. It always comes as a marvelous surprise when it arrives. Just like that "Etude" poem, you think, "Where did that come from?" A student will show me a poem and say, "Don't you think I ought to put a metaphor right about there?" As if you could go to Circuit City and buy one and plug it in. I am immensely grateful that I was given an imagination that has the associative side to it.

Tim Hofmeister: You have a wonderful way of sharing it in your poems. This partly has to do with what we are talking about, with that style. I also think about a device you use, which I think we have touched on. Where you say to a reader "you've seen how" and then you lead them into a scene. But you have tension there, too, a tension where you expect a person to say, "Yes, I have seen that."

Ted Kooser: You have to be careful with that kind of "lead-in" phrase. In the poem we're talking about—it's the one about the woman in the wheelchair, in which I say, "You've seen how pianists bend forward to strike the keys, then lift their hands." I can assume when I write like that everyone here has seen pianists do that. I wouldn't say, "You've seen how a man can repair a carburetor on a chainsaw." I couldn't expect you to know that.

There is another poem, the kind of poem that we've been talking about. A poem with an extended metaphor, that I sometimes read in public. It's called "A Washing of Hands." This is what happens to me when I'm working. I try to pay attention to what's going on. I was watching my wife at the sink washing her hands under the water and then flicking her fingers to get the water off.

David Baker: Great. Let's take a look at "A Washing of Hands."

> She turned on the tap and a silver braid
> unraveled over her fingers.
> She cupped them, weighing that tassel,
> first in one hand and then the other,
> then pinched through the threads
> as if searching for something, perhaps
> an entangled cocklebur of water,
> or the seed of a lake. A time or two
> she took the tassel in both hands,
> squeezed it into a knot, wrung out
> the cold and the light, and then, at the end,
> pulled down hard on it twice,
> as if the water were a rope and she was
> ringing a bell to call me, two bright rings,
> though I was there.

Ted Kooser: I love the idea of playing your way into that sort of associative stuff: just a braid of water. Those are the kinds of poems I really love to write because I am always so thrilled when they work. And let down when they fail.

David Baker: This poem again is a single conceit, or rather, a poem whose metaphor keeps transforming into another version of itself. There's the cocklebur, and then the seed of the lake, and then the tassel, the knot, the rope. These images aren't exactly cognitively connected; it's more about the magic, the leap of an associative imagination.

Ted Kooser: Yes, it's me following my imagination as it plays, and writing down some of that play, but not all of it. In a poem like that I will usually have deleted some of the play if it doesn't seem to enhance the effect. I like your use of the word *magic*, because when those metaphors come to me, unbidden, it feels magical.

David Baker: What do you see as the most helpful movements in contemporary poetry? You are right, earlier, when you point out so many fields and schools and types. A poetry for every audience. There is a loud din in the small world of poetry. What do you foresee?

Ted Kooser: I am not much of a scholar, and no cultural historian, but I hope time will somehow preserve the poems that have real meaning for broad groups of people, not just for literary professionals. Sir Thomas Beecham once said that he thought composers should write music that chauffeurs and delivery boys could whistle. Elsewhere he said that unless composers write music that organ grinders can play it will never be immortal.

David Baker: What are you working on now? I know—the "American Life in Poetry" project. But how about your poems? Are you writing? Do you see a new collection in the future?

Ted Kooser: I am slowly assembling a small stack of poems I'm pleased with, and the ones in the *Kenyon Review* are part of that, but I think it will be five or six years before I have another book ready. I don't want to publish anything that isn't at least as well done as *Delights & Shadows*. Right now, I could get just about anything published because my name is well known. But it would be stupid to use that celebrity as a way of getting inferior work published. Others have done that and it's a mistake.

Tim Hofmeister: I wonder if you have any final things you'd like to say—about your work, or the wider state of poetry?

Ted Kooser: Poetry has meant a great deal to me for almost fifty years, and I have been immensely lucky with my poems, to have them noticed and appreciated. I have a happy writing life and I am thankful.

The First Order of Wonders:
An Interview with Ted Kooser

William Barillas

Recent years have been good to Ted Kooser. He received two of the highest honors that can be given to an American poet: he served two terms as United States Poet Laureate (2004-2006), and he won the 2005 Pulitzer Prize for Poetry for his book *Delights & Shadows*. These accolades brought Kooser, who has had a long and distinguished career, to a much larger national readership. There is a kind of justice in these events, as Kooser has always written poetry with a diverse, nonacademic audience in mind. As Dana Gioia has said of him in *Can Poetry Matter: Essays on Poetry and American Culture*, "There is to my knowledge no poet of equal stature who writes so convincingly in a manner the average American can understand and appreciate." Accessibility, clarity, and the transformation of ordinary experiences by means of startling metaphors: These are the distinguishing characteristics of Ted Kooser's poetry.

It is also notable for its origins in small-town, rural Nebraska, where Kooser makes his home. He gives voice to a region known by many readers only in the fiction of Willa Cather, or perhaps the non-fiction of Mari Sandoz. In announcing Kooser's appointment as poet laureate on August 12, 2004, Librarian of Congress James H. Billington said, "Ted Kooser is a major poetic voice for rural and small town America and the first Poet Laureate chosen from the Great Plains. His verse reaches beyond his native region to touch on universal themes in accessible ways."

Although Kooser is a part-time professor of English at the University of Nebraska-Lincoln, he made his living as an insurance executive at Lincoln Benefit Life, writing poetry in the early morning and whenever he found a spare moment. Since retiring, he has survived a bout with cancer and continued to publish books of poetry, including *Flying at Night: Poems 1965-1985* and *Braided Creek*, his collaboration with Jim Harrison. His nonfiction includes two writing guides and *Local Wonders: Seasons in the Bohemian Alps*, which evokes the country near Garland, Nebraska, where he lives with his wife, Kathleen Rutledge, editor of the *Lincoln Journal Star*. His project as poet laureate, the poetry column, "American Life in Poetry," continues to appear in newspapers around the country and online at www.americanlifein-poetry.org.

William Barillas: Your poetry has done pretty well lately. You received the Pulitzer Prize and served two years as U.S. Poet Laureate.

Ted Kooser: It has been a surprising time for me. Ten years ago I didn't know if 1 would be alive in six months. 1 was really sick, and then all of this wonderful stuff happened. It's quite miraculous.

William Barillas: To begin, I'd like to ask about your early years in Ames, Iowa.

Ted Kooser: I was born in 1939, so by the time I was really awake to the world it was the postwar period, the Eisenhower years. Looking back, Ames seems idyllic, in a Norman Rockwell kind of way. We had huge elm trees and a park three blocks from where I lived where they had band concerts on summer nights. We had little makeshift parades on Memorial Day.

As a teenager I was obsessively interested in automobiles. I built hot rods and did a lot of drag racing. I didn't think much beyond that. It was all about hot cars and girlfriends, like in my poem "Hometown," where I describe myself wearing Levi's, boots with chains, a leather jacket, and duck's ass hair. Ames was populated with a lot of professors' families, whose children we called the popular kids. We hot-rodders were on the other side, getting in trouble, smoking cigarettes.

William Barillas: What started you writing as an adolescent?

Ted Kooser: One of my primary motivations was girls. I didn't have much else going for me. I didn't have athletic ability. I couldn't play any instruments in the band. I thought being a writer would make me interesting and mysterious.

William Barillas: Your first book, *Official Entry Blank*, was published in 1969. When did you start working on the poems that appeared in it?

Ted Kooser: Around 1959. l had a couple good friends, outsiders, in Ames. One was Jim Stevens, who went on to success in electronics and telecommunications in Seattle. The other was Jack Winkler, who was a history major. The three of us were interested in the Beat movement. Jim had a little house, and I spent a lot of my time there trying to be a beatnik. I wrote the first poems I was serious about while squatting on Jim's living room floor, drinking beer. In 1960 I was the editor of the student literary magazine at Iowa State; I published some things in that.

William Barillas: What led you toward writing about the life around you rather than more arcane subjects?

Ted Kooser: It was Karl Shapiro's influence, mostly. I had come to Nebraska because Karl was here; I wanted to study with him. I talked to him a great deal about William Carlos Williams. So Shapiro and Williams writing about ordinary life—they were my touchstones. If I was going to write about ordinary life and ordinary things, I was going to do it about what was right under my nose, which was the Great Plains and the life we have here.

William Barillas: Of all the poems in your first book, *Official Entry Blank*, only one made it into *Sure Signs: New and Selected Poems*, and that was "Abandoned Farmhouse." What distinguished that poem in your mind?

Ted Kooser: Of all my poems it's the one that appears most frequently in anthologies. It has stood the test of time. Many other poems in my first book are clearly derivative of Williams and other poets I was copying. But that one does seem very much my own. It's an experience I've had again and again, hanging around abandoned farmsteads and picking up things and looking at them.

William Barillas: The image of abandoned buildings on the plains appears in a number of your poems. ls it a metaphor or a synecdoche for the history of the Great Plains?

Ted Kooser: Who knows exactly why I was attracted to those things? For one thing I was an architecture major as an undergraduate; I was always interested in buildings. I have always drawn pictures of old farm-houses. In *The Poetry Home Repair Manual*, I tell a story about how import-ant reading Walter de la Mare's "The Listeners" was to me. It has a scene in which a man rides up to an empty house and hammers on the door and no one is there. There was a wonderful mystery about that poem that I liked. In a way, I've been rewriting "The Listeners" all of these years.

William Barillas: I'd like to ask about your desire to write for a wide audience. Where does that come from?

Ted Kooser: I like the idea of being of some use to a broad, general community, including people who live around me here in the country. I love the idea of writing poems the guy right down the road would ap-preciate. I've been thinking quite a bit about this lately. What is it about a popular song that makes people remember lines from it? Or even be able to sing the whole song? The music aside, it's that the lyrics supply useful language to people who may never have been able to articulate a certain feeling. They pick up on a phrase from a song, and it becomes a part of their personal vocabulary. I would like to do that in poems. I would like to provide language people can use in daily life.

I had John Prine come to the Library of Congress because I so ad-mire his lyric writing. He writes with tremendous respect about ordinary people. There's no sneering whatsoever in Prine's work. He has a wonder-ful song that goes, "There's a big old goofy man / Dancing with a big old goofy girl / Ohh baby / It's a big old goofy world." That could be done in a sneering way, but Prine does it with respect, and wonder, even. There are marvelous lines in popular music that as a poet I wish I had written. Kris Kristofferson has a line: "Maybe I'll never believe in forever again." That is the kind of phrase people all over the country could be packing around with them and using. I'd like to be of service in that way.

William Barillas: What qualities make for good poets, the kind of poets you admire?

Ted Kooser: Jim Harrison, who is one of my best friends: The per-sonal characteristic Jim has that makes him a very attractive writer is, he is an extraordinarily generous man. He wants to give something to the reader, something of use, but he never condescends. I like that about his work.

William Barillas: How did you get to know him and start a correspondence?

Ted Kooser: When he was working on his novel *Dalva*, he came to Nebraska to do research at the Historical Society. He was looking through boxes of old photographs there and John Carter, the photo curator, got to be friends with him and eventually introduced us.

William Barillas: Very few poets co-write a book with another poet. How did you and Harrison come to collaborate on *Braided Creek*?

Ted Kooser: We had no idea we were writing a book; we were just sending poems back and forth. At some point Jim mentioned we might have a collection. Although those poems appear to be sequential, I arranged them all. I had them on three-by-five cards in two long strips going into the bedroom and out to the far wall of the living room. I kept moving them around until I got them into an order that had a movement to it. One of the reasons readers can't identify which of us is writing what is that I didn't just alternate between Jim and myself. I used two by Jim, one by me, three by Jim, two by me—that sort of thing. We were so closely in tune that there are a few poems neither of us remembers who wrote.

William Barillas: The poems resemble haiku; each has two to four lines and conveys a single image or idea. How did the two of you get into that?

Ted Kooser: Both of us have been interested for years in the Asian poets. And there is a pithiness to haiku that works well in a letter. In the fall and winter of 1998 into 1999, I was also sending Jim the poems that turned into *Winter Morning Walks*. The two books developed at the same time. The intent with *Winter Morning Walks* was not necessarily to correspond, but to prove to myself I was well enough to write a poem every day and stick it in the mail.

William Barillas: Does *Winter Morning Walks* suggest poetry is about survival?

Ted Kooser: Poetry can be a way of identifying and preserving order in chaotic times. When I was desperately ill, trying to get back my health, writing poetry helped me identify a little area of order about the size of a postcard. I could make that much order every day out of my world, which was in great disorder. The same thing happened to many people who responded to September 11 by writing poems. I see that as their attempt to make order out of chaos.

William Barillas: You often take a seemingly ordinary subject and transform it through metaphor. Have you written a poem that achieves what you are after in using metaphor?

Ted Kooser: One of the better of that type is "Etude," in *Weather Central*, which I begin by talking about a great blue heron and then move into the image of a man in a blue suit at his desk writing a love letter. I reel in the metaphor at the end, with the man holding his pencil in the air like the beak of a bird. I often use that poem as an example of working with metaphor.

William Barillas: So it is a matter of introducing the connection, developing the actual subject, and then returning?

Ted Kooser: Yes. A metaphorical poem won't work if it just flies off and stays there. You have to ground it again; you have to pull it back. Writing with figures is like tying a knot in a rope. You begin the poem with one strand and then you tie in a little figure. Then you go a little farther and tie another little figure into it. Many failed poems are just catalogs of knots. The trick is to run a little thread through the whole poem so that when you get to the end, you pull the thread and all the loops unite into one big knot. After the reader has been captive of the comparison throughout the poem, he or she is released at the end of the poem.

William Barillas: What do people outside of the Great Plains most misunderstand about the region?

Ted Kooser: People say, "You have no culture out there," as if there is one culture everyone should share. But we have a marvelously rich culture here on the plains; it is just based on different things. We may not have the Museum of Modem Art, but we might have a beautiful

Catholic church in a small town, or tractor pulls and county fairs and small-town parades. It is just a different kind of culture. I don't know that many people out here hanker for something else. You could walk through Omaha, Nebraska, and talk to everybody on the streets and ask them how many people wish they could go to see the Bolshoi Ballet that evening, and you probably wouldn't find very many people interested in going. They have other things they want to do. People tend to be provincial wherever they are. They like what they have. People in Manhattan like what they have, and they have their own provincialism, just as we do.

William Barillas: How would you characterize people who live on the Great Plains?

Ted Kooser: Self-effacement is very important out here. We generally do not put ourselves forward. It is a culture of diffidence.

William Barillas: Soon after being named poet laureate, you executed something of a jujitsu flip on *The New York Times* interviewer who pestered you about not studying European poets. You replied, "Think of all the European poetry I could have read if we hadn't spent all this time on this interview."

Ted Kooser: Well, that interview is only one page in print, but we had been working on it for 10 days by e-mail. The way the interview was printed, it looks as if I am being impatient with her over a few questions, when actually we had been going on like that for days. A lot of people told me, "You really got her," but I wasn't being short. I really did like working with her. It was a very interesting process.

William Barillas: Her questions seemed to typify a coastal view of the interior. Many East Coast intellectuals are attached to Europe and are dismissive of the interior of the United States.

Ted Kooser: Yes, I think there is something to that. It is all part of modernism. T.S. Eliot said all art ought to build upon the art that went before. In order to make art you had to have a deep education. That thinking has been with us for about a hundred years now and will persist. It has a lot of vitality. But the audience I am after does not have that sophistication.

William Barillas: I have written about Midwestern cultural arche-types, such as the tinkerer—the person with practical knowledge about how to invent things, or build them, take them apart, or repair them. In the public imagination the tinkerer is embodied in Edison, Ford, and the Wright brothers, all Midwesterners, but it is also reflected in people's lives and in Midwestern writing. The title in your book, for ex-ample, *The Poetry Home Repair Manual,* strikes me as a very Midwestern way to think about poetry. Does that make sense to you?

Ted Kooser: Yes, I am very much a part of that tinkerer culture. When Jim Harrison met me, here at my house in Garland, one of the first things he said was, "I'll bet you have a couple buckets of bent nails in your barn you're going to straighten someday." And I said, "I do, as a matter of fact." When you live in the country, you don't throw anything away because on any given day you might need to find something and you're not going to drive 20 miles to the hardware store to find it. I have a barn full of miscellaneous stuff: pieces of furnace pipe, fittings, and tools of all kinds. I can fix just about anything myself if I have to. The air-conditioner repairman is here today because that is a little beyond my learning. Given time, though, I would take on an air condi-tioner just to see if I could figure out how to do it. I've built buildings; I've done wiring and plumbing. You're right; tinkering is very much a part of this culture.

William Barillas: In terms of the writing process, how is writing for you like tinkering, whether that be building something, repairing some-thing, or keeping spare parts? What would be the equivalent in your writing process of the bucket of bent nails in the barn?

Ted Kooser: For me writing a poem involves making use of available materials in the locality where I am. I'll make the poem out of whatev-er I can grab up. I'm not going to go to the library and check out *The Golden Bough* when I can make a poem out of available things. Some modernists would go to *The Golden Bough* and install something from it into the poem. I'm not interested in that.

William Barillas: Your newspaper column, "American Life in Poetry," which was your project as poet laureate, seems to have come out of the same ideas about poetry and audience. How did the column come about?

Ted Kooser: You can be poet laureate without doing any projects at all. But it seemed to me this was a great opportunity. For years Kathy and I had been thinking about how to get poetry back into newspapers. My laureateship gave me the authority to pursue that, and the column has been very successful; we are in more than 150 newspapers with a combined circulation of over 11 million readers. I took my idea of the average newspaper reader largely from my wife's experience in news-papers. I looked for poems that would be understandable to that kind of reader. I also looked for short poems because I know newspapers won't print a very long column; they don't want to give that much space. So I worked with 20 lines or less.

William Barillas: What other duties were required as poet laureate?

Ted Kooser: You give an initial reading in October to open the Library's reading series and a speech at the end of May. In February you select a couple of poets to receive the Witter Bynner Fellowships, which are $10,000 apiece, and you introduce the winners when they come to Washington to read. You can invite other people to the library to read as well, and be there to introduce them. Really, the duties are minimal. The rest of the work comes in correspondence and appearances and so on. I made a point right away to contact the National Council of Teachers of English to tell them I wanted to come to their convention. It was a wonderful experience, talking to English teachers about poetry. I went to the American Library Association meeting in Chicago as well. I've done quite a few traditional readings on campuses and that sort of thing. But I prefer to talk to people who are not already in the poetry camp, as a way of extending the reach of poetry. For instance, there is a lot of emphasis in medicine now on healing and the arts. So I arranged to talk to medical schools.

William Barillas: Do you read reviews?

Ted Kooser: No. I find them upsetting one way or the other. I feel terribly hurt by the critical ones, and the ones that praise me make me think, "Oh come on, this is way over the top. I'm not that good a writer." I have friends who are writers who don't read their reviews either.

William Barillas: By now you are beginning to get some scholarly interest. Do you give an eye to that?

Ted Kooser: Yes, but I find it amusing when people draw preposterous conclusions about my work. Perhaps they are right, but the ideas never occurred to me. Somebody wrote to me and said, "I noticed you often use the color blue in your poems. Why is that?" I responded, "I didn't realize I was doing that but it is my favorite color." It is logical that I would use it. In the issue of *The Midwest Quarterly* devoted to my work (Summer 2005, Vol. 46, Issue No. 4), there is an essay in which the writer says a person familiar with my writing can identify the poems I wrote in *Braided Creek*. Then the writer cites a poem that is not one of mine but one of Jim's. I think that is hilarious.

William Barillas: Would you talk about the genesis of a poem? I'm thinking about "Fort Robinson."

Ted Kooser: That is the place in northwestern Nebraska where Crazy Horse was murdered. It was also the scene of the Cheyenne outbreak of 1879. The army had captured Dull Knife and his Northern Cheyenne and kept them in a barracks in the dead of winter with no heat and very little to sustain them. On a very cold January night they broke out of the barracks and ran. They had some arms they had hidden under their clothes, but they were outgunned and many of them were killed.

Fort Robinson is now a historical park; it has all been restored. What happened was I took my young son on a vacation trip. When we pulled in, the grounds crew was poking the magpies out of the trees, I suppose because they mess on the sidewalks. The nestlings fell to the ground and the crew was stomping on them, killing them, and it was horrible. The matted bunches of feathers on the ground and in the grass connected with the memory of the Indians who had been killed there. The poem is a juxtaposition of two times. It is quite different from a lot of my work. Over the years people told me they remember that Fort Robinson poem, even when they don't remember anything else I've written. So it has a different effect. It is something of a history lesson, with a social message that is a little bigger than the topics I usually take on.

William Barillas: The poem ends, "We didn't get out of the car. / My little boy hid in the back and cried / as we drove away, into those ragged buttes the Cheyenne climbed that winter, fleeing."

Ted Kooser: *Fleeing*, of course, meaning my boy and myself as well as the Cheyenne.

William Barillas: Which of your recent poems has caused strong reactions at readings?

Ted Kooser: The poem "At the Cancer Clinic" is one. I read it a lot in public because it is an example of me standing on the outside of things looking in, not identifying myself with an "I," yet being a participant. It is based on an experience I actually had at the cancer clinic in Omaha, in an oncology waiting room, watching a cancer patient, a woman, being helped by two other women, who may have been her sisters. It would be easy to slip into irony in such a poem, but I counter the ironic impulse by saying, "There is no restlessness or impatience / or anger anywhere in sight." That is how it was; everybody in that room was on that woman's side. The part of the poem I like the best is the part that is most closely observed, how the woman watches "each foot swing scuffing forward / and take its turn under her weight."

I gave a copy of that poem to my doctor in Omaha, and he had it blown up and framed for the nurses' station in the cancer ward. It hangs on the wall, not in the patients' area but behind where the nurses are, where they put their stuff. I thought that was something; I had been of use with a poem. It was wonderful. There couldn't be a better way to be published. That's what I would love to happen with my work, to have somebody take it into their life and make some use of it. The doctor must have sensed that by where he put it. The poem is about the dignity of medical care. The nurses are not restless or impatient or angry with anyone. They are there to serve. So the poem honors them as well as the patient. I found the people in those waiting rooms were almost beatific in their affirmation of life. Here were people who had lost their hair, people who had to have parts of their faces reconstructed. But they glowed with a love of life that was marvelous. Plenty of people had given up and gone home to die. But the ones in the waiting room, who were working on it, who were going through treatment, really wanted to live. It radiated from them. I have no idea what happened to the woman in the poem, but she was a good example of someone who was struggling to live, leaning on a community to do that.

William Barillas: "At the Cancer Clinic" might be called a love poem for a community. That feeling for community emerges from many poems in *Delights & Shadows*, along with a kind of gentleness. They are quieter than many of your earlier poems. There is a new patience there.

Ted Kooser: Post-cancer, I've become much more patient and tolerant of all kinds of things. In Jim's new book of novellas, *The Summer He Didn't Die*, he cites someone who wrote that 80 percent of people are trying to live as best as they can and 20 percent are not. It serves the book he is writing very well, but I think a much greater percentage are doing the best they can. I went to a wedding 10 years ago in which the brother of the bride was a jailer from a county facility in Texas that processes all the guys who are on their way to death row at Huntsville, where they are executed by the hundreds. I asked, "How many of those guys are genuinely evil?" and he said, "Maybe two or three out of a hundred are evil. The rest just made stupid choices." I believe that most people try to live a good life, but they just screw up monumentally. They're up against enormous odds. But most people are trying to be good.

A Conversation with Ted Kooser

Chapman Hood Frazier

Chapman Hood Frazier: I noticed that the poem, "Four Civil War Paintings by Winslow Homer" was your only series of poems in *Delights & Shadows*. Tell us about how you composed these poems? Did you actually begin with "Sharpshooter"?

Ted Kooser: I don't often write about paintings because such poems require too much exposition. You have to take time to describe the painting and that sort of description is difficult to make engaging. But these four pictures interested me when I found them in an article in a magazine. I have no recollection of anything remarkable going on in my life at that time, nor what impelled me to write them. I do remember writing "The Sharpshooter" poem first. It was the easiest to describe, the painting being rather simple in composition. I wrote no other poems about Homer paintings because I was looking at only these four, in reproduction, and didn't look further. Since writing the poems I have seen a big retrospective of Homer's art, which I enjoyed.

Chapman Hood Frazier: In your first chapter, "First Impressions" from *The Poetry Home Repair Manual*, you write: "The titles and first few lines of your poem represent the hand you extend in friendship towards the reader." In this poem, you actually begin with the images of "waiting" that slow down the pace of the poem and delay our actual entry into the scene. Is this how you started this poem? Or did it begin with line 6 and you added these early lines later? Also, I love how you use 2nd person to bring the reader into the poem as a participant, especially as you move us to the unexpectedness of your last image. This point of view is quite different from the third person point of view that is apparent in the other poems.

Ted Kooser: I really don't recall the manner in which the poem developed. I revise extensively and a poem of that length can result from thirty or forty versions. I used 2nd person primarily because I wanted to include the "you" under the threat of the sniper.

Chapman Hood Frazier: In "The Bright Side" the images and similes that you use to describe the black soldiers portray them as objects: "like oily cannon rags" or "old harness." How did you arrive at these similes?

Ted Kooser: Simply, that's what they looked like. I have a habit of thinking in metaphor and these similes must have come to me in the process of trying to describe the pictures. Above, where I talked about the difficulty of having to use exposition, well, figurative language can help us tolerate exposition.

Chapman Hood Frazier: Do you find that all poems have an element of exposition that you as a poet must bring to the forefront? How is writing a poem like "The Sniper" or one of these about art different from how you write your other poems?

Ted Kooser: It's nearly always to furnish some information to the reader, and we can call that exposition. It has to be handled with great care because the more information a poet inserts in a poem, the more the poem sickens. Too much information and it dies. In these Homer poems I had to describe the paintings for my reader, thinking that without doing so he or she was in the dark. Writing about paintings is probably always like this. In "Musee des Beaux Arts," Auden had to describe that painting in which Icarus is falling into the sea so that readers not familiar with the painting could "see" it.

Too much information is the biggest risk in writing about history, too, as I learned when I was trying to write a long poem about the Black Hawk War of 1832. I knew a lot about the situation from having read a good deal, but I had to feed the knowledge into the poetry a little at a time. A big block of historical data would have stopped the poem in its tracks. David Mason's wonderful book-length poem *Ludlow* does a great job of managing history and is a model for this kind of writing.

Chapman Hood Frazier: "Prisoners from the Front" is a nice balance to "The Bright Side" in that you are showing three Confederate prisoners and how their body language presents a very different picture of the war. This portrait of insolence in the face of capture is strong and engaging. The very end of the poem moves us back to the artist, outside the scene and away from the portrait itself. How did you decide to end like that? Was that your first impulse or did it come much later during your revision process?

Ted Kooser: Again, I'm sorry, but I can't recall how the poem developed. I remember wanting to suggest the political dynamics behind the scene, so I would have been composing in that direction.

Chapman Hood Frazier: Do you remember how you composed "The Veteran in a New Field"? Do you listen to music or read other people's poems during your writing process?

Ted Kooser: Again, I have no specific recollection as to how the composition went, other than to underline the fact that I revise extensively. I most often write very early in the morning, from about 4:30 or 5:00 until about 7:00. I don't want any distractions, so of course I don't listen to music. Writing for me requires an intense, almost trancelike state of concentration. I begin poems then, and sometimes revise them over a period of several days, trying them this way and that. It helps to sleep on them, to let them show me their weak spots, which I can't immediately see but which become apparent with detachment.

Chapman Hood Frazier: Do you recall how long it took you to craft these poems? Did they all come at one sitting or did you write each one separately?

Ted Kooser: I'm sorry, I can't tell you how long they took. I wrote them separately, and when I'm lucky I can pretty well flesh out the first draft of a poem on the first day. Then I let them sit and look at them again in a few days.

Chapman Hood Frazier: Your poems often elevate the ordinary. Tell us, if you would, a little about how you grew up and what you consider to be some of the significant events in your life that have impacted you as a writer.

Ted Kooser: Well, I grew up in Ames, Iowa, and went on to college there. We tend to use the term "ordinary" to describe things that we look at or pass over hastily, because they don't immediately engage us. But behind the screen of the ordinary can be found unique and wonderful things. As to the significant events in my life, there were my two marriages, the birth of my son, being diagnosed with cancer, and so on. The deaths of my grandparents and uncles and aunts had a considerable effect on my life, and then the deaths of my parents, of course. I quit drinking in 1986 and I'd guess that that had more of an effect on the course of my life than just about anything else. I had never gotten in trouble from drinking, and may not have been a classic alcoholic, but drinking did waste a lot of my time and shaped the way I lived.

I wrote some poems when I was a little boy in grade school, but I think we all probably were doing that then, and I didn't really get serious about it until I was an adolescent. I was sort of an outsider as an adolescent. I had no athletic ability. I couldn't play a musical instrument, I could do none of the things that we used to say the popular kids could do, and I was very much on the outside. Somehow or other I got the idea that writing and painting would make me very interesting, that is, romantically interesting. It was mostly about girls. I think if you asked most people in the arts about their real motivation for why they got in the arts you would find that [romantic motivation] had a lot to do with it.

So I fell upon it with the single-mindedness of an outsider teenager and started writing and trying to look like a poet: wearing clothes that would look pretty ridiculous today. But at that time, in the 1950's, there were these beachcomber pants that tied with a piece of cord and had a sort of pedal-pusher length. And rather than real sandals we had plastic flip-flops (which are now back, of course), and I walked around with my brow furrowed so that people would take me real seriously (I have these permanent furrows as a result of that), and under my arm I carried big heavy books that I couldn't have read if I wanted to, but they looked really good and they would make my bicep look a little bit better.

I notice that this happens a lot in the arts and I've had students who act like this as well. They really want to be "the poet" before they get around to writing the poems, or they want to be the painter before they really do too much painting. It's a matter of taking on the identity and then realizing after the fact that you've got to do some work. In a way it happened with me. I thought, *Well, if I'm going to be this romantic figure as a poet, then I probably ought to be writing some poems*. So, I did a lot of that and went on to college at Iowa State, an old land grant engineering school in my home town.

Chapman Hood Frazier: So, did you follow your intuition at Iowa State and begin studying poetry writing or literature?

Ted Kooser: Well, not exactly. When I graduated from high school advisors were not terribly sophisticated. My high school advisor was the football coach, and at the end of my senior year he called me in and said, "Now Ted, you can draw and you've gotten A's in art. There are two things you could do with your life, you could be an art teacher or an architect." And I thought, "Huh, well maybe I'll be an architect." I was kind of shy about being a teacher.

So off I go into architecture school at Iowa State. You know, it was as if there weren't any other choices in life at all other than those two. And I forced myself through the basic architecture courses until I got to the first quarter of my junior year. They were on the quarter system then. I had already begun to have terrible difficulty with math and physics. It was the first day of a class called "Theoretical and Applied Mathematics," and there were two problems set up for us to do. One was a table with a hole in it and about 20 feet of a heavy log chain circling the hole. We had our slide rules, do you remember what a slide rule is? We were to figure out, given the weight of the links of the chain, when one began to lower the chain through the hole, at what point would it begin to pull itself through by its own weight?

Then, we were to figure out the rate of acceleration given a certain amount of resistance before it all fell through the hole onto the floor. That was one of the two problems for that day. The other one was a block of wood on a piece of rope, and we were to shoot into it with a certain muzzle velocity rifle that had a certain weight slug, and figure out how far the wood would swing in response to being impacted by the bullet. Then, we were to figure out the path of the bullet as it entered the wood given even resistance.

I sat there for about 15 minutes with everybody else writing around me and working their slide rules and doing all this stuff, and I just looked around and realized that I didn't have a clue about what to do. There's a lake on the center of the Iowa State University campus, called Lake Laverne, and I walked down to Lake Laverne, unsnapped my Dietzgen slide rule, threw it out in the middle of the lake, and dropped out of architecture school.

There was no English major at Iowa State at that time, because Iowa University was the liberal arts school, so I couldn't really get an English major at Iowa State. So I moved into what was called Distributive Studies because it was a way that I could get certified to teach high school English. So I did that and taught high school for one year at a little town near my hometown, and I didn't like it much. I was a skinny little guy, and my students were all bigger than me and I made the mistake of trying to make friends with my students. I mean that's the worst thing that can happen because they can take tremendous advantage of you. So I sort of ruined a year of high school teaching.

Chapman Hood Frazier: So, was it at that time that you went to the University of Nebraska to graduate school? What drew you there?

Ted Kooser: Yes, I was writing all this time, writing poems, and I decided well, maybe I could go to graduate school. I started applying, and the University of Nebraska in Lincoln accepted me. One of the reasons I wanted to go there was because of Karl Shapiro, a famous poet who had won a Pulitzer Prize and the Bollingen Award and had been the editor of the prestigious *Poetry* magazine. He was teaching at Nebraska, and I thought I could learn about being a poet from him. So off I go to graduate school and I had an assistantship (called a reading assistantship) that paid a pittance to help a professor correct papers. My professor was a scholar of Renaissance drama. The work bored me, and I suffered through a year of helping him. All I really cared about was writing poems, and Karl Shapiro was right there and he and I had become friends and we spent a lot of time together. But I didn't do anything else that I was supposed to do.

At the end of the first year of graduate school, my advisor called me in and, reclining in his chair and touching the tips of his fingers together, he said they were cutting me off and that they weren't going to renew my assistantship because my grades were bad and I hadn't even shown up for the Chaucer class at all. So, they threw me out of graduate school and I had to figure out something to do. My first wife had a high school teaching job, so we had some income, but I knew I had to do something. So I sat around for a couple of months and started looking in the Want Ads.

There was a management trainee job at a life insurance company which involved answering letters to policyholders. I applied and got the job. The personnel manager was, I soon learned, an alcoholic, and I think he saw in me someone who would have a drink with him after work. So they hired me for this job even though I had never had a business course, and I knew nothing about business. I knew nothing about insurance. I went to work there, but I still knew I wanted to be a writer. I decided, okay, you're going to have to earn a living, this is what you're going to do. You're going to go to work every day at the insurance company. You are going to put in eight hours, but before you go to work every morning, you're going to get up and write. So I got in the habit of getting up at 4:30 or 5:00 and writing until about 7:00, then I had to bustle around, get my necktie on (no "business casual," it was all suit and tie) and go to the insurance company. I rather liked this structure: the pay was good, I had good benefits, I was done at 5:00 every day (while my colleagues at the English Department would stay up all night correcting student papers). I just sort of fell into it, and I started taking a few classes at night at the University to get my masters degree. I worked at the first insurance company for eight years and the next one for about 25 years.

I still get up early in the morning. I've been retired now for eight years, but I still get up in the morning early and write every day. I sit in my chair with my cup of coffee and try to write and 28 days out of 30 I'm a complete failure at it. I write stuff that is just junk, but I figure if I'm not sitting there writing and the good one comes, I'm not going to get it at all. A very big part of being a success at anything is showing up for work. That's the way I felt about it. I began publishing poems in literary magazines when I was about 25. I published my first book when I was 30, which at 67 is now a terrible embarrassment to me, that first book. Every once and awhile I'll see a copy at a yard sale and I'll buy it, take it home, and hide it so somebody else can't see it.

This writing business you have to accustom yourself to is about failing again and again, and to not let that hold you up because if you keep at it day after day, after day, after day, eventually you'll get better. The same thing would be true if I had taken up longbow archery with the same zeal that I took up poetry writing: I could put forty arrows on a paper plate from 100 yards away. So that is what it's about, showing up for work. I may have some talent, a gift for metaphor and so on, that other people might not have, but generally my success is just the result of hard work over the years.

Chapman Hood Frazier: What influenced your decision to write poetry? Did you have teachers in school who encouraged you or a group of friends that you shared poems with? Who were the key poets that you felt influenced you as a writer?

Ted Kooser: Much of my impulse to write poetry came from my need to find ways of dealing with loss, so my feelings about the deaths that I mentioned earlier shaped some of my early work. I did have a couple of very good teachers in high school who encouraged my writing, and when I got to college I had a couple of friends I showed my poems to. By the time I was studying with Karl Shapiro I was reading many of the poets who were really my first teachers, May Swenson, William Carlos Williams, Randall Jarrell, and others. All of their poems had an effect upon me, May Swenson's in particular. She seemed to be able to write in any form and about anything.

The biggest challenge to me as a writer has always been to find time to write, to fit it into my life. And the greatest benefit has been to be able to establish small pieces of order, poems, from a life that can seem without order.

Chapman Hood Frazier: Who do you consider to be major influences on your development as a writer? Who has shaped your writing and what have you learned from them?

Ted Kooser: I mentioned May Swenson and Williams and Jarrell above. There was also my teacher and friend, Karl Shapiro. But it's important to note that I have read tens of thousands of poems and I'd guess everything I've read has in some minute way shaped my writing.

Chapman Hood Frazier: Who do you read today? Do you read literary criticism or what the critics say about your work?

Ted Kooser: I recently served on a poetry jury and read more than two hundred books. Of those, I liked about a dozen, but I don't want to name names. If a book has a poem or two that I like, and lots that I don't like, the two that I like make it a book I want to keep, and I have about four thousand poetry titles in my library. Because I have achieved some success as a poet, somebody sends me a book of poems nearly every day. I look at them all and write a note acknowledging receipt. Many of them I'll never open again, but I keep them, thinking that some day I may donate them all to a library.

I read very little literary criticism and never read anything written about me. I discovered long ago that it did me no good whatsoever. The criticism hurt me and the praise seemed overblown. It's been best to just ignore literary criticism. Nothing a critic might say is going to change the way I live or write. As to reading, I read all sorts of things from detective novels to books on nature to volumes of letters.

Chapman Hood Frazier: What is your advice for teachers of poetry in high school or college?

Ted Kooser: Teachers need to make poetry pleasurable. If a student finds poetry to be a chore he or she will never read it in later life.

Chapman Hood Frazier: In *Writing Brave and Free*, you discuss how a writer may find publishers for their manuscripts. Tell us about how you published your first book?

Ted Kooser: My first book was published when I was thirty, and it is something of an embarrassment to me now. All of the poems seem derivative of my early influences. A substantial portion of that book had appeared already in one literary journal or another, and that is the way most books of poetry are put together, from poems that have already proven themselves in literary publications.

Chapman Hood Frazier: When you were invited to become poet laureate of the United States, how did you first learn about the honor and how has it impacted you?

Ted Kooser: Yes, I got a call on a Friday evening, the 8th or 9th of August in 2004. My wife was in Washington, D.C. on journalism business, and I was trying to figure out what I was going to have for supper. It was maybe 10 minutes after 6:00. Phone rings, "Ted Kooser?"
"Yes."
"Ted Kooser, the poet?"
"Yes."
"My name is Prosser Gifford, I am the director of scholarly programs at the Library of Congress, and I am calling to see if you would like to be the next poet laureate of the United States." And I thought Holy Jesus. So, I am trying to respond to this and blabbering and making very little sense and he says, "You know, why don't I call you back tomorrow?" I got off the phone, began pacing around and couldn't get my wife on the phone. I noticed that I had two DVD's that we had checked out of the movie place in this little town about 12 miles from where we lived in the country. I thought, *okay, these are overdue.* They were due at 6:00, you're going to get in the car, drive to Seward, return the movies, and if you get there soon enough maybe they won't fine you 50 cents, or whatever it was. So, I go out to the car, and tell myself that I am going to think about being the poet laureate all the way over there and back. I go out to the car, put the DVD's on the seat, back out of the garage, and I rip the side mirror off on the center post of the garage. It's one of those mirrors that has a power cord so you can adjust it, and now it's hanging on the side of the car. I know right away that this is going to be expensive. So, already I have made a stupid mistake as a result of this poet laureate call. I get in the car and I drive to Seward and the

whole time I am thinking, holy Jesus, what is this going to be like? I mean traveling, going to Washington, doing all this stuff?

So, I pull into Seward and I think, huh, Bernie at the body shop is probably still working at this hour, these guys work late on Friday nights. I'll go talk to Bernie about this mirror. So I go out there and they did all this stuff with the computer and they looked it up and said it was going to be $138.00 and some change to fix this mirror. I thought, oh God, you know? Dumb, you know? All for the sake of two DVD's. I get back in the car feeling blue all the way home. I am feeling overpowered by being the poet laureate. I pull back in the garage very carefully, so as not to hit anything, I look down and the DVD's are still in the car. So it's like that, you know?

I knew that I was the first poet laureate ever to be picked from our part of the country, and I figured that I had better do it, and do a better job of it than anybody has ever done, because the eastern literary establishment had held a lock on it for a long time (with the exception of Bob Haas who is from California). Generally, it was all people from the Northeast corner who had been the poet laureates. I knew that people would be coming after me, because I wasn't one of them. But I just decided that for the next year or two (if they give me a second term) that I was going to do nothing but try to be good at this. And so I took it on with that spirit, and I probably made more appearances and did more interviews than anyone had ever done as poet laureate. I did things that were unexpected. I had the folk singer and songwriter, John Prine, come to the Library of Congress; the very first folk singer who had been on that stage since Woody Guthrie in 1936. I started a news-paper column that is still running and is free to any newspaper. In it, I present a short poem every week that I hope newspaper readers can understand with a little help, which includes a couple of introductory sentences by me. The column is running in almost 200 papers right now, and we have an estimated readership of 11 million, and I intend to keep it going even though I am no longer poet laureate.

The basic requirements for being poet laureate are pretty mini-mal. You have to give a reading of your work in October to open the library's season, and you give a closing lecture at the end of the year, and in between you have the privilege of giving away a couple $10,000 fellowships to poets you really admire. I gave one to Claudia Emerson who is at Mary Washington University, close by here. And then you can invite people in to do readings and this Prine invitation I did was one of those. I brought George Garrett from Charlottesville in to do a reading at my request.

But it's funded all by private donations, so there's no government money that goes into it, no appropriation. There is no connection, whatsoever, with the Executive branch. It's all Library of Congress; it's one of their programs. So it worked out, and for me, it was an opportunity to get the attention of a lot of people. It provided an opportunity for me to talk with people about what I thought about poetry. It allowed me to sort of push my agenda in a way.

Chapman Hood Frazier: That is quite a story. What is one poem that you have written that was, perhaps, challenging to write and something that you would like to be remembered for?

Ted Kooser: I wrote a 43 page essay about my mother's family, called "Lights on a Ground of Darkness." My mother was very ill with emphysema and heart trouble, and I decided that I would try to write about her family and give that to her before she died. And I worked on it hard for several months because I didn't know how much time I would have. It was an opportunity for me to take some very ordinary people. Like my grandfather, who was a farmer and ran a Standard gas station, and my grandmother, who was a homemaker and who lived on the edge of town and raised chickens, as well as my uncle who had cerebral palsy and lived at home with his parents. So I wrote this essay about the family with the idea that here was my opportunity to hold these people up into the light a little bit, that they might be forgotten otherwise because they were so ordinary. And every time anyone reads that essay, up into the light these people come for a little while. So it's a way of giving my people a little temporary immortality. And I think that piece is probably, to me, the most important writing I have ever done.

I was afraid to show it to Mother because I thought that it would make her terribly sad because all of these people were dead; she was the last survivor of the whole family. And that didn't happen at all. She was very pleased by it, which was a relief. But that's the kind of service that writers can do: you write about your family and it gives them a little bit of immortality. Maybe your memoir is never published. Maybe it's left in a manila folder somewhere and 75 years from now some grandchild comes upon it, opens it and reads about those long ago people, and all of a sudden they come to life. That is the kind of thing worth doing.

Memoirs

Ted's Box

David Baker

1976. People were hanging bunting. People were planning bright parades and writing speeches and preparing for the spectacle of the Bicentennial. It was early summer, early June, already scorching and dank with Missouri humidity, the world dripping green. I looked forward with a real happiness to a summer on campus at Central Missouri State University, my soon-to-be alma mater, the home of the "Fighting Mules." My minimum-wage job in the library had me sorting maps for the geography librarian, preserving rare 19th century land plats, cataloguing everything. I like organizing things. I like maps. My father was a surveyor and then a mapmaker for the Missouri Highway Department, and he taught me both skills, at least their rudiments. I like working alone with paper and plans and blueprints and books. And that summer I had plans of my own, to write poems, nonstop.

The library was a delicious place to work, since I could sneak away in long stretches or languish over lunch break in the rarely bothered shelves of the poetry section. Piling up books on a big wooden table, I'd read and write and daydream. I had grown up in central Missouri, mostly Jefferson City, about ninety miles from campus, and the poetry I discovered that summer enlarged by immense proportions my sense of the world and of people and of possibility.

How I loved Wallace Stevens. How exotic was his "Damned universal" language, chewy and sensual in the mouth. I loved to say "Chieftain Iffucan of Azcan in caftan / Of tan with henna hackles, halt!" and to feel and smell and hear the tropics in his languid meditations. Likewise, how moved I was by the restraint and eerie majesty of Mark Strand, whose lines, "Wherever I am / I am what is missing," were like spare keys to an enigmatic but wholly possible other world. And speaking of that other world: No other poet moved and sustained me like W.S. Merwin during those years. In 1977, in fact, I wrote my master's thesis—still at CMSU—on Merwin's books *The Carrier of Ladders* and *Writings to an Unfinished Accompaniment.* The layering of mythologies and sociologies inside his stark, rhetorical purity amazed me. I wrote dozens of poems that could have masqueraded as thrown-away drafts of minor Merwin works, all unpunctuated and comically over-populated by the famous wings and stones and bones of the deep-image school. The poems of Denise Levertov tutored me that summer as well. I loved her conscience, her footsteps, the accessibility of right living. I translated Follian. I parsed Hopkins. I unpacked the vocal gymnastics of Ashbery.

And then I found a slender drab-covered book called *Official Entry Blank*. What could the University of Nebraska give me, I wondered, that Antheneum and New Directions and Knopf could not? When I found Ted Kooser, in essence, I found the poet next door.

I found that poetry next door was not only possible but also plentiful. It was as if my uncle or neighbor had suddenly sprouted laurels. I kept digging and found Ted Kooser chapbooks and small press books— from Solo Press, Windflower Press, Pentagram Press—and then in them I unearthed a clarity and remarkable familiarity in the landscape and the language. For the first time I heard a real art crafted from the Midwestern idiom of my own tongue:

> The first few wounds are nearly invisible;
> a truck rumbles past in the dust
> and a .22 hole appears in the mailbox
> like a fly landing there.

These opening lines from one of Kooser's early poems, "Shooting a Farmhouse," are not remarkable for their dazzling complexity but for their simple precision. I have read some critical accounts of contemporary poetry that argue that such clarity—such a plain style—is a necessary feature of Midwestern aesthetics. The land is plain, the people are plain, so the poetry should be plain. It's all more honest and wholesome that way. At least that's the argument. I do not buy that argument as a blanket prescription, by the way. It seems easy, at best, and is potentially very condescending to the complexity of the people and their lives and the land. And it seems limiting to the vast capabilities of the art and imagination. But in Kooser's particular case, the sparkling sharpness and selective turns of language aren't merely plain; somehow they create a powerful, suggestive kinship in me. His is an art of miniature precision and clarity.

Notice how quickly "Shooting a Farmhouse" commences, the attack already underway; the truck "rumbles" by; and then comes the surprising detail of the bullet hole in the mailbox. But the real magic is the fourth line. What prudent line-break Kooser gives us after "mailbox." The subsequent simile feels perfect, and perfectly set up, arrived at. Why? First of all, the literal correspondence between a .22 hole and a fly is exact: the right size, the right shape (never exactly round), the right color (shadowy black). But the suggestive image also carries further resonance, the way one fly, then many flies, might congregate on a decaying organic body, gathering for the slow feast of decomposition. He's able to suggest a long-reaching timeline of loss through this single minute detail.

One of Kooser's best skills is the creation of such images and metaphors. Poem after poem bears the rightness of both familiarity and surprise. In a poem from his new book, *Delights & Shadows,* Kooser depicts a simple act in "The Necktie":

> His hands fluttered like birds,
> each with a fancy silk ribbon
> to weave into their nest,
> as he stood at the mirror
> dressing for work, waving hello
> to himself with both hands.

This whole poem, one sentence, six lines, one conceit. The two hands (or birds) are adorning their neck (nest) with ribbon. So simple, and yet the man's reflection gives him back a complex image. He seems a little proud of his fancy display, a little comical, and a little lonely, waving to himself with both hands. He's caught himself there, revealed.

Three evenings ago at dinner, my friend, the poet Linda Gregerson, described coming to Kooser's poems only recently. What she admired most was their "yield." She meant, as she described it, that despite their brevity and apparent simplicity, his best poems provide a significant gift. But she meant something else, too. The poems embody and enact a kind of generous patience. They await, they hold still, they yield, in order for the world to be revealed or the subject to be fully illuminated.

That's precisely right. Kooser's poems work through illumination more than transfiguration. To see the thing being seen: that is his goal.

And to see the thing being seen, we must see its counterpart—its meta-phoric other—as precisely this: a representation or likeness of the thing itself. Look at these parts of other Kooser poems, to see what I mean about rightness:

> The cat has fallen asleep,
> the dull book of a dead moth
> loose in his paws.
>> (from "Sitting All Evening Alone in the Kitchen")

> There's a click like a piece of chalk
> tapping a blackboard, and the furnace
> starts thinking: *Now, just where was I?*
> It's always the same stale thought
> turned over and over...
>> (from "Furnace")

And in "Snakeskin," the subject at hand is at once "a dusty tunnel echo-ing / with light," "a glove of lace," and "a long train / cross[ing] a bor-der." And now it holds only a "ghost of a wind." How rich, appropriate, and illuminating are these figures.

This is something I was thinking about, marveling over, again last summer during another Kooser reading-spree. I read poets this way—in devoted slices for a few days of nights—back and back again. I spent three intense evenings with Kooser, and then I wanted to try my hand at a poem like his. I wanted the stanza, the clarity, the unselfish rendering of a simple object. I wanted a tight, lean poem with no narrative, but rather an image-driven poem, in short lines. Nowhere to hide. Mostly I wanted to try to capture the precision of his variety of metaphor. So I wrote "My Father's Tacklebox":

> Its hinges creak
> and the box gapes open,
> revealing two straight rows
> of lures, bobbers, stringers,

> and hooks still sorted by size—two rows,

> like a mouthful of teeth,
> beneath which lies
>
> his hunting knife
> thick as a tongue
> and furred with rust,
> but it's not talking.

It took me several days and drafts of tinkering to manage the lines and details and concision. But writing the poem was one thing.

Then I did something else. I sent it to Kooser.

We have never met, though we have exchanged a few letters over the years. I wrote this time, in my letter, some words about his just-released *Delights & Shadows,* and I included my poem as a friendly tribute or thank-you.

When Kooser's reply arrived a couple of weeks later—he had not yet been named Poet Laureate—I was surprised and happy to hear from him. He was glad, he reported, that I had found and enjoyed his new book, and was pleased to see my poem. But then he did something more generous than that. In the kindest way, he let me know that I had not got the ending right, not quite. Or, rather, while my ending was just fine, there might be a better way to configure the details. With the simple flick of a line, he suggested, look at the way the poem might more effectively conclude:

> his hunting knife
> furred with rust
> and thick as a tongue
> but it's not talking.

One of Kooser's special skills is the handling of image and metaphor, then another is his sense of endings, their closures, captures, illuminations, the box clicking shut. Here is what Kooser sensed that I did not. The tacklebox is rather like a head—a skull, mute but still full of teeth. This is most evident in the last line where it isn't "talking." In my earlier version, though, I had not attended fully enough to context and syntax of these finishing details. First, the knife must be rusted, then the rust will thicken, and then the simile should come—of the tongue, and speech. Kooser's order of things, and not my first version, understands and clarifies this procedure. It arrives more fully this way. It makes more complete, a more revealed, sense.

That's why he was right. But I'd like to make one final adjustment to the poem. I wish to change its title from "My Father's Tacklebox" to "His Tacklebox." I'd be pleased if Mr. Kooser shared this little box with my father. They'd like each other, I believe.

To Ted, From Two Cow

J. V. Brummels

Sometime near the end of the 1970's, when his wonderfully named Windflower Press was perhaps in its most active period, Ted Kooser sent me one of his famous picture postcards—a copy of an antique print of a westward moving wagon train on one side and on the other a brief announcement in Ted's careful and compact hand. What he had in mind, he wrote, was *The Windflower Home Almanac of Poetry (Illustrated)*. He was looking for poems with a lot of "eye" and not much "I."

Ted Kooser's reputation was already widespread twenty-five years ago, particularly among poets my age grounded in the Moderns. His poems were brief and imagistic, like William Carlos Williams's, though often sharper. When his subject was relationships, the poems could possess an edge like Robert Frost's darker poems. He was an insurance executive, and the association with Wallace Stevens was inevitable.

Several of his poems were (and are still) on my short list of all-time favorites—"Abandoned Farmhouse," with its clear subject, perfect details and haunting refrain; the darkly funny "Tom Ball's Barn"; and the edgier, meaner poems like "The Widow Lester" and "Grating a Brain."

Ted also had a knack for book titles. What better to call a first book of poems than *Official Entry Blank*? And was there a better title ever for a book of poems than *A Local Habitation & A Name*? It's the heart of the passage in *A Midsummer's Night Dream* in which Shakespeare gives us poets our marching orders: "And as imagination bodies forth / The forms of things unknown, the poet's pen / Turns them to shapes, and gives to airy nothing / A local habitation and a name."

A perfect title, and a perfect book to help lift the pejorative weight from the appellation "regional" and move poetry in a fresh direction. At the time of the book's publication, the "schools" of the '50s—Black Mountain, New York, Beat—no longer told us much but history, and pretty much every poet—except Ted—was Confessional. A few years after *A Local Habitation & A Name* appeared, Ed Field's mass-market paperback *A Geography of Poets* pointed in the direction Ted had already gone. Soon, small-press anthologies and journal numbers devoted to "place" began to plop down like fat raindrops in farmyard dust.

Not only had Ted been writing poems of place and geography for a decade or longer before anybody much thought it wise, he'd also been publishing those of others through Windflower, most notably in *Alvin Turner As Farmer* and several subsequent collections by William Kloefkorn.

In short, I knew Ted's work well enough that the "I/eye" distinction he drew told me what he was looking for. Or, more precisely, I knew what he wasn't looking for. Some years earlier I was privileged to attend a Philip Levine reading, during which he told a story: It seems the printer of Levine's first collection called him to say that, though only partly through the typesetting, he'd used his last uppercase "I."

The anecdote stayed with me because it was funny and because I used (and still do) "I" in poems (and prose) like some people use "huh" or "like" in conversation. I knew I was in trouble. Still, the opportunity to have my poem included in an anthology edited by Ted Kooser represented too much opportunity for a young poet to ignore. So I sat down and wrote a poem prompted by a drive I'd taken the weekend before. Ted included it in *The Windflower Almanac of Poetry (Illustrated)*. In the years since, it's been reprinted, exhibited in calligraphy, won me compliments and generally drew more attention to itself than most of my other poems. That's been both gratifying—for the obvious reasons—and awkward, because its strengths stem entirely from the pleasure I'd taken in knowing Ted's poems. (I readily take the blame for its weaknesses.) I've often speculated that it is more Ted's poem than mine, and this is a grand opportunity to send it back his way:

APPLE HARVEST ALONG THE MISSOURI

Someone or something is holding its breath:
A couple travel silently down the road,
the kids finally quiet in the back seat;
the bank of clouds to the northwest
no longer advances on the sun;
the river pauses for an orange barrel

snagged in the branches of a fallen cottonwood;
the breeze is taken in by the orchard;
in a sorting shed a man recalls a fragment
of a tune his father used to whistle,
a woman remembers a poem
she was taught in school.

In a moment the wind comes up in the leaves,
the barrel moves out into the sun and current,
a car turns into the lane to buy cider.
In the shed two hands reach for the same small winesap.

Tuesdays with Ted

Twyla Hansen

In the fall of 2002 I was no longer working full-time so I enrolled in Ted Kooser's graduate poetry class at the University of Nebraska-Lincoln. I'd known Ted for years and admired his writing; this was my chance to learn what the master had to say.

I wasn't an English major but had taken a few writing classes over the years. It quickly became evident this would be no ordinary workshop. On the first day Ted told us this would be our only meeting together; for the rest of the semester, we'd meet him individually in his office for an hour each week, and that we should bring something new to look at each time. So each week from late August to early December, I walked from my part-time job on campus to his spare office on the second floor of Andrews Hall at 3:30 on Tuesdays, its south window overlooking the library, the Willa Cather native plant gardens and the tops of trees surely changing from green to yellow to red.

The format seldom varied. After a little chitchat, I handed him a new poem and he read it to himself for the first time in front of me. We were not allowed to read our poems aloud, because "it would influence my perception of [the poem]." Then he'd comment on a line or a word or the entire poem itself. He wanted to make sure the poem was free of anything that might trip up a reader, stand in the way of understanding what the poem was trying to say. He missed nothing and questioned everything. What I learned—this fine-tooth comb reading of my own new writing and others', encountering the inevitable early draft rough spot—was to ask myself WWKD—What Would Kooser Do? If brevity is the soul of wit, then it was clear I was becoming a witty writer: for that semester, at least, my poems became shorter.

To fill in for a class lecture/discussion, he sent e-mail messages, sometimes in the form of general thoughts on what we had been writing, to illustrate a point by using his or another writer's poem, or anything else that came to his mind about writing. Every few days these messages "from Ted Kooser" arrived to my In-box, addressed to me and the other eleven students I didn't know, plus two other people who wanted his weekly wisdoms sent to them, too. I have a feeling that many of these WWKD wisdoms are included in his latest book, *The Poetry Home Repair Manual*.

He made us all proud. I heard the U. S. Poet Laureate news on NPR while traveling home on I-80 from Colorado and yelled out loud, which startled my husband who was driving and evidently in another world. But it was just the best news I'd heard in such a long time.

Inhalations

William Kloefkorn

It is not the poem I choose to return to that most compels me; it is the poem that returns to me, again and again, without its being sought after or invited, that I most admire

Ted Kooser's "The Blind Always Come as Such a Surprise" is such a poem. On the off-chance that the reader is not familiar with this poem, I'll present it here in its entirety:

> The blind always come as such a surprise
> suddenly filling an elevator
> with a great white porcupine of canes
> or coming down upon us in a noisy crowd
> like the eye of a hurricane.
> The dashboards of cars stopped at crosswalks
> and the shoes of commuters on trains
> are covered with sentences
> struck down in mid-flight by the canes of the blind.
> Each of them changes our lives,
> tapping across the bright circles of our ambitions
> like cracks traversing the favorite china.

I first read this poem in 1974, the year that it appeared in a book-length collection, *A Local Habitation & A Name*. Since then, the poem has found its way into my mind on a number of occasions, as if it were a touchstone against which I might measure my own degree of surprise when confronted with someone or something that challenges my sense of self-importance and inflated pride. In my judgment, the poem reflects Kooser at his inhalation best, by which I mean a poem he must have written while inhaling, slowly and deliberately, the thin air of distinctly appropriate figurative language. Consider, for example, the "great white porcupine of canes," a metaphor that joins canes to porcupines, and, in joining, suggests the portentous nature of the surprise. The metaphor is apt and, for me, especially foreboding, not because I am an expert on porcupines, but because once upon a time I watched a dog in the Nebraska sandhills attack a porcupine, whereupon it took three men and a boy to restrain the dog while the dog's owner, wielding an oversized pair of pliers, extracted at least two dozen quills from the canine's lips, tongue, and nose.

Consider, next, the simile that follows the metaphor: "coming down upon us in a noisy crowd/like the eye of the hurricane." Kooser gives the blind an "eye" by way of his comparison, and the reader, already surprised—or, in my case, stunned—shudders: There, but for the grace of good luck and circumstances, go I. The images that follow the simile continue to underscore both the surprise and the fear; dashboards and shoes "are covered with sentences/struck down in mid-flight by the canes of the blind." Anyone who has driven a vehicle, and has braked to permit a blind person to cross the street, knows at least two things: 1) the braking might well have been sudden enough to cause whatever was being said to have been broken off in mid-sentence, and 2) whatever was being said, though surely of international importance, could not be remembered and thus returned to by the one who did the braking. Very quickly "international importance" is relegated to the low shelf it probably deserved before the humbling occurred.

Shortly thereafter, Kooser's "bright circle of our ambitions" suggests, metaphorically, that our aspirations move not linearly but in a "bright circle" which further suggests that, though sighted, we might not see clearly enough to avoid the tedium of "bright" as perhaps in "unseen" repetition. A lesser poet—that is, a poet more given to displaying himself than in preserving the integrity of the poem—might have alluded to, say, the blind soothsayer Tiresias; but Kooser chooses to go with "bright circle" and "ambitions," both of which are appropriate to his down-home, and self deprecating ("our" includes the poet as well as the reader) irony.

Close on the heels of this metaphor is a second simile: "like cracks traversing the favorite china." When Kooser modifies "china" with "favorite," he resonates with those readers who know what it means to have been raised in a home where good china was decidedly the exception, not the rule. In such a household the question, "Does anyone know where the *good* scissors are?" means that the family can afford only one truly quality pair of scissors, as in that same family the "favorite" china is rare and thus rarely used (it spends most of its rarified life in the oak buffet that was handed down from Aunt Vivian, whose maternal grandmother, who favored Vivian over Ruby, gave to Vivian several years before she, the maternal grandmother, passed away, the old woman scorning the leaving of a will, she had so little to leave anyway, fearing that Ruby might contrive to snatch away this heirloom from under the nose of the more deserving Vivian, and so on). So the favorite china, one piece or a dozen, spends most of its days and nights in such a buffet, and when a crack or two traverses the face of one of the dishes, or a platter, the imperfection is looked upon with a very genuine sense of loss and dismay.

I am not saying that a poem's success depends wholly upon the experiences that the reader brings to it, but neither should those experiences be wholly discounted. Kooser's poem succeeds—and mightily, I believe—because of its compression and its fresh and unassuming figurative language.

Several years ago (by "several" I mean more than three decades), I sent Ted Kooser a thin sheaf of poems, thin because the sheaf contained all of the poems I had written, and when we met in his home to talk about them I learned, or began to learn, the extent to which Kooser appreciates the compact poem. There were several more or less long poems in the group, the longest being just under four pages. But the poem that chiefly caught his eye was the shortest one, "After Ten Winters":

> I stand alone
> At the foot
> Of my grandfather's grave,
> Trembling to tell:
> The door to the granary is open,
> Sir,
> And someone lost the bucket
> To the well.

His preference for the poem surprised me; I thought he might want to spend more time talking about the seven or more ambiguities so skillfully embodied in one of the longer efforts. But he didn't. Instead, he said a few things about this short and simple poem, and when a final beer had been inhaled and the conference was about to end, he asked if he might publish "After Ten Winters" on one of his Windflower Press's postcards. Without a lot of hesitation, I said yes. It was my first ever publication.

It is possible that pity (for the frail duration of the evening) clouded Ted's critical judgment—pity and, perhaps, that final beer. But I like to believe that his reaction was chiefly a reflection of his high regard for the concise poem that at least attempts not to fall into the lowest literary pit of them all—the sermon. In any case, I thanked him and having declined another final beer I took my sheaf of poems in hand and went home.

Another indication of Kooser's splendid preoccupation with conciseness—aside from many of his poems, which of course are the primary indicators—is his inveterate love affair with the brief messages on old postcards (*found* poems, I think they are called), several of which are included in *A Local Habitation & A Name* with "The Blind Always Come as Such a Surprise." Many of Kooser's poems deal with the subjects of aging, disability, abandonment, estrangement, death, so it is not surprising that the long-lost words of someone probably long deceased should compel him to haunt junk and antique stores with the hope of resurrecting some of those dusty inscriptions. Here is one, dated August 27, 1919:

This picture is of
the hoghouse here.
We have been having
a rain this morning
and fore-noon but
I guess it is about
over now and dinner
will soon be ready.
Yesterday there
was a man supposed to be
a patient here found dead
in the hog-yard.
Had hung himself
with a wire about Thurs.
I got my hair

cut this forenoon
and day after tomorrow
is shave day but I
won't get shaved until
next Thurs. Once in two
weeks is all I get.

Not much space on a postcard, not a lot of opportunities for smooth transitions, not enough wiggle-room to inform the reader which of the subjects is paramount and whether the two weeks pertains to shaving or to something else. Kooser appreciates the wryness and the ironies that such forced juxtapositions induce, and as humorous as these connections might sometimes be, Kooser, I believe, is drawn to them also because they were written by someone who now is rather permanently dead. Perhaps an even more melancholic example is this postcard, dated December 31, 1914:

Dear Velma, Hope
you are having a
fine time. Enjoy
life while you can
for when you get old
you can't. Happy New
Year to you. From
Grand Pa.

Or this one, dated October 6, 1908:

I wish you girls had
been over to hear the
singing this evening
it sure was dandy.
But I suppose you
do not care to come
to Bennett at night again.

The touch here (I assume intentional) is the phrase "at night," just as the touch (or one of them) in Kooser's "The Blind Always Come as Such a Surprise" is "favorite."

I said earlier that Kooser's short poems must have been written when he was inhaling, when the lungs are filling and the chest expanding, a slow inhalation that permits nothing short of the clearest air to enter. What happens, then, when the poet exhales?

Just this: The poems become more expansive, less metaphoric (though not oblivious to metaphor), more casual. "Abandoned Farm-house" is a good example. Another, one of my favorites, is "Father," a two-page tribute to Theodore Briggs Kooser (May 19, 1902-December 31, 1979). In the poem, Ted addressed his father directly:

> You spent fifty-five years
> walking the hard floors
> of the retail business...

The following ten stanzas (four lines in each stanza) speak of his father's work, of his relationship with the customers (Kooser asks if he remembers a certain teacher, and his father responds, "I certainly do;/ size ten, a little something in blue."), and only near the close of the poem does Kooser indulge a simile: His father, "posing as customers," goes

> strutting in big flowered hats,
> those aisles like a stage,
> the pale manikins watching:
> we laughed till we cried.

Kooser inhales more frequently than he exhales: he seems wary of over-extension. But on certain occasions, and in special contexts, he lets the air out, completely out, and the longer poem occurs. "Father" is maybe the consummate example. Not far behind is "Abandoned Farm-house," mentioned above, and to complete the trinity I would add "So This Is Nebraska."

I return to these poems, and to others, because they return to me; each time I read them, I am surprised anew. Several years ago, sitting on the cool cement of the front porch, I noticed a flower that suddenly and unexpectantly had popped up near a bush of lilacs at the head of the driveway. *Surprise lilies*, my wife called them, and I agreed. Their sudden appearance brought Ted Kooser's "The Blind Always Come as Such a Surprise" to mind, and before the next day ended I had written a poem that respectfully I dedicated to my first publisher. With respect I rededicate it here:

SURPRISE LILIES

The blind, my friend writes, always come
    as such a surprise. And so too
        these lilies

appearing suddenly on the last dog-day
    of summer, their stems
        delicate

and as slender as the legs of that
    translucent girl in the
        seventh grade

their petals a color I can't come up with.
    Lavender, for my wife tells me,
        or maybe orchid.

I prefer both—lavender into orchid—lavender
    for the sound of three
        syllables,

orchid for my grandmother's laughter
    each time she stumbled
        saying it. So

I sit on the front porch at high noon
    studying the lilies, their
        frail effrontery,

their silence, so far-flung and absolute.
    Tonight not even a full moon
        will be sufficient

for me to see them. With a length of sumac
    I'll tap my way to where
        I'll hope to find

them, until—surprise!—the solitary leaf,
    the howl, the sudden
        snow.

A Sunday Afternoon
with Ted Kooser and the Gaffneys

Glenna Luschei

I wish I could remember everything in my literary life as well as I recall the fascinating conversation in the living room of Wilbur and Libbey Gaffney on a warm summer afternoon in Lincoln. My old writing teacher from my university days wanted me to meet a rising young poet, who turned out to be good looking Ted Kooser with his distinctive flat Nebraska accent. I remember that especially because we read poems and his captivated me. I asked if he would send poems to my magazine *Cafe Solo,* which before the year, 1974, was over, would be a request to publish his book.

Our conversation that afternoon stood out to me because it centered on words, especially words that had to do with sticky substances. I was planning a trip to Alaska (where my marriage was falling apart) the next day. Talking about airstrips led to the word *tarmac,* a black sticky substance, which is nearly universally misused according to my now up-to-date web site. Airport runs are made of concrete, not tarmac but perhaps they were in the days of the Wright brothers? On second thought, wasn't Kitty Hawk a sand base?

Tarmac led us further into sticky black *macadam,* and then to *antimacassar,* an item which probably never figures in drawing-room conversations these days, but which Libby actually had pinned to the cushion of her rocking chair. They are something like doilies which keep hair ointment from soiling the chair. It also refers to a sailor's collar.

"But what is Macassar?" asked Ted. *Macassar* was the best word of all. Sometimes hair pomades were made of palm or coconut oil but the true Macassar was made from the glang glang ebony tree (Cananga adorata) endemic to the Island of Silowesi in Indonesia. Ahhh. The Macassar wood is pure white until the heart is reached. Ah-haaa. What a rewarding revelation!

I left feeling stimulated and hopeful that afternoon with a sense that my future, a future of words and their meanings was still before me.

The fascination with words still bonds Ted and me together. A poem I recently sent him mentioned my grandmother's "Roads to California" quilt. He looked up the quilt and sent me a picture of it.

Through the decades Ted and I have corresponded with poems. He became a counselor to me during my divorce and new marriage, also through some literary wrangles. I learned from him not to take life too seriously but he seemed to take my own torments to heart. He knew the pain of losing my mother and later my daughter.

He published my poem "Back into my Body" in his magazine, *Salt Creek Reader:*

> My mother is dying. I give her a bath,
> swollen belly and one nipple gone
> where I bit down as a baby.
>
> My mother is pulling silk from the cocoon
> not to lose the thread.
> She's larva again.
>
> I'm taking her back into my body.
>
> She's taken her hands from my shoulders.
> No longer yells, "straighten up."
>
> Death has come to take her back
> and only the well cast blame.
>
> Only the beautiful hide their breasts
> and you naked as a spool
> have folded the linens one last time
> and touched the cranberry glass.
>
> In the fight for your antiques,
> leave me nothing I'm alive
> and strong with you back in my spine.

I lift you from your bath
and dry and love you.

So much has happened in between but nothing will ever beat the thrill of discovering poetry and life with Ted Kooser fifty years ago.

P.S.: I was one of the people who received a valentine from Ted every year. One year, we all composed valentines to mail in return.

Mine was a haiku ending with the line: "Ai Yai, Cowboy Ted."

Teasing Out the Lies, Stitching in the Life: Ted Kooser's Poetry Writing Seminar University of Nebraska-Lincoln, Spring 1988

Paul McCallum

By the time I'd enrolled in the Poetry Writing Seminar, I considered myself the proud master of the "loose thread" poem. Such poems force readers to light upon that one element that doesn't fit with the rest—an incongruous detail or a lone bit of irony—give it a mental tug, and then gasp in shock and admiration at how this single anomaly gives the lie to the whole poem, and of course to their own expectations. The fact that my readers either never detected the loose thread, or else pulled the wrong one, or else didn't pull the right one hard enough was vexing, but also vaguely satisfying.

Three of my loose thread poems were to be discussed during our seminar's second meeting. Before then, however, we received notice that the scheduled instructor would not be teaching the class after all. Instead, it would be taken by a part-timer whose full-time job I understood (erroneously, it turned out) was selling insurance: Ted Kooser. He certainly *looked* like an insurance salesman that first evening, in his jacket, tie, and wingtips, and a weariness of expression well suited, I thought, to a profession that preached the folly of indulging hope at the expense of prudence.

The first poem I read to the class depicted a young couple falling into bed giggling and having happy joyful sex. The line—"Yes, but I hear the sparrows screeching"—was the loose thread. Despite appearances, all is not well in the relationship. After I read it, Kooser stared over half-lenses at the poem, which he held at nearly arm's length. "Paul," he began at last, "suppose I'm not ornithologist enough to know this nocturnal habit of sparrows. How am I to have a chance with this poem?"

My second offering, in which the narrator roughs up a beggar, an ironic allegory intended to suggest Christ's humiliation by the complacently respectable of this world, fared much worse. My classmates missed the loose thread and were horrified that I could endorse violence against the homeless. I gaped like a carp. Kooser, in a *there-there* tone, observed that irony was probably not something to be attempted by the unpracticed.

Kooser was openly scornful of my final poem, an attempt at psycho-spiritual communion with my grandfather. Clearing his throat, he boomed out six lines in an exaggerated Edward R. Murrow newsreel voice exactly as I'd heard them in my head as I wrote them. Now they seemed not dramatic and solemn but silly—each stressed syllable a rumbling belch, eructations posing as the voice of Time. Kooser had taken only twenty minutes to quietly dismantle my poetic prejudices and predilections.

Kooser never saw our poems before we read them in class. He usually said nothing for some minutes, staring impassively at the page before him as the group gaggled about what "worked for" them or what they "had problems with." Then suddenly, sometimes cutting into another's comment mid-meander, Kooser would lay bare the elaborate machinery of artifice puffing away behind the façade. This was pulling the loose thread indeed: one good yank and the entire garment unraveled.

By the time I read a poem in class called "Sea Turtles," I'd abandoned coded cluing. My description of hundreds of turtles laying their eggs on Costa Rican shores under the moonlight was clear enough, it seemed to me, as was the ironic fatalism with which the newly hatched young "skitter to/ The waiting/gulls," and the implied parallel between the turtles' lot and that of the two lovers who witnessed their doomed struggle.

"Paul, what makes you think we can see hundreds of turtles and thousands of eggs and then thousands of hatchlings more easily than a single turtle and one egg and one hatchling? Suppose you tried this—." And Kooser read the poem aloud, substituting singulars for all my plurals. He was right. It *was* easier to visualize one turtle, one hatchling, one gull, and consequently easier to build an emotional response.

Kooser had little patience for poems that strove after grand effect, or that resorted to abstraction and editorializing. "Here," he'd say in such cases, sometimes with amusement, sometimes with a disappointed sigh, "is where the poet comes sweeping on stage with his cape and hat to explain it all." The affective power of a poem, he stressed, resides in well-chosen, well-rendered images that the reader can see clearly. Kooser made the point indelibly one evening by having each of us cite a detail descriptive of an abandoned farmhouse. We conjured up an old car on blocks, a sagging porch, broken windows, a shutter hanging by a single nail, peeling paint—all commonplace, as Kooser no doubt expected. "Now," he said, "suppose we show an empty potato chip bag blowing about in the front yard." The effect was startling: the unexpected detail made all the stock images seem suddenly fresh, as if we were seeing such a place for the first time.

From that night on, "Throw in the potato chip bag" became our shorthand for saying more was needed to engage the reader's imagination. Other Kooser sayings became shorthand as well. "Pick the puppy up in the middle" meant that we had missed the central significance or were trying to finesse what needed to be said outright; "throw in the alligator," that we needed more energy in our images, diction, or rhythm.

I tried to put these prescriptions into practice. By midterm, I noticed that my approach to writing poetry had changed; I had become a defensive writer, in two senses. Before I turned in a poem now, I ran through a mental checklist of things I needed to put in (potato chip bags and alligators among them), and things I needed to excise: clichés, sentimentality, Latinisms, abstractions, inadvertent rhyme and alliteration, hamfisted manipulations, all superfluous images, lines, and words. I was learning, in short, to see things through Kooser's eyes and was becoming a more considered reader of my own work. But I was also becoming defensive in the way one drives defensively, anticipating that the guy in the grey Buick will run the light or that the blonde ponytail jogging with her Lab-mix will suddenly chase her dog into traffic. There was no escaping the fact that I couldn't expect my readers to look out for me; I had to accommodate them. Even a hasty scan of the page had to yield enough that was intelligible, new, and meaningful to seem worthwhile. And if I were lucky enough to catch the reader's attention, there had to be something beneath the surface that was also accessible and rewarding.

The trouble with being defensive is that there is never any reason to write a poem other than wanting to. And the poet's wanting to can almost always be traced to ego. "Pay attention to me," says the poet to the reader, "and I will show you something worth your while." It's a wholly reasonable demand, for readers are busy and have no reason to read a poem instead of changing a tire or doing the dishes. And if it's absurd to intrude on their attention, how absurd to insist on one's eccentric, idiosyncratic notions of a ruined abbey or an upscale dinner party on a warm October evening?

Late in the term, Kooser delivered to us the short sharp kick in the shins. Certain species of well-crafted, enjoyable poems—here I fancied he glanced over at me—will have no chance whatsoever of finding a publisher. Well then: the surest way not to vex readers and editors is to write no poems at all. Yet what is one to do with the inklings and intimations that come unbidden and demand expression?

Here I was at a stop, impelled and restrained by the same impulse. What was there to do but write a poem about my conundrum? And so I wrote about an old man who "shadows the page" of the poem being written, points "with fingers / smudged with ink and nicotine," and says, "You're lying—here—here…."

> Old Man's smirk can mock the truth of any line;
> his fingers can make each knot a tangle to be cut away.
> But when Old Man sleeps, the line he'd scrap as tinsel
> can be woven in, the thread whose glint teases
> the poem into the words, stitches in the life.

When I read the poem to the class, I was certain my classmates would pounce on the allegorical figure of Old Man, on the unspecified properties of the glinting thread, on the sheer self-centeredness of the piece. But they were silent. Perhaps they merely waited to take their cue from the Old Man at the end of the table who had been chastening and exposing and deflating all of us all term and who now resided in each of us: No poem worth reading without him; no poem at all without finding a way to cheat him.

On this night in late April, it happened that Kooser was willing to let himself be cheated.

"Solid work," he said.

Portraits of Kooser

Mark Sanders

The Man at Home

In September 1977, I drove to Lincoln, Nebraska, where Ted Kooser lived in a big, turn-of-the-century house on Washington Street. I was nervous: he was my first poet.

The previous summer at Kearney State College, I had composed a research prospectus on Nebraska poets—Kooser among them. "An excellent topic," Dr. Pierce wrote on my paper. After class, she told me to pursue it: "This is necessary. Some of these poets are going to be important." I hedged. "You lack confidence," she said. "Call the poets up, write to them." I'm not certain what my "subjects" thought when, from the bowels of west Nebraska, the phone calls came, yet they accommodated someone who had not earned accommodation.

I pulled alongside the Washington Street curb ten minutes early and sat studying the intricate leaf-painting Kooser had done on his house beneath the upper eaves. Don Welch, my friend and poetry-mentor at Kearney, had told me about Kooser's brief occupation as a painter. There had been a crisis in Kooser's graduate studies under Karl Shapiro's tutelage. Kooser loved poetry so much he took all his studies with Shapiro, failing to make progress on his master's degree by taking the "appropriate" academic coursework. Called into his advisor's office, Kooser was informed he was being let go. Kooser's wife, Diana, working to support their family of three, was upset, according to Don's recall. And Ted, well, he had to find work and became a painter instead of a professor. (Don had also been a student of Shapiro's in the early 60s; he talked about conversations he and Shapiro had at the urinals in Andrews Hall at the UNL campus). Eventually, Kooser stepped from brush and ladder to life insurance.

How much of this narrative was accurate I couldn't know; I was an impressionable small town kid and willing to accept whatever I was told. Kooser's example was a cautionary tale. My mother hoped I would be a grade school teacher; my father wanted an architect. Art was dangerous and beat a path to poverty and hardship.

Eyeing the paintwork on his house, I thought—despite how nice it looked—Kooser's choice to change careers was probably the right thing. No one could earn a living painting—

How that thought caused me dread. I was thinking in the box, as my parents did. I wanted badly to live outside that box, to write, to publish. Here was proof: I was parked in front of a poet's house, anticipating conversation about poetry, looking for answers and validation. Normal people didn't do such things.

I knew Kooser through a few letters and phone calls, but mostly through the poetry of his first collections. His letters were disdainfully short, curt, without the beauty of image which softened the familiar tone of his poetry. They were insurance-man memos, always signed, *Hurried*. Kooser terrified me. I suspected he did not like me (though we had not met), that he was merely tolerant. My coming here was a violation of a poet's privacy, of someone unlike me, sure of his words, sure of his place.

I wonder how long Kooser stood inside his living room, watching me out the window. I imagine him, now, standing in stocking feet, sipping a cup of coffee, grinning sardonically at the kid who feared to move.

At 9 o'clock sharp, I left my car and made my way up the porch steps. Before I could ring the doorbell, Ted opened the door. "Sanders?" he asked, extending his hand. "I'm Ted Kooser. Come on in."

Soon, I was seated on an old rocking chair and setting up my tape recorder. He brought me a cup of coffee, and, having never interviewed anyone before, I fumbled and apologized for fumbling. He sat on his sofa and drew his legs up to recline. He was relaxed. Too relaxed. I was a cat—all tense and sinew. And then his cat jumped on me, from behind, the whole height from the floor to my shoulders. His claws took hold. The chair rocked deeply back. I flailed arms to catch my balance, nearly knocking over a floor lamp. Ted said, "Are you allergic to cats?"

I shook my head.

"Then he won't hurt you."

Toward the interview's end, I asked, "Why do you write poetry?"

His answer: "My psychologist tells me I write poetry to find someone to love me. I think he's probably right." When his new wife Kathy made noise in a back room, he confessed poetry brought them together. He recounted how one morning he stood at his office window, watching people file up and down the sidewalk, the cars going by. A most beautiful woman walked past, arresting his attention. He watched until she disappeared, yet she remained on his mind all day. Later, he said, at five o'clock, the same woman passed, going the other direction, moving down the sidewalk, moving out of view.

This happened over several days. Finally, Ted said, he had to know who she was. He followed her home, saw which mailbox she took her mail from, and, under darkness of night, left poems in her box. He attached a note, with his name and phone number: "If you like my poems, maybe you'd like me. I really am quite harmless." She called, they talked long, they met, they married. Good instinct.

Ted read me several new pieces during that morning meeting, and we also talked about my own poetry. I had sent him a self-made chapbook, entitled *1:10*; he had typed four pages of commentary and told me he feared he was too harsh, but not to feel too badly about that. If I kept writing, I would get better. He said I needed to find my own voice, not the voice of my teacher nor the voice of Kooser nor the voice of Bill Kloefkorn, whose work I was also studying. "Find Sanders," he said.

The Maker of Books

In 1978, I decided to start a small press. I took the idea to my professors at Kearney State, and all but Don Welch told me not to bother. One professor, in particular, was quite angry. "You're encroaching on the journal I founded," he said. "There's not enough poetry to go around." Then, I took the idea to Ted Kooser. Before I ever knew Kooser as poet, I had known him as small press editor. His Windflower Press had published the early books of Kloefkorn and Welch—among the first books of poems I ever owned, and I much admired what he had done with the *New Salt Creek Reader*. I wanted to do that sort of thing.

I told him I thought I'd call it Sandhills Press, after the region where I had lived as a boy and because of its approximation to my own last name. He had told me to find Sanders; the Sandhills was the ground from which I had come—best to start there. His return letter gave me confirmation: the press name was "wonderful," he wrote. Then, he gave me ideas on where to find typesetters, printers, how to price the books, how to sell them. Thus began the 30-year history of my presswork.

T-shirt Entrepreneur

In August 1981, Ted Kooser put together the first gathering of Nebraska writers, the Tin Camp Writers' Picnic. Although I then lived in southwest Missouri, I journeyed home to join the festivities. Tin Camp was way-west Nebraska, in the Sandhills, near the little towns of Sutherland and Paxton, home of the legendary Ole's Big Game Bar and Lounge. These communities were two little watering holes, outposts, in the center of the Great American Desert, where the twenty or so Nebraska writers, some with family members with them, showed up to camp for a weekend—among them, J. V. Brummels, Paul Shuttleworth, Bill Kloefkorn, Shirley Buettner, Susan Strayer Deal, Liz Banset, Judith Sornberger. All we had was tall sky, cottonwoods, buffalo gamma grass, a cold stream etching its deep name into the soil, and colder nights that had us huddling in sleeping bags inside our tents. One of Don Welch's sons said, "I guess the cold is something you have to get used to."

When I arrived at Tin Camp, Kooser greeted me. He wore the Indian beadwork around his neck that he had worn for the back cover photo of *A Local Habitation & A Name*. And, as always, he called me Sanders. "Hello, Sanders," he called, "Good to see you."

We ate hot dogs, chips, drank beer, soft drinks, sipped pan-boiled coffee over an open fire. Ted sold Tin Camp Writers Picnic and Windflower Press T-shirts: "Support the arts, take a poet to lunch." At night, when the locusts sang, we stood around the bonfire and read samples of our own poetry. I read "American Flyer" and sucked a fly down my throat. Kooser later told me that my poem was a Kooser poem. "Find Sanders" rang in my head.

Kooser and I visited about a book proposal I had in mind, an extension of the 1977 research I had published on him, Kloefkorn, and Welch. I envisioned a big book, of interviews, poems, critical commentary. All three men were at Tin Camp, and all three liked the idea;

Kooser's reaction was especially welcomed. The Pitt Series had just published *Sure Signs*; a poet doesn't do much better than that, and I was still awestruck. Ted told me about a young writer with a sound critical acumen, a New York businessman named Dana Gioia. Gioia had written a review of *Sure Signs* for the *Hudson Review*. He wanted Gioia to write an essay on his work, if I could get him. I did. Gioia's significant essay on Kooser first appeared in *On Common Ground* in 1983.

Professor Poet

By 1987, I had returned to Nebraska to pursue a Ph.D. at the University. Though I had been away for seven years in Missouri, I maintained my connections to my Nebraska fraternity of writers, yet more and more separated myself from their earlier influence. I was finding Sanders. Ted Kooser and Charles Woodard were collaborating on a book entitled, *As Far as I Can See*, and Ted accepted a poem of mine, "Self-Portrait," for the anthology. At last, I had written a poem that Ted liked.

In 1989, as my last course in the doctoral program, I took a poetry writing seminar. I had avoided creative writing courses those three years; Ted had once cautioned me against becoming "Dr. Poet." "Do an academic degree," he advised.

The professor scheduled to teach the class bailed after the first meeting. Dr. Link, head of the English program, called me to his office. "We have to find another teacher for the class," he said. "The previous one says he can't teach Sanders anything." Dr. Link explained he had asked Ted Kooser to step in as a visiting lecturer. Was that all right with me? Of course it was.

During one meeting, Ted told us that his former teacher, Karl Shapiro, had said that all good writing had to have an alligator in it. Something should surprise the reader, shock and bite him. I've used that alligator in my own creative writing seminars to encourage my students to dare. It was a lesson I learned well for myself, too: I wrote some good poems in that class. And, to this day, I have noted that Ted Kooser no longer calls me Sanders. Perhaps that I found Sanders allowed him to use my first name.

Colonel Carter

In 1998, I was invited to the Nebraska Literature Festival at Wayne State College. I had hoped Ted would go, so I called him from my home in south Texas to visit with him. Ted was ill. He had had cancer, chemo, an operation, and could barely speak. Yet, he wanted to visit. I told him I was planning a set of broadsides for the festival, not unlike the broadsides he had done with *The Salt Creek Reader* back in the early 70's. I explained I would do line drawings, as he had done in *Grass County*, to accompany the poems. Could I use "Beer Bottle," "Laundry," and "Snow Fence"? He agreed.

What was going to be a collection of one dozen cards quickly grew to 42, all with one poem and one of my line drawings. It was fast work, completed in less than three weeks. Because Ted could not attend the festival, I sent him the entire set. He wrote back to say what a handsome collection it was and gave my press, now doing the Main-Traveled Roads chapbook series, a helpful donation. He also gave me an essay manuscript for the series, *Riding with Colonel Carter*, which I published shortly thereafter. In the essay, Ted alludes to Robert McCloskey's *Lentil*, a book I remembered from my childhood mornings with Captain Kangaroo. Lentil does a good deed, saves the day, and gets to ride with Colonel Carter. In the essay, Ted writes how he feels like Lentil, getting to ride with Governor Bob Kerrey.

I sent McCloskey a copy of *Colonel Carter*. Ted heard from him, in a letter that evidenced how much he appreciated Lentil's evocation. Ted also sent me a photocopy of that letter for my own archives.

And, like Lentil, I appreciated getting to ride along with both Mc-Closkey and Kooser.

Old Friend

I next saw Ted Kooser at Nebraska City, the fall of 2001, at a fete honoring Don Welch and William Kloefkorn's contributions to Nebraska letters. I was invited by the Nebraska Center for the Book to give testimonial remarks, as was Ted, as were about a dozen other writers. The governor, Mike Johanns, was there, as well. One of the things I said that night was how, had it not been for Kooser and his Windflower Press, we might not have had any reason to honor those two men. I said what I came to say, and it was passionate (I believe) and honest—Don and Bill have meant much to me. Yet, I also knew Ted Kooser should have been so honored. He has meant so much to so many of us.

Before Ted left for home—it was past his bedtime, Kathy said— he autographed a copy of his *Journey to a Place of Work* for me. There's a picture of Ted on the front cover, an insurance man in suit and tie, and he drew a cartoon bubble over to the side of it. "For Mark, old friend," he wrote inside the bubble.

For more than 20 years, he had seen me find myself, find my voice, my work, my confidence. He was "old friend," indeed.

Three More Encounters

I recall the occasion of Ted's receiving the Pulitzer Prize, as some-times people recall significant historic events, tragic or pleasurable. Details remain vivid, for example, of the occasion when John Kenne-dy was assassinated, when Oswald was subsequently killed, when the Beatles appeared on *The Ed Sullivan Show*, when Bobby Kennedy was shot, when Martin Luther King was shot, or when John Lennon was shot outside the Dakota. I know exactly what I was doing the first time I heard Jimi Hendrix's *Are You Experienced*, Frank Zappa's "Mon-tana," Grand Funk Railroad's *Grand Funk*. Such memories are endless. Kooser's winning the Pulitzer is prominent among them. David Baker had just finished his poetry reading at Lewis-Clark State College in Lewiston, Idaho, where I was professor of creative writing. Several of us—Kimberly Verhines, Northwest writers Robert Wrigley and Claire Davis, among others—were sitting at the Red Lion Inn, eating appe-tizers and drinking. David was the one who received the message, and the news he shared was exciting. We toasted Ted's success, and I made a joke: Ted Kooser's mentor, Karl Shapiro had won the Pulitizer in 1945 for *V-Letter and Other Poems*; 60 years later, his student received the award. By my calculations, because I took a poetry seminar with Ted in 1989, I figured my turn at the prize would come in 2065, at a youthful 110 years of age. The future seemed bright.

*

I sent Ted a copy of my book, *Conditions of Grace*, upon its publica-tion in 2011. Not long after, I received a note which I now keep close so I may return to it when my writing mood needs bolstered; the note reads, "I'm proud to have this book in my library." I make much out of small gestures, as Ted makes much out of small things, and the note is among my highly regarded mementos. A few months later, I received word that Ted wanted to include one of the poems, "The Cranes, Texas January," in his "American Life in Poetry" column. This remains a celebratory moment.

*

The last time I saw Ted (though I hear from him occasionally via email) was in November 2015, when he attended a reading of poetry I did at the University of Nebraska; his coming to the reading was a tremendous compliment, and I appreciated the generosity he showed me—the weather was horrible and pouring down cold rain. Snow seemed imminent. I was surprised anyone showed up at all. Ted had to drive into Lincoln from Garland in that weather, and I doubt I would have given myself the same courtesy. He was waiting for me outside the room where I was reading, and we visited about a number of topics before and after, ranging from concern about our friend Don Welch, who was quite ill, to my recent edited work, *A Sandhills Reader*, in which Don, Bill Kloefkorn, and Ted played an important role—they were among my first encouragers, way back in 1977 when they indulged my poetic inquiries, and they were among the first poets I published on my Sandhills Press imprint. I handed Ted his contributor's copy that evening.

The Love of the Well-Made

Don Welch

> Poets' real biographies are like those of birds . . .
> their real data are in the way they sound.
> —Joseph Brodsky, *Less Than One*

In the 1960's, about the time James Dickey was extolling the merits of the "unwellmade poem," I approached my car in the parking lot of the university where I was teaching, only to find a student had its hood up and its battery caps off. He was using a straw to extract acid that he was dropping on his new tennis shoes and that, by eating holes in them, was making them "unwellmade."

When I realized what he was doing, I told him I thought his shoes were also too white, and that he should take them over to the gutter, where there was muddy rainwater, and to wallow them around a bit. "Good idea," he said, and as I drove off, I noticed he was well into the act of making them grungier.

Ted Kooser has never bought into the idea of the unwellmade poem, nor into the cultural irony, long ascendant, that ratty is up. One of my favorite poems of Ted's illustrates this more clearly than I can:

LOBOCRASPIS GRISEIFUSA

This is the tiny moth who lives on tears,
who drinks like a deer at the gleaming pool
at the edge of the sleeper's eye, the touch
of its mouth as light as a cloud's reflection.

In your dream, a moonlit figure appears
at your bedside and touches your face.
He asks if he might share the poor bread
of your sorrow. You show him the table.

The two of you talk long into the night,
but by morning the words are forgotten.
You awaken serene, in a sunny room,
rubbing the dust of his wings from your eyes.

(Delights & Shadows 58)

Here the sensitivity of the anapests, as muted as they are by Ted's sure ear, are a perfect counterpart to something small, yet intricate, drinking like a deer at the edge of the sleeper's eye. And, later, to the almost casual haunting of the figure touching the face of the dreamer. If we can tell great poetry by its rightness, here it does not miss the mark, its art drifting first to the right, then back to the left, like an inerrant occurrence. Like the rhyme of "sorrow" and "table" at the end of the second stanza, so simply dissonant, so slightly emphatic, so surely made. Or the poem's preponderance of muted vowels (sleeping?) which open in the last two lines to the higher-pitched "a," "e," and "i."

So too Ted's handling of the four-beat line, with all its old echoes of what was once called common or hymnal measure. More familiar, less ceremonial than the more organ-toned five-beat line, it places great emphasis upon nouns and verbs, while undressing itself of adjectives and adverbs. Typical of Ted, it achieves its resonance through simplicity, its honest use of language, which is the ultimate political act.

The best poems, like "Lobocraspis griseifusa," drop like plumb lines through the wreckage of our lives, holding us still as our blood runs on, asking us to be true to their moments. After we finish reading them, we are both equal to and true. We are the sum of sounds we've never listened for, whose gravity is the point of our lives.

Commentary
& Criticism

A Review of
Official Entry Blank

Greg Kuzma

Official Entry Blank is an impressive first book, much neglected, coming at a bad time from the University of Nebraska Press as they succumb to the financial pressures of publishing poetry, as they close out their poetry series. Perhaps the book has suffered from insufficient advertising or distribution as a result—I have seen only one review of it, and that in *Prairie Schooner*. Or perhaps coming out of the "heartland" as it does it has been written off as a regional work.

Not that the book escapes being regional, but it is so only in matter not in vision. Kooser writes of the demanding land, its delicate changes that only a Midwesterner might note, its conservative often backward people:

BIRDSBEESBIRDSBEESBIRDSBEESBIRDSBEES

Jane's mother didn't mention it to Jane
because *her* mother hadn't mentioned it
when *she* was Jane's age. God forbid!
The secret stayed under their bridal trains.

When John was young, *but old enough to know,*
his father blushed and whispered down to him
the secret. John ran; John told Jim,
and they touched each other: vertigo.

Jim was a nudging Best-Man, John looked bold,
and Jane was tight and worried (some could tell).
Their parents kissed them and wished them well.
Now John is impotent and Jane is cold.

It's the old story, the one they tell out here, but clearly told with an awareness of ironies, clearly with wit and an industrious technical skill. Here is a description of motorcyclists (from "The Iron Bachelors"):

> Chromey as surgery and loud as gods,
> the motorcycles lope along the streets,
> swinging their heavy heads with loneliness—
> the iron bachelors are dangerous tonight.
> They are as desperate as acne, quick
> as innocence, and brittle as a wish.
>
> . . .

The images here are active. They are so much involved with the rest of the language that it is unfair to talk of Kooser, no matter how much "style" one can fault him for, as simply a skilled technician. These poems may not brood, but they penetrate. The details are telling.

Of the poems I like a good deal, "Lament," "For Karl Shapiro," "The Corpse of the Old Woman," "The Closet Zoo," I especially admire "Rooming House":

> The blind man draws his curtains for the night
> and goes to bed, leaving a burning light
>
> above the bathroom mirror. Through the wall,
> he hears the deaf man walking down the hall
>
> in his squeaky shoes to see if there's a light
> under the blind man's door, and all is right.

Untitled Introduction to
A Local Habitation & A Name

Karl Shapiro

For all its guff, William Carlos Williams' dogma of the Local remains the touchtone of what authentic American poetry we have. Whitman tried the Local on the heroic scale, mapping the continent. Nothing very local there but at least he dared the idiom to come into being. And despite the adversary esthetic of the Modern, the programmatists, the pseudo-revolutionaries, the doom-sayers, the boors of protest and cant, an idiom, a language, emerges.

Programmatic or national (anti-American) poetry is the easy way out, the low road to the laurel. Everyone is sick of it except of course its practitioners, people who exploit poetry in the name of social progress.

The quest for the idiom goes on, and where it is heard most clearly is the Middle West, the womb of so much American creativity. In Kooser's poems there is that dry and patient irony of the plainsman, that deceptive quietism, that dark humor, the lover's quarrel with nature, and overall the landscape, itself rigid and infinite. Few poets have captured the spirit of place as well as he, that place in which people are almost incidental, and speak out of postcards. The bitterness of Masters and Sherwood Anderson is gone, replaced by glimpses of the office man, the gas station attendant, the tattooed lady in the carnival, still-lifes of people, camera stills. There is a clarity and purity in these poems that suggest the great photographers or artists like Hopper. One leafs back and forth through these poems with a strong feeling of *déjà vu* but not of nostalgia. And one contemplates them like mandalas.

So that in the end one thanks him for his gifts of honesty and lucidity, the sharpness of focus, and that mysterious quality of voice which confers significance upon his material. Reading these poems a foreigner would know and ken Kooser's land and the spirit of it.

On Ted Kooser's
Not Coming to be Barked At

Lex Runciman

Understand just the title of this book by Ted Kooser, and it is like putting a key in a lock. For the phrase "not coming to be barked at" is, in its own way, a kind of affirmation. And what Kooser gives us, in poem after poem, is affirmation. Even here in the poem "Fort Robinson":

> When I visited Fort Robinson,
> where Dull Knife and his Northern Cheyenne
> were held captive that terrible winter,
> the grounds crew was killing the magpies.
>
> Two men were going from tree to tree
> with sticks and ladders, poking the young birds
> down from their nests and beating them to death
> as they hopped about in the grass.
>
> Under each tree where the men had worked
> were twisted clots of matted feathers,
> and above each tree a magpie circled,
> crazily calling in all her voices.
>
> We didn't get out of the car.
> My little boy hid in the back and cried
> as we drove away, into those ragged buttes
> the Cheyenne climbed that winter, fleeing.

Even here something is salvaged and learned. For a few lines at least, it is that winter, we are Cheyenne.

Kooser's voice and tone is almost always subdued—down home and ordinary. It is a voice that seems to come precisely from the country it speaks of, from Nebraska, cornfields, wheat. It has that calm, and sweep of distance. Yet even within this almost flat tone, and perhaps because of it, Kooser's poems have a greater impact than one might first suspect:

THERE IS ALWAYS A LITTLE WIND

—for Debra Hulbert

There is always a little wind
in a country cemetery,
even on days when the air stands
still as a barn in the fields.

You can see the old cedars
stringy and tough as maiden aunts,
taking the little gusts of wind
in their aprons like sheaves of wheat,

and hear above you the warm
and regular sweep of wheat being cut
and gathered, the wagons creaking,
the young men breathing at their work.

Pentagram Press has printed a handsome book, and Ted Kooser has filled it with poems that matter. The best of them will stay with you for a long time.

Ted Kooser: Searching for Signs

George von Glahn

As some of his reviewers have pointed out, Ted Kooser is deceptively easy to read. He uses few if any unusual words, his poems are all relatively short, and his impact seems refreshingly free of subjective obscurities. Yet he is somehow deep and rich. Those readers who possess the normal baggage of academic criticism should be forewarned of this. His simplicity is lucid rather than superficial.

That very ease with which he communicates intimate meaning has meant for me, however, that the impulse to say something *about* Kooser's poems has not come often since I got my first look at them. But that in itself constitutes a discovery about them—the latest of many. What I have mainly done instead is read them delightedly to friends and relatives every chance I could get, mainly from his last collection, *A Local Habitation & a Name*. As I suspected and hoped, the response to such readings has nearly always been some sign of pleasure, sometimes through surprise and sometimes through recognition. The only exception, which I also expected really, came from west coast people who seem to have a very hard time acknowledging even the tangible existence of a place mysteriously known as the plains. To them it is simply not the sort of place that one can get excited about or from where poetry would be expected to come. In general it has been my experience that Kooser offers a rich and rewarding sense of "place" for those who are willing to accept the modesty of Kooser's demands and have enough awareness not to be trapped in their own pretenses to sophistication.

What basically are Kooser's demands? Only two, as I see it. First, the same openness to subtlety of immediate response on which any poet depends, and second, a previous encounter with the midwest experience, on whatever level, actual or mythical. This last may appear to limit fatally the scope of his audience, but not necessarily. He really demands only the memory of what it feels like to be in the midst of an emptiness that somehow calls into question, or reduces to actual absurdity, any object or person that happens to invade it. Thus arises the implied loneliness in the title *A Local Habitation & a Name* and in most of the opening notes of that book as well. The fundamental mood is captured perfectly in the closing three lines of "A Place in Kansas": "Not a single white sail of a meaning / broke the horizon, though he stood there for hours. / It's like that in Kansas, forever." To write in and of such a region requires special gifts of honest, lucid, and courageous perception. Kooser uses these deftly and manages to transcend the merely local, not only by his sure feel for image and metaphor but also, and essentially, by peopling his landscape with vivid, albeit silent, and precariously balanced characters.

Given this kind of place to work with, Kooser must necessarily deal with interior vision rather than exterior description alone. Thus he reaches for his ideal essence of the "place" through capturing brief instants of life in the souls of the people who inhabit it, some of them nameless or only implicitly present, others named, and still others known only as anonymous voices in brief postcards. And it is this human presence, mute for the most part though it is, that allows these poems to transcend "nature" poetry and become true rural poetry.

Character, and frequently tragic character, is his true subject. This is true even of those poems which appear at first to be about animals only. One of my favorites is "How to Foretell a Change in the Weather." It masterfully and subtly builds into an excited emotional pitch that has almost biblical, prophetic overtones. Nature is not worshipped here; it is known, observed—and feared for its ultimate mystery and uncontrollability. In the face of its power one can only watch and feel its signs as they are given: legends, fables, old wives tales are all born of it.

> Rain always follows the cattle
> sniffing the air and huddling
> in fields with their heads to the lee.
> You will know that the weather is changing
> when your sheep leave the pasture
> too slowly, and your dogs lie about
> and look tired; when the cat
> turns her back to the fire,
> washing her face, and the pigs
> wallow in litter; cocks will be crowing
> at unusual hours, flapping their wings;

hens will chant; when your ducks
and your geese are too noisy,
and the pigeons are washing themselves;
when the peacocks squall loudly
from the tops of the trees,
and the guinea-fowl grates;
when sparrows chip loudly
and fuss in the roadway, and when swallows
fly low, skimming the earth;
when the carrion crow
croaks to himself, and wild fowl
dip and wash, and when moles
throw up hills with great fervor;
when toads creep out in numbers;
when frogs croak; when bats
enter the houses; when birds
begin to seek shelter,
and the robin approaches your house;
when the swan flies at the wind,
and your bees leave their hive;
when ants carry their eggs to and fro,
and flies bite, and the earthworm
is seen on the surface of things.

Kooser's mood in this simultaneously amusing and exciting rural pastiche defines one of the major poles of his sensibility. He lives the role of the passionate and awake searcher for signs to announce or proclaim, and he finds them in fragments all over his native landscape in both people and the animals people relate to. This attitude will not allow for a consistency of pattern, and Kooser knows that and is willing to accept it. But he does possess something equally valuable, at least for his early stage of development: a kind of dominant attitude or mode of perception around which he scatters various attempts at experimentation that tentatively define other modes, but into which he never strays too far. Most of his inspiration comes in the form of sharply focused "bits" of experience that depend for their success on complete and fresh honesty. These bits are not, however, at all like those "vortexes" of Ezra

Pound that so strongly influenced the early imagist school. The ragged edges of an involved and alive viewer's emotions are too evident for us to place Kooser comfortably among those stern, objective, and rather cold classicists. Nor does Kooser share the metaphysical concerns of Wallace Stevens. No, Kooser is at once simple, profound, and emotional. In every bit of Kooser's experience that he managed to mold into something communicable, there is an implied flux—one is always made aware that in the next micro-instant the experience will be gone, despite its being captured in language. Kooser sees everything in the process of either becoming or dying, even symbols. And that is the opposite pole of Kooser's sensibility, the awareness of the constant threat that the signs will be meaningless.

The perception of that threat, along with the courage to ignore it, is the root of ultimate honesty. Such honesty, incisive and even brutal, as we find it, for example, in "Another Old Woman," must be understood as largely the result of a "process" insight into life, an insight that cannot help but illuminate life's basic tragic and ambiguous character:

> Oh, how horrible it has been to have been alive!
> It has been like one train meeting another in the night;
> the face of some strange man in the window opposite
> looking hungrily forward into your past
> while you are carried recklessly into a country
> made up of things that he has soiled,
> both of you cold and uncomfortable, moving at terrible speed.

To arrest this "terrible speed" and yet retain the awful realization that it cannot be done is Kooser's urgent yet perilous poetic enterprise. If the urge of his thought is to see a pattern in the signs of passing and tell what he sees, the emotional corollary is the temptation to despair in the face of its inevitable fragmentation and evanescence. Life in time in the midwest, perhaps most aptly captured in the image of trains or cars passing through the flat endlessness, has a peculiar, sordid, and lonely quality. It is brought explicitly to consciousness in a poem like "Late Lights in Minnesota":

> At the end of a freight train rolling away,

a hand swinging a lantern.
The only lights left behind in the town
are a bulb burning cold in the jail,
and high in one house,
a five-battery flashlight
pulling an old woman downstairs to the toilet
among the red eyes of her cats.

The light-signs of life in the emptiness of the land, the jail, the house, and finally the old woman herself, are all at the same time signs of silence. Only the poet speaks of such things, and he does not say more than he must. Kooser writes about death, abandonment, emptiness and estrangement, yet with an admirable reticence. He avoids the heavy-handedness of someone who secretly enjoys what he says because, as Hemingway puts it, he hasn't had to pay for his emotion. The genuineness of Kooser's emotion is certified by his consistent and pervasive appreciation for the unspectacular quality of silence that hangs over these conditions of human life wherever and whenever one comes to realize the impact of their existence. The final stanza of "Abandoned Farmhouse" is a fine instance of this appreciation.

Something went wrong, says the empty house
in the weed-choked yard. Stones in the fields
say he was not a farmer; the still-sealed jars
in the cellar say she left in a nervous haste.
And the child? Its toys are strewn in the yard
like branches after a storm—a rubber cow,
a rusty tractor with a broken plow,
a doll in overalls. Something went wrong, they say.

As a further result of this sensitivity to the quality of estrangement, Kooser generally prefers to express experience without an imposed pattern, thus allowing himself to share in the risk of fragmentation. That is why his own sense of permanence always seems put in jeopardy by each experience he tries to express. He feels the presence of the blind, for example, as "tapping across the bright circles of our ambitions / like cracks traversing the favorite china." Putting his hand on his son's head, he grows suddenly older. He sees a buzzer by the side of his bed in a rented room, a buzzer that "once brought a nurse." This buzzer is the "odd reality" for him. "Waking through broken dreams, / I've pushed it in the night but no one comes." Only once in a while does this kind of experience become generalized into something approaching self-pity, as in "They had Torn Off My Face at the Office" and "Grating a Brain." Not that these two poems do not have an impact of their own. What they lack is the sense of the concrete presence of perception, the found sign of the "odd "reality," that is characteristic of Kooser at his best.

In general, Kooser's sensibility does not function at its best in a city environment, or when he allows his personal life into the poem. He himself seems to sense this, for in *A Local Habitation & a Name*, he relegates most of the non-rural poems to the last fourth of the volume and puts them under the separate title "Other Depots." Many of these poems are entertaining and have a recognizable Kooser irony about them. Yet they lack the sense of place that gives Kooser his real value for us. An excellent example of what I'm talking about is "Anniversary," one of the poems, incidentally, that got a particularly good response from my California friends.

> At dinner, in that careful rouge of light
> of five or six martinis, you could pass
> for Ginger Rogers; we could dance all night
> on tiny tabletops as slick as glass
> in flying, shiny shoes. As Fred Astaire,
> my wrinkles grow distinguished as we dine,
> my bald spot festers with the growth of hair,
> I grow intelligent about the wine.
> But such high life is taxing; urgencies
> excuse us from the table. Hand in hand
> we seek the restrooms, trembling at the knees,
> and find our grins grown horrid in that land
> of flare-lit, glaring mirrors. Through the wall
> you flush your toilet like a lonely call.

This is not at all the effect of the lonely light on the end of the freight receding into the night in "Late Lights in Minnesota," clever as it is. To be sure it does convey Kooser's sharp and painful sense of discontinuity between appearance and reality. But hard reality in the flush of the toilet is not a function of "place" as it is in his best poems. In "Anniversary" artificiality is dominant and reality a remote though cutting suggestion. In the other the reality of the land, the place is dominant, and the artificiality of the lives that inhabit it becomes a function of that dominance. "Anniversary," to put it bluntly, is to "Late Lights in Minnesota" as Whitman's "O Captain, My Captain" is to "When Lilacs Last in the Dooryard Bloom'd."

In such comparisons we can see that the relationship of fragmentary experience to pattern is only one of the polarities of Kooser's vision. At a lower level of abstraction the basic tension in his view of reality translates into the interaction between the land and the human beings who live on it. It is by no means a happy relationship. "Cherry County, Nebraska" illustrates quite graphically Kooser's feeling for this tense and estranged condition.

        Eight crows
        by the road
        eating a dog

        their wings
        wash up
        in the wind

        like surgeon's
        hands their beaks
        look dirty

        to the drivers
        too far off
        to see.

The birds are the meaning of the land; the cars (and their drivers) are not. Too alienated from it to read its truth, the drivers can only see the gore as dirt. And they secretly see the land that way also as they speed by it on the artificial pavement. They see only the beaks and miss the "wash up" of the wind in the wings. The people grasp limited, encapsulated meanings that miss reality.

Sometimes Kooser keeps this sense of precarious human existence in the midst of the larger irrational presence of the land to the barest minimum and yet by metaphorical suggestion keeps the humanity-land polarity in live tension. "Spring Plowing," for example, reveals by its point of view the poet's sympathetic focus on the animals and yet at the same time reveals the alien threat. Spring, conventionally described in sunlight, is now seen at night, all human activity for the moment in abeyance, and yet present as the underlying cause of all the movement.

> West of Omaha, the freshly plowed fields
> steam in the night like lakes.
> The smell of the earth floods over the roads.
> The fieldmice are moving their nests
> to the higher ground of fence-rows,
> the old among them crying out to the owls
> to take them all. The paths in the grass
> are loud with the squeak of their carts.
> They keep their lanterns covered.

Life is either fugitive or predatory, as it is in most of Kooser's poems, or rather life is both fugitive and predatory. And strandedness and alienation remain in the atmosphere even while the people are resting.

> One doctor in a Piper Cub
> can wake up everyone in North Dakota.
>
> At the level of an open upstairs window,
> a great white plain stretches away—
> the naked Methodists
> lying on top of their bedding.
>
> The moon covers her eyes with a cloud.

The sense of precarious balance here finds its real expression in the land's almost embarrassing silence. Any sound, but especially mechanical sound, immediately reminds one of the more usual condition. One feels somehow that even the sound of a human voice would be as startling an anomaly in the Kooser prairie landscape as the sound of the lone Piper Cub. The people, unidentified except by the single abstract but also loaded word *Methodist*, must be imagined perched on rather than settled into the land's hugeness. The mood of "A Hot Night in Wheat Country" just quoted is echoed in a poem like "Houses at the Edge of Town" in which Kooser again captures the silence and implacability of natural growth and the tentative nature of the human existence near it. As he suggests, the land functions like the sea.

> These are the houses of farmers
> retired from their fields;
> white houses, freshly folded
> and springing open again
> like legal papers. These are houses
> drawn up on the shore of the fields,
> their nets still wet,
> the fishermen sleeping curled in the bows.
> See how the gardens
> wade into the edge of the hayfield,
> the cucumbers crawling out under the lilacs
> to lie in the sun.

As these examples indicate, the silent, embattled, somehow overwhelmed interior lives evoked in these glimpses of experience are often not even given names, and when they do have names they have little else. They remain, despite the occasional privilege of a name, examples of anonymous, finite existence that at best may give us a slightly more focused feel for the essential ambiguity and tragedy of human life. "My Grandfather Dying" reveals the ambiguity the poet feels in his simultaneous awe and helplessness in the presence of the powerful honesty of fact. The poet's own identity is experienced only during a fleeting moment of curious echo before it is overwhelmed once again by nature: "I leaned down to call out my name / and he called it back. His breath

/ was as sour as an orchard / after the first frost." And at the beginning of the same poem we see with the poet down past the skin of the dying old man into a deeper meaning in his death, one that transcends identity.

> I could see bruises or shadows
> deep under his skin, like the shapes
> skaters find frozen in rivers—
> leaves caught in flight,
> or maybe the hand of a man reaching up
> out of the darkness for help.

In "Tom Ball's Barn" the character of Tom himself is all but non-existent. The real subject is the barn and the almost animated vitality it takes on as it first self-destructs and then receives the completely passive Tom Ball as he falls dead onto the board pile that is the barn's last remnants.

> The loan that built the barn
> just wasn't big enough
> to buy the paint, so the barn
> went bare and fell apart
> at the mortgaged end of twelve
> nail-popping, splintering winters.
> Besides the Januaries,
> the barber says it was
> five-and-a-half percent,
> three dry years, seven wet,
> and two indifferent,
> the banker (dead five years),
> and the bank (still open
> but deaf, or *deef* as it were), *and*
> poor iron in the nails that
> were all to blame for the barn's collapse
> on everything he owned, thus
> leading poor Tom's good health
> to diabetes and
> the swollen leg that threw him
> off the silo, probably

dead (the doctor said)
before he hit that board pile.

One other named character, Nels Paulssen, deserves some "Notes" from
Kooser on the occasion of his death "at the ripe old age of 90."

> A harvest
> of nail parings,
>
> a wagonload
> of hair—
>
> over his ashen
> fields,
>
> no dust
> in the air.

These lines define perfectly the kind of polar relationship between man
and land that Kooser characteristically holds in tension when he manages
to capture one of his moments from time. If he is battling on the one
hand to discover some semblance of pattern in the midst of fragmen-
tation, the pattern he does find is itself an ambiguous, unreconcilable
polarity. The people in these poems neither belong to the land nor does
the land in any true sense belong to them.

In short Kooser finds himself unable to get close enough to ei-
ther the land or the people perched on it to enable him to resolve what
amounts to an intimacy problem. His subject consequently becomes nei-
ther the land and its animals nor the human being, nor even himself,
but rather the tragic discontinuity between them all. And while we are
all quite tired, I am sure, of seeing artistic reflections of the wasteland,
somehow it will not go away. And Kooser refuses to offer himself or us
the occasional cosmetics we are only too eager to have. Thus each of
his evanescent pictures stands as a spiritual-psychological microcosm of
the American macrocosm, but at a naturalistic depth where all the sur-
face veneer is removed and life is bared in all its rawness, boredom, and
terror. At this depth, which Kooser finds already revealed to him in the

common life of the region, one is finally forced to decide which he will side with, the human beings or the land. And although Kooser tries hard to avoid the choice, realizing that either one is essentially fatal, he lacks the necessary strength in himself to reconcile the two poles. Thus he himself becomes alienated and disappointed, unable to celebrate rather than to lament the reality he sees. Such is the source, I suspect, of the undertone of sadness in these poems. He sees the brokenness of people in their leavings, their spiritual signs as it were, in broken deserted farms, in plastic gas stations run by ex-cons, and the like.

The genuine emotional depth and richness behind this tension is certified for me in the sure way Kooser's form is shaped as a function of this theme of alienation from the land, of the finite tragically engaged in fighting off the presence of the infinite, the abyss of death. The form he achieves is really an example of heroic poetic self-sacrifice, for the really remarkable quality of the writing is the extent to which, in his best work, Kooser is able to keep himself out of it. That to many, I realize, is no poetic virtue. Yet given his dilemma there is no other way for him to go. He must practice "letting-be"; that is, he must practice the only truly meaningful form of love, despite the fact that he is bound not to succeed.

This letting-be is expressed in still another polar tension: on the one hand, Kooser is, as I have said, on a passionate search for "signs" to announce; but on the other hand, he is extremely reluctant to elaborate on these signs, almost as if he fears to destroy by his presence the reality of what he finds. The result is that Kooser must live under the simultaneous threat and temptation of silence. It is easier, after all, not to write about or announce a sign at all, and yet *not* to announce it is to jeopardize one's human identity. We *are* the experience we can report to others. Silence preserves the purity of the experience from our inevitable distortion in the telling of it, but it also threatens us with the oblivion of knowing much yet ourselves being unknown. Kooser, it seems to me, is vitally sensitive to this fundamental tension.

How does this threat of silence, that is also a temptation, express itself in Ted Kooser's forms? The answer to this is readily apparent to anyone who reads through a complete volume of his poems, not only *A Local Habitation & a Name*, but his earlier collections as well, *Official Entry Blank* (1969), *Twenty Poems* (1973), *Grass County* (1971). It is the peculiar quality of "foundness" in his best work. That is, one gets the distinct feeling that the poems are transcriptions of anonymous writings by some anonymous consciousness that had no intention of producing art. Yet Kooser has come along and recognized the pathos and irony in them and by placing them in a volume intended to be poetry has made them into art by that act of recognition. An excellent example is "Landscape with a Single Cedar":

> The March wind's having its little joke
> with death; a wreath bounds through the headstones,
> throwing flowers.
> >   Not so funny,
> somebody's circled a child's fresh grave
> with toys—flags, pinwheels,
> a yellow plaster rabbit. On its bottom
> is carefully scratched *Are Bobbys Rabit.*

The poet provides the context, but he does not really provide the words as such. He "found" them in the profoundest sense of releasing their meaning through recognition. Thus Kooser unconsciously modifies the well-known Archibald McLeish formula from "Ars Poetica," "A poem should not mean but be," to something like, "A poem should not be made but found."

In fact Kooser punctuates his arrangement of poems in *A Local Habitation* with found postcards from various years. A few examples are enough to bring out the quality of these postcards in the context of the concerns already discussed. One, for example, is titled "Postcard: April 1, 1913":

> *All kinds of*
> *water here the*
> *creeks are run-*
> *ning bankfull*
> *almost imposs-*
> *ible to get a-*
> *round. Your card*
> *at hand last night.*

Another is titled "Postcard: March 1, 1910":

> *I hope this will find you*
> *feeling much better and getting*
> *stronger every day. Have thought*
> *of you so many times*
> *and felt sorry you had to suffer*
> *so much. But I know you*
> *will be able to appreciate*
> *good health when you get*
> *strong again, and that is something*
> *to be thankful for. People*
> *who haven't been sick really*
> *do not realize how fortunate*
> *they are. Thought you would like*
> *a picture of this curious rock.*
> *It is about six miles from here.*

Some of these found cards are ironically amusing, others redolent of background tragedy and loneliness, but each reflects something of the life of the people living an uncertain existence. Our sense of kinship is heightened without its having to be forced or pointed out to us.

Yet when we reflect further we notice that each voice is touching on the edge of inarticulateness, for all the latent power of what its communication suggests. Each has made the effort to break silence but not by much. That is why Kooser seems to me to be groping for some authentic western form of the haiku, not haiku in its strict form but in its essence.

More than by any overt theme, Kooser conveys his sense of vulnerability through the quality of this peculiar laconic directness that seems to stand within the felt presence of some much greater and more powerful silence that is about to overwhelm it. Nebraska indeed is a place where one is reminded of vulnerability. Karl Shapiro says in one of his poems that it is a place where Californians bitch about the lack of progress and New Yorkers step on the gas in a panic. Kooser has allowed himself to be emersed in this vulnerability down to the level of the speech it somehow generates; then he lets it be and wonders at its meaning. Thus Kooser refuses to participate in the great plastic American dream of conquering vulnerability. For this refusal he pays the necessary price of insecurity; but much has also resulted from it for which we must thank him.

The question that now comes to mind is about Kooser's next direction. Will his vision trap him into the role of mere spectator of the flux, himself standing still in order to see it? Will he manage in future volumes of poetry to elude this common graveyard of promising poets? There is some evidence that he does sense what might provide the power he needs to move from ambiguity to affirmation, at least on some level. The poem "Red Wing Church" that opens *A Local Habitation* not only announces the basic condition that will form the context of the poetry that follows it but also the loss of a spiritual dimension that is still another part of the condition and whose recovery is vital:

> There's a tractor in the doorway of a church
> in Red Wing, Nebraska, in a coat of mud
> and straw that drags the floor. A broken plow
> sprawls beggar-like behind it on some planks
> that make a sort of roadway up the steps.
> The steeple's gone. A black tar-paper scar
> that lightning might have made replaces it.
> They've taken it down to change the house of God
> to Homer Johnson's barn, but it's still a church,
> with clumps of tiger-lilies in the grass
> and one of those box-like, glassed-in signs
> that give the sermon's topic (reading now
> a birdnest and a little broken glass).
> The good works of the Lord are all around:
> the steeple-top is standing in a garden
> just up the alley; it's a hen-house now:
> fat leghorns gossip at its crowded door.
> Pews stretch on porches up and down the street,
> the stained-glass windows style the mayor's house,
> and the bell's atop the firehouse in the square.
> The cross is only God knows where.

Kooser seems to capture a glimpse of an urgent realization that one feels becoming more powerful among aware people in our symbolically fragmented age—that we have to become dumb before we can learn to use names and words faithfully again, before we can rediscover the eloquence of great symbols of the age, including the cross. In Kooser's poetry that realization dawns on the reader as an extension of the peculiar reticence that has always come naturally to the plainsman.

Ted Kooser

Shawn Leary

In the area of predictable dullness, insurance underwriters are often grouped with the likes of statisticians and accountants. Ted Kooser, however, is a credit to his maligned profession. Ted Kooser is anything but boring.

Home from a structured day at work, the poet sits on his living room couch, strokes Jesse, his cat, and smiles at walls and out windows. Kooser's art appears to imitate his life: within a rather formal structure exists a truly free spirit.

Born in Ames, Iowa, in 1939, Kooser received his bachelor's degree from Iowa State University. After dropping out of graduate school in English at UN-L to take a job at a Lincoln insurance company, Kooser founded *The Salt Creek Reader*, a literary quarterly. Kooser's magazine, which he edited throughout its existence, from 1967 through 1975, was the recipient of several national grants.

Kooser is currently the editor and publisher of Windflower Press, a small concern specializing in the publication of poetry. Windflower Press has published work by Nebraska poets William Kloefkorn and Don Welch, among others, as well as two books by Kooser himself (*Grass County* and *Hatcher*).

"The visible activity among Nebraska poets has increased tremendously over the past 10 or 15 years," Kooser observes. "There's more money available now for small literary magazines and that sort of endeavor, which could account for the change," Kooser says. "UN-L's *Prairie Schooner*, of course, has existed for many years, and by publishing work by Nebraska poets, the magazine has allowed us to keep in touch with the directions we're all taking."

"But there has been, recently, a definite resurgence of interest in poetry, I suppose," Kooser muses, "that poetry has become more fashionable than it used to be. People like Leonard Cohen, Allen Ginsberg, and Bob Dylan became folk heros during the Sixties, and the interest they created through the poetry of their lyrics has persisted."

In 1976, Ted Kooser received a writing fellowship from the Literature Panel of the National Endowment for the Arts. Kooser used part of that grant to produce a book that must have come as a surprise to the Endowment: *Hatcher* is an "illustrated novella," a collection of captioned engravings in which Kooser presents the story of Hatcher, his absent protagonist, who was "forever the fool of love.... maddened by the erotic."

Asked to characterize his more conventional work, Kooser pauses, turns his head, and looks at the wall for a few minutes. "The details I include in my poems are more realistic than surrealistic," he says, finally, speaking slowly, choosing his words with great care. "The general subject matter is whatever is close to me. It's strongly visual, descriptive poetry, and structurally measured, if not formal in style. I seldom write in the first person," Kooser observes, "and I pay a lot of attention to structure, to form. Each poem I write is strikingly different from the next... though it may not appear so at first glance," Kooser asserts.

A DEATH AT THE OFFICE

The news goes desk to desk
like a memo: Initial
and pass on; each of us marks
Surprised or Sorry.

The management came early
and buried her nameplate
deep in her desk. They boxed up
the Midol and Lip-Ice,

the snapshots from home,
wherever it was—nephews
and nieces, a strange, blurred cat
with fiery, flashbulb eyes

as if grieved. But who grieves here?
We have her ballpoints back,
her bud-vase. One of us tears
the scribbles from her calendar.

(reprinted from *The Periodical of Art in Nebraska,* spring 1976)

Ted Kooser has published poems and criticism in many national and regional literary magazines; his books include *A Local Habitation & A Name, Not Coming To Be Barked At, Old Marriage & New* and *Hatcher.*

The Sense of Measured Compatibility
In Contemporary Nebraska Poetry

Mark Sanders

William Kloefkorn, Ted Kooser, and Don Welch are "regional" poets following one of the first rules in writing: they write about what they know, which is frequently Nebraska, its people, towns, landscape, weather, and language. In a 1977 letter Kooser stated, "An author must write about things that are familiar to him. If a man lives in a particular landscape, it is only natural that he will write well about the locale which he knows, breathes, and inhabits."

Although these poets are regional in locale, they show various and fluctuating attitudes toward the Nebraska setting. Knowing the place in which they live and write, and bringing their own temperaments to bear upon it, they produce what Kloefkorn calls "a measured compatibility" with that subject matter. Welch calls it "a whole poet thrown into his verse." In Robert Frost's terms, it might be described as "a lover's quarrel with one's environment," which Kloefkorn says is

> a condition I am 'at home' with. And most poets, I suspect, indulge such a quarrel, wherever they do their writing, however deep or shallow their roots. Poets who write from an environment that is essentially rural tend to be specific in their imagery, I believe, no doubt because they cannot avoid such privileges as the sweet stench of sorghum and the greens and yellows of early wheat and ripened corn. There is not much that hits deeper than the incredible fact of birth, and writers in the midlands are never very far from seed.[1]

What the poet harvests is a measurement of his compatibility, an understanding acquired from his living in a given locale. This "sense of place," as Kooser has stated it, finds these three Nebraska poets sometimes reacting harmoniously to the salient features of the locale, sometimes uncovering harsh, negative features, and sometimes combining a complex compatibility and incompatibility with those features.

Lyric poetry often poses the writer in harmony with Nature. He achieves a sense of belonging, in which he experiences the truths in Nature of innocence, youth, and fertility. It is as though the simple rural life can heal the illnesses of civilization. Such poetry is a poetry of satisfaction, and there are many examples of this type in the work of Kloefkorn, Kooser, and Welch. Two from Kooser's *Not Coming To Be Barked At* are "In The Corners Of Fields," and "So This Is Nebraska."[2]

In this first poem, "In The Corners Of Fields," there is a progressive awareness that Nature does, indeed, provide satisfaction.

> Something is calling to me
> from the corners of fields,
> where the leftover fencewire
> suns its loose coils, and stones
> thrown out of the furrow
> sleep in warm litters;
> where the gray faces
> of old *No Hunting* signs
> mutter into the wind,
> and dry horsetanks
> sprout fountains of sunflowers;
> where a moth
> flutters in from the pasture,
> harried by sparrows,
> and alights on a post,
> so sure of its life
> that it peacefully opens its wings.

Kooser works like a diamond-cutter, beginning by dissecting the "corners of fields" into images of "loose coils" of fencewire, the "stones thrown out of the furrow," and the old, gray *No Hunting* signs which "mutter into the wind." The cut is completed by the small, delicate images of the moth, alighting on a post, peacefully spreading its wings. Throughout the poem there is an abundance of words which suggest comfort: the fencewire sunning its coils, the warmth of litters, the moth's quietude, even the fountains of sunflowers, flowing in dry horsetanks. And although the "gray faces of old *No Hunting* signs" disturb the warm, comforting landscape, the traditional idea that Nature is a redemptive force is brought out "In The Corners Of Fields." For there, as the moth attests, one need only hunt to become sure of his life.

Redemption by going to the land may also be seen in "So This Is Nebraska," where you can drive:

> along
> with your hand out squeezing the air,
> a meadowlark waiting on every post.
>
> Behind a shelterbelt of cedars,
> top-deep in hollyhocks, pollen and bees,
> a pickup kicks its fenders off
> and settles back to read the clouds.
>
> You feel like that; you feel like letting
> your tires go flat, like letting the mice
> build a nest in your muffler, like being
> no more than a truck in the weeds,

where your joyful impulses continue until:

> You feel like
>
> waving. You feel like stopping the car
> and dancing around on the road. You wave
> instead and leave your hand out gliding
> lark-like over the wheat, over the houses.

In "So This Is Nebraska," the reader becomes the driver, and the redemptive impulse slows the driver down, makes him "feel like letting" his "tires go flat," and makes him forget about the hurry of conventional driving. For the moment, anyway, the driver belongs to the environment, and his measurement is a satisfied one.

The assurance of the good life in nature or rural areas may also be found in Kloekforn's *loony*. For instance, when loony is in the small town café, he can feel that:

> Everything is in its place at Selma's,
> even loony:
> how when he sits down
> the puzzle comes together,
> and will again tomorrow
> and tomorrow.
> Listen:
> this is something not so small to have,
> and something very large to look for:
> cup and spoon and coffee steam,
> the hands of Selma from behind the counter.
> And he must be the loony
> who cannot be thankful
> for the merest order:
> who can only know that
> life is good
> when life is over.

In this poem, loony has found his place, knows that he fits into the scheme of small town life like a puzzle piece. In another place, loony's absence might not be noticed. But at Selma's, he belongs, makes the picture complete. Though he is retarded, he knows that such a feeling of belonging is "not so small to have," and that it is "something very large to look for." As Kloefkorn said in regards to this poem, "My loony says that the *true* loony is the one 'who can only know that / life is good / when life is over.'"[3] In other words, loony is optimistic. He believes life is good *now*, and that other men, those incapable of being "thankful for the merest order," those who feel "life is good" when death occurs, are those who are the *true* loonies.

Loony's assurance of the good rural life may also be found in his country baptism, for he realizes a satisfaction which might otherwise be overlooked.

> The preacher squatted me
> into the water and said

In the name of the Father
and of the Son,
and of the Holy Ghost,
Amen,

and I did feel different,
we both naked
in a stream in a pasture,
a brown cow
chewing its cud at us
from across the
clear rocky water.

And even later,
drying in the sun,
I did feel different,
as if I had just waked up
on a cool morning
to find myself
not alone.

Loony's baptism is a simple ceremony, as implied by the cud-chewing cow and the pasture setting. Though simple in ceremony, the baptism affects loony considerably. He realizes the act has changed his life. He feels different, and it is a satisfied feeling for the sacrament has made him one with all others in the rural community. Like the rest, loony is baptized in the same pasture stream, united by the same Holy covenant. And even more important, loony experiences an Adamic sensation like waking up "on a cool morning," finding himself "not alone." In either case, loony is assured that he belongs, and that feeling is good.

This sense of belonging may also be seen in Don Welch's "Gifts and Myths: 2,"[4] where the environment has the rudimentary means to settle all problems:

Today the snow settles all questions.
Don't ask how it turns the corners
of windows into oval portrait frames

> or why the cattle out there look as if
> they are going mad at the mouth
> or the windmill cries to be let loose.
> Even if you ask why I've lived long enough
> to accept it, you'll get no answer.
> But I'll tell you this: today my hands
> are as sweet as cellar onions;
> they don't have to ask if they're mine.

The weather may be hostile, but there is a comfort to be found on the plains. There is no need to ask any questions for there is a physical satisfaction which must be felt to be known. This satisfied feeling comes only from living "long enough to accept" the environment's occasional hostility. Like onions stored in a cellar, once it is accepted, a house may provide a womb-like sense of comfort or security. "Gifts and Myths: 2" is similar to Kooser's "In The Corners Of Fields," and Kloefkorn's poem about loony in the café. In each case, there is a sense of security, a sense of physical satisfaction. In each case, though in different capacities, one may feel assured of his place in life.

Welch's love poem to his father, "Lines For My Father" (*Dead Horse Table*), is also such a poem, one that finds its happiness in bringing the past to the present:

> I love you, old man, in our time.
> The shotgun cradled in your arm,
> the marbled wood,
> the varnished sky.
>
> The milo's cut.
> The fence holds leaves.
> The thicket has its quail and
> the final green.
>
> We walk.
> We clot in time.
> The fence sings birdless
> in the wind.

The picture of a father and son hunting may "clot in time," but it is a picture to be remembered fondly forever. Not surprising, this fond memory occurs in a rural setting, a place in which both men sense who they are.

Not only does Plains poetry deal with one's sense of belonging, it also describes the despair of not belonging. It measures loneliness, hardships, and disappointments, where the landscape often destroys well-being, producing sterility, decay, and death. For example, in Kloefkorn's *Alvin Turner As Farmer*, Alvin Turner discovers:

> There is always the rock:
> That, first and last, to remember.
> The rock, at times at dusk the rabbit,
> Robbing the garden in its own leaden way.
> And I remember how once
> I lost time deliberately,
> Reining the team to a stop
> And raising the rock high to crush it.
> Underhoof it had wanted to trip
> Even the full-rumped mares,
> And I stood there in the furrow
> With the rock raised above my head,
> Powerless at last to reduce it
> Or even to lose it to sight.
> Yet I tried. (For in those days
> I had not learned to say
> *There is always the rock.*)
> I threw it into the soft plowed ground
> And dreamed that it disappeared.
> How many times then it rose with the rain
> I cannot say, nor can I boast
> That ever its usefulness
> Was fully cause for its being:
> The fences failed to deplete it,
> And it collared the hogs but partially.
> Yet somehow I expected yesterday's blunted share

> To be the last. That part which I cannot see,
> I said, cannot reduce me.

The poem implies tedium: "There is always the rock: / That, first and last, to remember." To bring this across, Kloefkorn employs hard images: the rock, like a rabbit, "robbing the garden in its own leaden way," the inability to crush or hide the rock, and yesterday's blunted share. Turner even admits to himself that there was a time when he "had not learned to say / *There is always the rock,*" and had felt that if he tried to bury the rock, the part which he could not see could not reduce him. But after years of struggling in the fields, he knows better, knows that the rock will always be there, and that (even if he refuses to acknowledge its existence) it can and will reduce him. The sounds, too, suggest the difficulties Turner has working rock infested fields: the *k*'s and *g*'s in words such as *rock, collared, garden,* and *crush;* and the softer stops, the *p*'s and *b*'s, in words such as *rabbit, stop, blunted,* and *tip.* The *s* sounds further intensify the softer qualities of the poem in words such as *dusk, soft,* and *share,* as do the *r*'s in *raising,* and *rain.* The harsh sounds describe Turner's work. The soft sounds, Kloefkorn's attitude toward the back-breaking worker.

Kloefkorn's poetry not only examines man's hardships, such as Alvin Turner's, it often measures life's disappointments. One disappointment is the often cruel loneliness felt by young and old alike. Such is "Ruby," in Kloefkorn's *Uncertain The Final Run To Winter:* "One of Christ's unwanted many, / Ruby rotted right along with the porch swing," knowing "the good Lord never gave her anything: / Not even, mind you, a decent pot to pee in." Ruby's loneliness makes her bitter, and this bitterness increases, and before it is finished, she rocks herself in the swing like "a stillborn child" into the late hours of the night. Another example, this one from *ludi jr,* expresses the extreme anger an adolescent feels when he loses a close friend. Ludi's friend has drowned, and his reaction to the news is "that I never want to see / that dirty reckless two-timing piss-complected / son of a bitch ever / again." In either case, there is a certain despair in loneliness, certain bitterness.

Kooser's verse also contains lonely moments. In "The Widow Lester" (*A Local Habitation & A Name*) an old woman reflects, "I was too old to be married, / but nobody told me." She speaks of the pain she endured so many years as she caught wedding bouquets, but never married, herself. "Then," she says, "I met Ivan, and kept him, / and never knew love." Married, but unrequited, she says "How his feet stuck in the bed-sheets! / I could have told him to wash, / but I wanted to hold that stink against him." Forced by her loneliness into an unfavorable marriage, she sees Ivan drop dead in the field, and finishes hanging her wash before looking to him.

There are other similar measurements of disappointments in Kooser's poetry, instances often all too familiar. "Tom Ball's Barn" *(A Local Habitation & A Name)* is one example in which the land produces disappointment, even destruction:

> The loan that built the barn
> just wasn't big enough
> to buy the paint, so the barn
> went bare and fell apart
> at the mortaged end of twelve
> nail-popping, splintering winters.
> Besides the Januaries,
> the barber says it was
> five-and-a-half percent,
> three dry years, seven wet,
> and two indifferent,
> the banker (dead five years),
> and the bank (still open
> but deaf, or *deef* as it were), *and*
> poor iron in the nails that
> were all to blame for the barn's collapse
> on everything he owned, thus
> leading poor Tom's good health
> to diabetes and
> the swollen leg that threw him
> off the silo, probably
> dead (the doctor said)
> before he hit the board pile.

Though there are other circumstances involved, the environment plays the biggest destructive role. It is the "nail-popping, splintering winters" and summers which make the barn fall apart. Indirectly, it is the environment which causes Tom Ball's failing health and diabetes, as well as his death.

Welch's poetry is not without such measurements either. "Anton Pilic" *(Dead Horse Table)*, for example, deals with the inevitable separation initiated by the environment's severity and culminated in death:

> You have to wear a road to make it yours, he'd said
>   over the wilted lettuce, apple butter, and side
>   pork late one summer.
>
> They'd looked across the supper table at each other
>   while the darkness aged around them like canned
>   meat in the cellar. The Aladdin lamp bleached
>   the dark hair of her temples. The potatoes grew
>   to white buttes on his plate.
>
> He'd let his eyes settle on her shoulders, half in light,
>   half in dark, well, not so much settle as linger,
>   then slide down the cords of her arm.
>
> This was the arm that carried cream to Rhone's store.
>   He'd asked her why no bread and gravy—strange
>   how he remembered that—what did arms and gravy
>   have to do with the darkness all around them?
>
> Now as he sits here thirty years from then, he's
>   wondering why he told her she'd have to wear
>   a road—good lord, she'd done it till the socket
>   stayed in place that held the cream can, done it
>   till she forgot the hurt and sang back to the king
>   birds on the wires, even done it till her soul
>   smelled like gravel after rain.

> When he goes to town today, he'll remember her so much
>   every stone'll speak Ruth. Ruth Ruth—Ruth Ruth,
>   they'll say, and when he drives faster, Ruth Ruth Ruth.

Separation is felt throughout the poem, beginning with the remark, "You have to wear a road to make it yours," for it is this which becomes Ruth's burden, resulting in her destruction. Separation is also indicated when the couple stare through the dark at each other, a darkness which ages with the couple "like canned meat in the cellar;" as well as the thought that Anton cannot let his eyes settle upon his wife any longer, but only linger, and "then slide down the cords of her arm." The actual separation culminates with Ruth's death, one which results from the gradual erosion caused by the environment. Anton has worked his wife hard, so hard, in fact, her arm's socket stays in place. He has worked her until she no longer feels pain, and until she wears a road.

These are just a few of the measurements of despair found in poetry by Kloefkorn, Kooser, and Welch, whether it is the hardships of farmers such as Alvin Turner, Tom Ball, or Anton Pilic's wife, or the loneliness felt by young and old. The themes are universal as there is suffering in all walks of life. As measurements of one's compatibility, however, we find the environment in the country sometimes destructive.

There is one final measurement, one far more complex than the ones previously mentioned. It is one that treats capability with incompatibility, good times with bad times, the sense of belonging with a sense of loneliness in the same poem. This final measurement is one that strikes a balance of two worlds, one not of complete satisfaction nor of complete dissatisfaction. As Kloefkorn wrote, "Who can love *anything* completely over an extended period of time?" With this in mind, Kloefkorn says "The writer must retain that sense of wonder characterized by the child and that sense of rebellion made famous by the adolescent—and in the process he must keep his adult f-a-c-u-l-t-i-e-s intact." The poet, Kloefkorn continues, "must at times appear to be a trifle loony, a trifle ludicrous. And sometimes more than a trifle misunderstood."[5] A poetry which blends opposites "becomes complex," according to Don Welch, "and this complexity is the result of emotions and intellect 'marrying' themselves together."[6] To get there, Welch says, a poet must make his verse push as far as it can, right up to the edge of things.

One such example from Welch's poetry would be "Dry Creek" (*Dead Horse Table*):

> Dry Creek starts anywhere.
> It runs its sand in no motion.
> There are no fennels in its channel
> when it comes out of the hills toward Upland
> a mile west of town. Bending
> and spreading out Loeshen's, it looks
> ferny before it pulls back again
> to what its notion of strand is.
>
> It sings no song. It barely says
> its tongue.

Furthermore, since it is a *dry creek,*

>   no one notices
> what attracts no notice.
> Two miles east of town it flows
> into the Republican.

Welch relies heavily on the sound of the line, as the lines serve as an extension of the content. Dry Creek is so sluggish, "It runs its sand in no motion." The lines are like that. Many are short. Others are long and meandering, as a creek would run: "Bending / and spreading out Loeshen's, it looks / ferny before it pulls back again / to what its notion of strand is." The sense of good belonging is there; in the rural images, and the unique qualities of the creek, the idea that time stands still as does the creek. But then there's the juxtaposition of contraries. Dry Creek is a good creek because it exists, it is a bad one because its existence lacks life. Dry Creek "sings no songs," it "barely says it tongue," "it starts anywhere." The uniqueness is there, but there is a lack of identity apparent in these examples. In starting anywhere, it lacks what other creeks possess, for "no one notices / what attracts no notice." The creek's only movement is no motion, and since it is dry, it makes no sound as it flows its empty course. Empty, and with barely an identity in Nature, it further loses its identity when "two miles east of town it flows / into the Republican," yielding itself to the omnipotence of the ideal river.

Kloefkorn's "ludi jr, as the hired hand, pays dearly for what he is paid for" (*ludi jr*) serves to marry the worlds of innocence and maturity. It is rural, but does not lend itself to the traditional, accepted belief that one may become redeemed in that setting. Ludi's soul is not purged by his environment, but is dirtied, reduced to bestial instincts.

The confrontation takes place in a hog-yard. After several unsuccessful attempts at trying to catch the hog, ludi finds himself bathed in hogshit *but* gains the essence of hog:

> in the boots hog
> in the hair hog
> in the nose hog
> in the eyes
> down the back
> between the lips
> against the tongue
> adrift all up and down the spine
> hinged in the knuckles
> in the elbows in the knees
> in the bend and snap of the ankles
>
> hog
>
> knowing but not thinking that no word
> not even hog hog hog hog hog
> can backflush the bowel that is truly hog
> like brother cannot itself
> as either sound or squibble
> be what the brother knows
> under the skin in the bone

to be

that no smell however stout
can do it either
no snort no grunt no squeal

What all this means is that ludi jr

no less than god
must earn his keep:
must become the essence of hog

Once he acquires this essence, ludi is able to catch the hog, and cuts its throat. His job is finished, and he takes his fill of the hog's blood in exaltation of his deed. The poem is a symbolic exploration of ritual. Ludi jr is searching for his manhood, and the search, itself, is a struggle with animal nature. As an innocent, ludi fails miserably in his attempts. But once he takes on the essence of a hog, after he is baptized in hogshit, he is able to "earn his keep." If Nature is redemptive, the poem is extremely ironic. Once he is initiated, ludi is cleansed of his innocence, and is purified by manure. He takes on the essence of hog, and reacts like one. Only then is he mature enough to do the job, mature in a world that usually thinks bestial behavior in humans is either uncivilized or childish.

One final example in which Nebraska poetry strikes a balance of two worlds is Kooser's "My Grandfather Dying" (*A Local Habitation & A Name*):

I could see bruises or shadows
deep under his skin, like the shapes
skaters find frozen in rivers—
leaves caught in flight,
or maybe the hand of a man reaching up
out of the darkness for help.
I was helpless as flowers
there at his bedside. I watched
his legs jerk in the sheets.

He answered the doors,
he kicked loose stones from his fields.
I leaned down to call out my name
and he called it back. His breath
was sour as an orchard
after the first frost.

In this poem, there is a juxtaposition of young and old, of life and death, of vitality and decay. Traditionally, a rural poetry dealt primarily with youth, and how Nature retains youth. In contemporary regional poetry, the old become more important. If Nature retains vitality, somehow it has passed this old man by. The old man, like ludi jr, has at one time been initiated into maturity, has bathed in hogshit. Like Welch's "Dry Creek," his worth is his existence, even though that existence is in peril. There is also a fine touch of irony in the poem. Kooser leaves the grandson living, not fully aware of maturity's hazards, nor how his own life will become "sour as an orchard after the first frost."

Perhaps there is another point being made. Rural life is good for those who are young, but all too often, the elderly find themselves confined to it, as if it were a prison. Tom Ball, of Kooser's "Tom Ball's Barn," stays with the land as long as he can, through failing health, until his death. Welch's Vallie from "Two For Vallie" (*Dead Horse Table*) works her garden until she has a stroke at the age of 70, widowed and alone. And Kloefkorn's "Aunt Dora" (*Uncertain The Final Run To Winter*) tries in vain to keep her innocent optimism despite varicose veins and cancer, believing it could be worse even at the time of her death. Kloefkorn writes:

and thus she disappeared,
her last breath sucking deep to start again
that certain fiction.

"That certain fiction" is a curious ambiguity. In the context of regional poetry, the fiction might be that death is a beginning. The elderly in these poems understand that Nature more often destroys than creates, but as they die, their places are taken by individuals not yet indoctrinated. But they, too, will soon learn, for as Kooser said: "there is a certain thing I used to call the weight of the weather, in which I sort of metaphorically said that the sky actually had physical weight, and that old people on the Great Plains, the reason that they begin to bend over, was because they had been bearing the weight of the weather all these years.... The sky out here on the plains, metaphorically, is attempting to squash everything flat, and eventually it does."[7]

Though the terminology and images of these poets are related to a rural area, Kloefkorn feels these need not limit the poem. "The rural details can be used to suggest universal impulses . . . . I wouldn't want to write a poem just about a plow, for example. Not a plow per se. But I wouldn't hesitate to use a plow to write a poem about human endurance. And I would hope the reader, wherever he is, could identify with the endurance, even though he, perhaps, has never been behind a plow."[8] Though rural, the impulses transcend the region, and are felt across the country: people dying, people enjoying life, people getting caught into the scheme of the larger Nature. Each of these are measurements of one's compatibility to his region, though the region itself is not the *only* factor. As Welch said, "Every writer has to use the material that he finds fascinating, is comfortable with . . . . What he always hopes is that he's going to use the particular—call it the regional, if you will—so well that it will become good poetry for people out of the region."[9] The result, then, is that "a good poem makes you at home with its subject, it invites you in, asks you to get inside its atmosphere, to breathe it, live it, to wonder with it."[10] This lets the reader go beyond the region, perhaps even occasionally beyond the measures of the poet's *own* compatibility.

NOTES:

[1] Personal letter written by William Kloefkorn to Mark Sanders on September 15, 1977.

[2] Poems quoted in this discussion come from the following editions of collected poems of Kloefkorn, Kooser, and Welch, unless otherwise noted:

Kloefkorn, William. *Alvin Turner as Farmer.* 1972;rpt. Lincoln, Nebraska: Windflower Press, 1974.

_____. *loony.* Springfield, Illinois: Apple, 1975.

_____. *ludi jr.* Milwaukee, Wisconsin: Pentagram Press, 1976.

_____. *Uncertain The Final Run to Winter.* Lincoln, Nebraska: Windflower Press, 1974.

Kooser, Ted. *A Local Habitation & A Name.* San Luis Obispo, California: Solo Press, 1976.

Welch, Don. *Dead Horse Table.* Lincoln, Nebraska: Windflower Press, 1975.

[3] Kloefkorn letter.

[4] Don Welch, "Gifts and Myths: 2," *Platte Valley Review,* 4, No. 1 (1976), p. 73.

[5] Kloefkorn letter.

[6] Personal letter written by Don Welch to Mark Sanders on August 19, 1977.

[7] Stated by Ted Kooser in an interview with Mark Sanders at Lincoln, Nebraska, on August 19, 1977.

[8] Stated by William Kloefkorn in an interview with Mark Sanders at Lincoln, Nebraska on October 15, 1977.

[9] Stated by Don Welch in an interview with Mark Sanders at Kearney, Nebraska on September 17, 1977.

[10] Welch letter.

Poetry Chronicle

Dana Gioia

Ever since I lived in Minneapolis, where local connoisseurs informed me in most matter-of-fact tones that the Walker Art Gallery was generally acknowledged to rival the Uffizi, that the Guthrie Theater summer stock outclassed the Salzburg Festival, that the IDS building downtown ranked with Chartres, and that Mary Tyler Moore was the new Garbo, I have been suspicious of Mid-Western cultural boosterism. Therefore, over the past few years when three Nebraskans I met independently recommended the work of Ted Kooser, a poet who works as an insurance underwriter in Lincoln, I smugly made the resolution to remain in blissful ignorance. Now confronted with a review copy of *Sure Signs,* a first-rate collection of Kooser's new and selected poems, I abhor my snobbism and repent in dust and ashes. As penance I promise to skip the cartoons in the next five issues of *The New Yorker* and talk for five minutes to the next insurance man who calls up during dinner.

Kooser is a master of the short poem. Only two of the eighty-nine poems in *Sure Signs* run longer than one page, and their average length is only about a dozen lines. Within these narrow bounds Kooser seems ready to try anything. His poems are most often bizarre, surrealistic anecdotes, little stories where details and metaphors acquire an unruly life of their own. Kooser obsessively sees things as people (ladders as men, mice as refugees, a furnace as an old man), and it is not unusual for one of these things to get up and walk away with the poem. So many of the poems have surprising twists that one never settles into that sort of drowsy half-attention that too much dinner or too much poetry can bring on. I found it impossible to put *Sure Signs* down until I had finished the entire book. It was like sitting next to a box of chocolates before dinner. I kept intending to put the book down to finish later, but kept sneaking one more poem until there were none left. I suspect that praising a book of poems for being so readable will cause much suspicion in certain parties. I can only direct the skeptical to the book itself and ask if they can find fault with a collection alternately so delightful and mysterious and always so unassuming.

What is especially refreshing about Kooser's work is the originality of its imagery. Nowadays when most poets plug in "striking, original" images as mechanically and predictably as their grandparents plugged in standard rhymes, it is a pleasure to read a poet like Kooser whose imagination is naturally metaphorical. When this gift for metaphor combines with Kooser's eerie sense of humor, the results are usually memorable, as in "Spring Plowing":

> West of Omaha the freshly plowed fields
> steam in the night like lakes.
> The smell of the earth floods over the roads.
> The field mice are moving their nests
> to the higher ground of fence rows,
> the old among them crying out to the owls
> to take them all. The paths in the grass
> are loud with the squeak of their carts.
> They keep their lanterns covered.

Notice how conventionally this surprising poem begins. The first five lines, which could have been written by any competent poet, scarcely prepare us for what follows. Kooser compresses several implicit metaphors into the next four lines before ending with a sinister, enigmatic image. Yet the poem never becomes clumsy or crowded. This macabre smoothness is Kooser's distinctive touch. On the very next page in "Sitting All Evening Alone in the Kitchen" one finds the same smooth, simple surface covering a complex organization of symbols:

> The cat has fallen asleep,
> the dull book of a dead moth
> loose in his paws.
>
> The moon in the window, the tide
> gurgling out through the broken shells
> in the old refrigerator.

Late, I turn out the lights.
The little towns on top of the stove
glow faintly neon
sad women alone at the bar.

My only complaint is that the book gives no clue to how the po-
ems are organized. Are they arranged chronologically, randomly or under
some organic principle I have not discerned? Still this small confusion
cannot hamper the enjoyment of such a unique and unassuming talent.
Learn from my mistakes. Pull down thy vanity and read Ted Kooser.

Excerpt from Omnibus Review Including *Sure Signs*

Mark Sanders

Probably the best and most even collection of the six [reviewed here] is Ted Kooser's *Sure Signs*. Kooser has long been recognized for his acute eye for detail, his ability to take the natural and cut it down, facet by facet, until it creates for the reader an insight in the familiar that is new. It would be impossible for me to do any justice to the merit of the collection by touching only one or two isolated poems in the book as this is essentially *The Greatest Hits of Ted Kooser*. The selections come primarily from his earlier collections and provide the reader in one volume so many of his best poems, it seems unreasonable to objectively consider the diversity of subject, theme, and style in the limited space provided here. What I can do as a paltry alternative is offer one poem, "In the Corner of Fields," as representative of Kooser's exactness and texture:

> Something is calling to me
> from the corners of fields,
> where the leftover fence wire
> suns its loose coils, and stones
> thrown out of the furrow
> sleep in warm litters;
> where the gray faces
> of old *No Hunting* signs
> mutter into the wind,
> and dry horsetanks
> spout fountains of sunflowers;
> where a moth
> flutters in from the pasture,
> harried by sparrows,
> and alights on a post,
> so sure of its life
> that it peacefully opens its wings.

So many of the poems in *Sure Signs* are like this one in that Kooser pays special attention to the small object. Despite what some might claim is a pastoral theme that runs throughout the collection, other of the poems portray ambivalence toward the region, and sometimes hostility toward it (reminiscent of Frost's "lover's quarrel"). There is always, though, that thick and appropriate texture; as in this poem, Kooser illustrates restfulness in terms of fence wire sunning "its loose coils," the stones "sleep in warm litters," and the moth, escaping its harried world, "peacefully opens its wings." The reader appreciates that honesty in detailing. It places the reader in the midst of the poem so he or she can feel, live, and breathe in the surroundings, making it a part of themselves. I assume this is what most readers of poetry are looking for. I certainly find that here.

The Anonymity of the Regional Poet

Dana Gioia

I. THE PREDICAMENT OF POPULAR POETRY

> Ordinary thoughts and feelings are not necessarily shallow,
> any more than subtle or unusual ones are necessarily pro-
> found.
>
> —Edwin Muir

Ted Kooser is a popular poet. This is not to say that he commands a mass public. No contemporary poet does—at least in America. Kooser is popular in that unlike most of his peers he writes naturally for a nonliterary public. His style is accomplished but extremely simple—his diction drawn from common speech, his syntax conversational. His subjects are chosen from the everyday world of the Great Plains, and his sensibility, though more subtle and articulate, is that of the average Midwesterner. Kooser never makes an allusion that an intelligent but unbookish reader will not immediately grasp. There is to my knowledge no poet of equal stature who writes so convincingly in a manner the average American can understand and appreciate.

But to describe Kooser merely as a poet who writes plainly about the ordinary world is misleading insofar as it makes his work sound dull. For here, too, the comparison with popular art holds true. Kooser is uncommonly entertaining. His poems are usually short and perfectly paced, his subjects relevant and engaging. Finishing one poem, the reader instinctively wants to proceed to another. It has been Kooser's particular genius to develop a genuine poetic style that accommodates the average reader and portrays a vision that provides unexpected moments of illumination from the seemingly threadbare details of everyday life.

If Kooser's work is visionary, however, it is on a decidedly human scale. He offers no blinding flashes of inspiration, no mystic moments of transcendence. He creates no private mythologies or fantasy worlds.

Instead he provides small but genuine insights into the world of everyday experience. His work strikes the difficult balance between profundity and accessibility, just as his style manages to be personal without being idiosyncratic. It is simple without becoming shallow, striking without going to extremes. He has achieved the most difficult kind of originality. He has transformed the common idiom and experience into fresh and distinctive poetry.

But what does an instinctively popular poet do in contemporary America, where serious poetry is no longer a popular art? The public whose values and sensibility he celebrates is unaware of his existence. Indeed, even if they were aware of his poetry, they would feel no need to approach it. Cut off from his proper audience, this poet feels little sympathy with the specialized minority readership that now sustains poetry either as a highly sophisticated verbal game or secular religion. His sensibility shows little similarity to theirs except for the common interest in poetry. And so the popular poet usually leads a marginal existence in literary life. His fellow poets look on him as an anomaly or anachronism. Reviewers find him eminently unnewsworthy. Publishers see little prestige attached to printing his work. Critics, who have been trained to celebrate complexity, consider him an amiable simpleton.

It is not surprising then that Kooser's work has not received sustained attention from academic critics. In an age when serious critics have begun to look on themselves either as creative personalities hardly less important than the authors they discuss or at the very least as great interpretive artists—the Van Cliburns of poetry—without whose skilled touch literature would remain as mute as an unopened score, there is little in Kooser's work that would summon forth a great performance. There are no problems to solve, no ambiguities to unravel, no dizzying bravado passages to master for the dexterous critic eager to earn an extra curtain call.

What can a critic meaningfully add to the attentive reader's appreciation of this poem, for instance, which is one of Kooser's more complex pieces:

THE BLIND ALWAYS COME AS SUCH A SURPRISE

The blind always come as such a surprise,
suddenly filling an elevator
with a great white porcupine of canes,
or coming down upon us in a noisy crowd
like the eye of a hurricane.
The dashboards of cars stopped at crosswalks
and the shoes of commuters on trains
are covered with sentences
struck down in mid-flight by the canes of the blind.
Each of them changes our lives,
tapping across the bright circles of our ambitions
like cracks traversing the favorite china.

One can enumerate its small beauties—the opening image of a blind person (or persons) entering an elevator to the slight alarm of other passengers, the unexpectedly surreal equation of a porcupine's quills and the white tipped canes, the sharp observations of how normal people pause uncomfortably when they notice the blind or disabled, the rhetorical trick of referring to the blind collectively, which gives them a mysterious, sexless, ageless composite identity, or the haunting final simile. But aside from cataloguing these moments, there is little a critic can provide that the average reader cannot, because the difficulties this poem provokes are experiential rather than textual. It poses none of the verbal problems critical methodologies have been so skillfully designed to unravel. Rather it quietly raises certain moral and psychological issues that the professional critic by training is not prepared to engage or resolve.

Paradoxically, the simpler poetry is, the more difficult it becomes for a critic to discuss intelligently. Trained to explicate, the critic often loses the ability to evaluate literature outside the critical act. A work is good only in proportion to the richness and complexity of interpretations it provokes. Finding little challenge in Kooser's poetry, the enterprising critic is tempted to dismiss it. Surely poetry so simple must lack depth. While admitting to a certain superficial fascination, the critic qualifies his admiration by exploring the author's limitations, which

in itself becomes a compelling critical activity. While defining a po-
et's limitations is a legitimate critical pursuit, limitations in themselves
are not necessarily shortcomings. Even the greatest authors have blind
spots: Milton had little gift for comedy; Wordsworth a relatively narrow
technical range. To find a limitation does not necessarily invalidate an
author's achievement. Criticism should make meaningful distinctions,
not apply irrelevant standards.

Kooser does have significant limitations as a poet. Looking across
all his mature work, one sees a narrow range of technical means, an
avoidance of stylistic or thematic complexity, little interest in ideas,
and an unwillingness to work in longer forms. In his weaker poems one
also notices a tendency to sentimentalize his subjects and too strong a
need to be liked by his readers, which expresses itself in a self-depreca-
tory attitude toward himself and his poetry. In short, Kooser's major
limitation is a deep-set conservatism that keeps him working in areas
he knows he can master to please his audience.

Significantly, however, Kooser's limitations derive directly from his
strengths. His narrow technical range reflects his insistence on perfect-
ing the forms he uses. If Kooser has concentrated on a few types of
poems, he has made each of these forms unmistakably his own. If he
has avoided longer forms, what member of his generation has written
so many unforgettable short poems? If he has not cultivated complex-
ity in his work, he has also developed a highly charged kind of simplic-
ity. What his poems lack in intellectuality they make up for in concrete
detail. If he occasionally lapses into sentimentality, it is because he
invests his poems with real emotion. Even Kooser's self-deprecatory
manner betrays a consistent concern for the communal role of the
poet. He will not strike superior poses to bully or impress his audience.

Limitations, however, are not necessarily weaknesses. Having cata-
logued Kooser's conspicuous limitations, one cannot help noticing that
they are more often sins of omission than commission. Discussing
them may be an interesting critical exercise, but it is useful only insofar
as it sharpens one's understanding of Kooser's particular strengths. It
may seem obvious to say, but it is surprising how often some otherwise
intelligent critics forget, that a writer is better judged by how success-
fully he works with the material he includes than by what he omits.

Kooser's achievement is in the consummate skill with which he handles the self-imposed limits of the short imagistic poem, the universal significance he projects from his local subject matter.

If Kooser's particular achievements as a poet don't fit comfortably into current critical standards, how then is one to judge the extent of the achievement? Here I would submit four simple criteria. After reading carefully through Kooser's work, one should consider the following questions. First, there is the question of quality. Has the author written any perfect poems, not just good poems but perfect ones—on whatever subject, in whatever style, of whatever length—which use the resources of the language so definitively that one cannot change a single phrase without diminishing the poem's effect? And if there are perfect poems, how many? Second, there is the question of originality. Are the author's best poems different from those of any preceding poet? Can one hear a distinctive personality or sensibility behind them that is either saying something new about the world or speaking in such an original way that it makes one see familiar parts of the world as if for the first time? Third, there is a question of scope. How many things can an author do well in his poetry? How many styles or subjects, moods or voices can he master? Fourth, and finally, there is the question of integrity. Do the author's poems hold together to provide a unique and truthful vision of the world, or do they remain isolated moments of illumination?

There are other criteria one might use, but, at the very least, this test helps distinguish a superb poet from one who is merely good. And it is a test that highlights some important ways in which Kooser surpasses some of his more highly praised contemporaries. Kooser has written more perfect poems than any poet of his generation. In a quiet way, he is also one of its most original poets. His technical and intellectual interest may be narrow (indeed, in terms of limited techniques, he shares a common fault of his generation), but his work shows an impressive emotional range always handled in a distinctively personal way. Finally, his work does coalesce into an impressive whole. Read individually, his poems sparkle with insight. Read together, they provide a broad and believable portrait of contemporary America.

II. POPULAR POETRY AND REGIONAL IDENTITY

> All events and experiences are
> local, somewhere.
>
> —William Stafford

Popular poets always reflect the general taste and values of a particular time and place, even when those values are at odds with the high culture of the age. Robert Burns's folkish simplicity stands in sharp contrast to the cosmopolitan polish of his eighteenth-century contemporaries, just as Kipling's dance-hall exuberance sounds jarringly unlike the subtle orchestrations of the *fin-de-siècle* versifiers around him. Popular poetry draws its distinguishing vitality from the particular milieu it shares with its audience. It presents a more relevant world to this constituency than do the traditional *topoi* of high culture. Rooted in specifics ignored or excluded from mainstream culture, popular poetry therefore often assumes a regional identity. It represents the values and aspirations of a body culturally, politically, and often geographically separate from the ruling class of a nation.

Not surprisingly, therefore, Kooser's popular sensibility expresses itself most clearly in its regional loyalties. Kooser writes about the countryside, weather, towns, and people of the Great Plains. His regional perspective determines not only the subject matter of his poetry but also its texture and thematics. His language, imagery, ideas, attitudes, even his characteristic range of emotions reflect the landscapes, climate, and culture in which he has spent his entire life. To many critics such regionalism still equals provincialism, especially when the region in question is the Middle West. As it also becomes apparent that his work deals more with prosaic small towns and agricultural countryside than the conventionally poetic urban or natural landscapes, his parochialism simply becomes too much for most critics to bear.

Regionalism is ultimately a political term, a dismissive label applied to literature produced in and concerned with areas outside the dominant cultural and economic centers of a society. Classifying a work as "regional" implies that it cannot be judged by "national" standards. It suggests that certain subjects will be of only local interest. Where there are politics, however, there are also coups and revolutions. Sometimes a type of regional writing attains prominence because a new regime has come into power in the literary capital. The rising reputation of Southern literature in America, for example, neatly matches the influx of Southern writers and critics in the late forties into New York and the Ivy League universities.

In most industrialized countries there is also a pervasive urban bias against agricultural areas. In America that prejudice is focused on the Midwest, especially the Great Plains states, which are seen as flat, characterless, and provincial. Unlike the South, an older rural society that defiantly clings to its traditions, or the Southwest, which boasts a continuity of Spanish and Indian culture that has remained relatively intact amid its recent development, the Great Plains was settled later than most other areas of the country. Its economy is also less diversified, its population more widely scattered, and its people less ethnically heterogeneous, consisting largely of assimilated Northern Europeans (Kooser is of German descent). To the outsider there is less obvious local color—no accents, no dramatic social problems, less various scenery—although ironically it is this same uniformity that gives the Great Plains a distinctive cultural identity.

One would think that after Yeats and Faulkner, Joyce and Svevo, Verga and Cather, Cavafy and Hardy, regional writing would no longer be perceived as a second-class artistry practiced by those incapable of presenting the world at large. But although regionalism has become irresistibly attractive as an abstract concept in seminars studying "The Southern Literary Consciousness" or "Poetry and the Irish Revival," it meets with stern resistance when applied to uncanonized regions. The same professor who spent three years researching the facts of Yoknapatawpha County would usually never consider reading a novel by Wright Morris or Leonardo Sciascia. The regionalism celebrated in the universities usually centers on a few familiar territories, which have been described by such a long line of writers that they have been as thoroughly mythologized as Ilium or Rome, rather than the general notion that literature should be rooted in the reality of a particular place. In some cases, like rural Southern fiction or Los Angeles detective writing, one almost wonders if such writing can even still meaningfully be called regional. The local elements have become so thoroughly universalized through continual use that a skillful foreigner might be able to use them convincingly as purely literal patterns. After all, there is a point where the local becomes the universal. Parnassus was once only a small mountain near Delphi and Pan the local deity of impoverished rural Arcadia.

Midwestern critics have not helped the reputation of regional writing. Disenfranchised by a cultural establishment based largely in New York and New England, they have too often lost the objectivity that distance from the literary marketplace should allow. In retaliation to Eastern presumption they have adopted an unconvincing kind of regional boosterism, making extravagant claims for local writers of limited gifts. While one cannot excuse metropolitan critics for ignoring or undervaluing the work of important regional writers, neither can one sympathize with regional critics for applying looser standards to local writers than to those of national reputation. Regional favoritism is the worst kind of provincialism and eventually undermines the credibility of all local reputations. Here, Midwestern critics could learn from Southerners. While there is no region in America second to the South in the intensity of its literary self-esteem, Southerners have had a long and distinguished tradition of native critics who judged regional writers without losing perspective. Southern critics like Allen Tate, Cleanth Brooks, Robert Penn Warren, Randall Jarrell, John Crowe Ransom, or, more recently, Henry Taylor, George Garrett, Fred Chappell, and William Jay Smith have often discussed their regional writers without lowering their standards.

To some degree, Kooser's reputation has suffered from all of these factors. Rather than viewing his regional roots as a source of authenticity and exactitude, some critics have seen them as parochialism. His local subject matter has been labeled quaint; his affection for the particulars of his native landscape declared sentimental. His insistence on creating a poetic language out of plain Midwestern speech has been construed as a lack of accomplished technique; his deliberate simplicity as folksy ignorance. In short, critics have considered his regional loyalties as limitations. Even more important, however, by labeling Kooser a regional rather than national poet, the majority of critics have missed his grand overriding theme—the gradual disappearance of American rural culture. Focusing on the Great Plains states, Kooser has captured one of the century's great changes, the shift from country to city, from farming to business, from traditional family life to ambiguous personal independence. In hundreds of precise vignettes Kooser has created a poignant mosaic of this cultural transition no less relevant to Abidjan or Osaka than to Omaha or Des Moines. But by stereotyping him as a regional artist, even his admirers have failed to recognize the breadth of his themes. He has been reduced to the product of their expectations.

III. THE DEVELOPMENT OF A REGIONAL POET

> A poet's hope: to be
> like some valley cheese,
> local, but prized everywhere.
>
> —W. H. Auden

Ted Kooser's poetic career reveals some of the problems faced by a regional writer who does not either immigrate to a major literary center or join the university network. Born in Ames, Iowa, in 1939, Kooser has spent his entire life in Iowa and Nebraska. He attended Iowa State University, where he majored in English Education. Upon graduating in 1962, he taught high school for a year and then entered a graduate program in English at the University of Nebraska. After one year he stopped full-time study to begin a temporary job in insurance while finishing an M.A. at night. He has worked in insurance ever since and is currently a marketing executive at Lincoln Benefit Life. Thus, Kooser has been doubly alienated from the American literary establishment. First, he has lived only in two agricultural Midwestern states far removed from the centers of literary opinion. Second, he has spent the past twenty-five years working in business, cut off from the academic communities that support most regional writers and provide them with a professional network of colleagues, readers, and reviewers. This isolation would have destroyed most young writers' determination, but in Kooser it nourished an unusually strong sense of independence and self-sufficiency.

Kooser began his publishing career very conventionally, however, with *Official Entry Blank,* his wryly titled first book, which appeared in 1969 as part of the University of Nebraska's short-lived "Poetry from Nebraska" series. Not a precocious volume, *Official Entry Blank* showed a modestly talented young poet trying out a variety of contemporary models as he searched for his own characteristic style. Yet although the volume contained an example of almost every fashionable kind of workshop poem of the period, from heroic couplets to haiku, even those exercises usually gave glimpses of the author's smooth to haiku technique and engaging personality. It was an entertaining but curiously unfocused volume, which showed Kooser still writing under the influence of many older poets, most noticeably William Carlos Williams and Karl Shapiro, who had been Kooser's teacher.

Coming upon *Official Entry Blank* in 1969, one would have been hard-pressed either to predict Kooser's subsequent development or to define his individuality as a poet. Reading these poems today, however, one can occasionally hear Kooser's characteristic voice amidst the diversity of borrowed styles. Sometimes humorous, sometimes sober, it is never strained or sarcastic, for Kooser (unlike Whitman and his followers) is a truly democratic poet who addresses the reader as an equal. He never assumes the pose of prophet or professor instructing the unenlightened. He is intimate without being private, never obscure but also never public. He speaks as one would to an old friend. This tone of quiet trust, which characterizes Kooser's best poetry, may explain why the poet claims to dislike reading his work in public. His poems, he has commented, belong "on a page, not in an auditorium." Conceived in solitude, his poems are best encountered without the theatrical distractions of a public performance.

In *Official Entry Blank* one also notices Kooser's sharp eye for images. Again and again, he catches some tiny detail from everyday life that masterfully evokes a larger scene. He does not yet know how to frame these details for their full effect, but his observations often give these early poems, whatever their faults, an arresting freshness and immediacy. And in a few instances, like "Abandoned Farmhouse," he casts them in a form that foreshadows the best of his later work.

Official Entry Blank was the only immature or derivative book Kooser ever published, but, ironically, it was also the only one for the next eleven years with a university imprimatur. After its publication Kooser disappeared into the gulag of small regional presses. Printed in tiny editions, his books and pamphlets cultivated a small local audience—for some titles probably not more than a few dozen readers. Unnoticed in New York and Boston, they were sometimes reviewed by small and often ephemeral regional magazines like *Great Lakes Review,* *Raccoon,* and *Dacotah Territory.* More often they were not reviewed at all. But slowly Kooser's reputation grew in the Plains states, though readers and critics elsewhere were not generally aware of his work until the publication of his new and selected poems, *Sure Signs,* in 1980.

Two years after *Official Entry Blank,* Kooser issued a tiny pamphlet with his own illustrations. Self-published by his newly created Windflower Press, *Grass County* announced its intentions to combine "the author's illustrations with his poems in an attempt to more completely convey that vision of the Great Plains introduced in *Official Entry Blank.* Those readers with eyesight sharp enough to decipher its microscopic typeface would have found that the pamphlet actually lived up to its blurb. In *Grass County*'s eight short poems Kooser had found the proper subject and form for his poetry. Here, for example, is "Tom Ball's Barn":

> The loan that built the barn
> just wasn't big enough
> to buy the paint, so the barn
> went bare and fell apart
> at the mortgaged end of twelve
> nail-popping, splintering winters.
> Besides the Januaries,
> the barber says it was
> five-and-a-half percent,
> three dry years, seven wet
> and two indifferent,
> the banker (dead five years)
> and the bank (still open
> but deaf, or *deef* as it were), *and*
> poor iron in the nails that
> were all to blame for the barn's collapse
> on everything he owned, thus
> leading poor Tom's good health
> to diabetes and
> the swollen leg that threw him
> off the silo, probably

dead (the doctor said)
before he hit that board pile.

No single element in "Tom Ball's Barn" is new to American
poetry, and yet the combination of these elements strikes a unique
note. Without breaking from the past, Kooser had developed a new
and personal way to describe the world of the Great Plains, especially
the undramatic but tragic lives of its rural people. He had also found
a way of universalizing its landscape and stories without losing their
local character. He managed ordinary spoken language without making
it sound dull and undistinguished.

"Tom Ball's Barn" has another importance in Kooser's career. It
is the earliest successful example of the character poem—a kind of
poem that would subsequently account for much of his best work.
The model for Kooser's character studies were obviously Edwin Ar-
lington Robinson's Tilbury Town portraits and Edgar Lee Masters's
Spoon River Anthology—which remain the two touchstones of American
regional poetry—but, as "Tom Ball's Barn" demonstrates, he handled
his material very differently. Kooser's portraits have a relentless lineari-
ty in their exposition, which endows them with their peculiar speed and
powerfully dramatic simplicity. This linearity, however, is balanced by
the typically laconic and indirect presentation of the central character.

Syntax is the key to Kooser's expositions. Written in one long sen-
tence, "Tom Ball's Barn" moves quickly through a series of simple
observations that the reader immediately understands but has no time
to assimilate before his attention is pushed ahead to the next fact. This
speed also gives each fact a certain inevitability, as if mere sequence
were logic, so that at first glance the callous "thus" in line 17 really does
seem to explain Ball's death. Likewise, the reader is immersed in the
narrative situation so quickly that he has no time at first to notice the
unusual way Ball's story is told. The poem is almost over before Ball
is introduced. He is not shown directly; rather he is characterized by
the things around him, especially the unpainted barn, whose decay and
eventual collapse mirror his own fatal fall. Seen here explicitly for the
first time, this equation between people and their property will become
a major preoccupation of Kooser's poetry.

That Kooser was unaware of the possibilities he had uncovered in *Grass County* is evident from his next collection, *Twenty Poems* (Best Cellar Press, 1973). This pamphlet shows Kooser uncertain of his direction. While in a few poems, especially the character sketches like "The Failed Suicide" and "Selecting a Reader" (a charming portrait of an ideal reader, who is sensible enough to reject him), Kooser develops the methods he had discovered in *Grass County*, most of the new poems are facile exercises in conventional styles. Here Kooser sometimes explores his characteristic themes but in ways that dilute their effectiveness. There is also a series of macabre poems that matter-of-factly describe weird events—"Grating a Brain," "They Had Torn Off My Face at the Office," and "A Dead Man Driving a Car." Superficially effective, these poems trivialize Kooser's real talent. By affecting the blasé tone, the placeless setting, the surreal methods of San Francisco and New York poets, he lost the compassionate authenticity that characterizes his most vital work.

This lack of direction did not last long. The next year Kooser consolidated his achievement in *A Local Habitation & a Name* (Solo Press, 1974). Here, for the first time, he revealed the full range of his talent. Collecting about two dozen of his favorite earlier poems, he added fifty new pieces, including half a dozen perfect poems of unmistakable originality. This volume proved that the intermittent successes of his earlier books had been no fluke. Ranging in tone from comic to tragic, from gently nostalgic to savagely satiric, these new poems, which include such signature pieces as "Spring Plowing," "The Widow Lester," "The Blind Always Come as Such a Surprise," and "A Place in Kansas," showed Kooser capable of handling diverse material in a masterfully personal way. His mastery, however, was of a consciously modest variety. He had chosen the short poem as his medium. All of his poems were shorter than a page, most of them under ten lines. Seen together in bulk for the first time, however, they went beyond a series of dazzling miniatures and formed a memorable composite. All drawing their inspiration from the world of the Great Plains, they re-created that world as effectively in verse as any American poet had done before. Few people on either coast were paying attention (except the maverick William Cole, who in his chatty column in the *Saturday Review* called Kooser his "favorite young poet"), but the Great Plains had just produced a poet of national importance.

To show how far Kooser had developed in a few years, one need only compare two short poems that use similar material. First, here is "Haiku for Nebraskans" from *Official Entry Blank*:

> Telephone wires whine
> in the claws of red-tailed hawks—
> frightened mice screaming

In only seventeen syllables, this piece displays many of the conventions of the Sixties' workshop poem. Technically competent but uninteresting, it is written in a notoriously easy foreign form that announces its fashionable independence from traditional English metrics. Having been scrupulously compressed to the point of small ellipses, the language is sharp but lackluster. The situation is conveyed visually, the structure of the poem being merely an equation between two images. The content is as unsurprising as the style. The poem begins with an easy contrast between nature and technology (though the technology has been animated—"whining" as it does). Although the ending pretends to be tough and elemental, it is actually cryptically sentimental. Although this poem is skillfully constructed, it ultimately shows no particular virtues to distinguish it from the work of a hundred other poets. Nor does Kooser use his tired images in any way that makes the reader see them with fresh eyes.

Now read "Spring Plowing" from *A Local Habitation & A Name*:

> West of Omaha the freshly plowed fields
> steam in the night like lakes.
> The smell of the earth floods over the roads.
> The field mice are moving their nests
> to the higher ground of fence rows,
> the old among them crying out to the owls
> to take them all. The paths in the grass
> are loud with the squeak of their carts.
> They keep their lanterns covered.

This perfect little poem has no exact precedent in American literature. Deceptively simple on first hearing, it bears sustained attention, and is ultimately satisfying on either a purely naturalistic or imaginative level. Not only is it more technically skilled than the earlier haiku (in the naturalness of the language, the complexity and originality of the imagery, and the structure of its development), but, more important, this poem opens the reader's eyes to the world—albeit some tiny part of a specifically Midwestern world. It enlarges our humanity in ways the earlier poem did not. It will be difficult to drive by a freshly plowed field without thinking of the vulnerable creatures it displaced.

The expository structure of "Spring Plowing" also shows how expert Kooser had become since *Official Entry Blank*. The poem's unexpected movement from ordinary observation to compassionate illumination illustrates Kooser's special achievement as a poet who can endow everyday subjects with a fresh and mysterious resonance. "Spring Plowing" begins conventionally with a description any competent poet might have written, but the first five lines don't prepare one for what will follow. As the poet adjusts his focus from an overview of the field to a close-up of the mice, the scene is suddenly transformed from a naturalistic description to a fantastic, humanized vision of the fleeing animals. Kooser compresses several implicit metaphors into the next four lines, and then ends with a sinister, enigmatic image. The language is highly charged but never clumsy or crowded. The metaphorical trick of transforming mice into threatened refugees is fresh and surprising. Only nine lines long, this poem accomplishes a complex but seamlessly executed shape.

Kooser's next book, *Not Coming to Be Barked At* (Pentagram Press, 1976) solidified his reputation as an important regional poet. (The strange title of this book comes from an incident in the Finnish national epic, the *Kalevala*, but it is also a typically self-deprecating Kooserian gesture to the reader.) By now Kooser was fully conscious—even if his critics were not—of the position he had created for himself in American poetry as the master of the short, colloquial, imagistic poem. Having perfected his technique, he began broadening his thematics, exploring more fully the world of the Great Plains. *Not Coming to Be Barked At* not only contained many of Kooser's best poems, such as "The Very Old," "Late February," "In a Country Cemetery," "Visiting Mountains," "So This Is Nebraska," and "Shooting a Farmhouse," it also demonstrated the consistent high quality that distinguishes his work. Virtually every poem has some particular virtue to recommend it, and page after page in poems like "Snowfence," "The Afterlife," "North of Alliance," "Old Soldier's Home," "Sitting All Alone in the Kitchen," "Living Near the Rehabilitation House," and many others, the reader feels the presence of a rich, naturally poetic imagination. The individual poems were short, but cumulatively they created a powerful picture of a real life in a particular time and place.

In his best poetry up to this time Kooser usually maintained a certain distance between himself and his subject. Most often he acted the part of a seemingly impartial observer who stamped his personality on the situation indirectly by choosing the details that he presented or omitted. Sometimes in more openly personal poems he put himself in the action of the poem, but he balanced his direct involvement by deliberately understating the emotional elements of the situation. In *Old Marriage and New* (Cold Mountain Press, 1978), Kooser tried to develop a more openly autobiographical kind of poetry. Writing about the failure of his first marriage and the promise of his second, he carefully established a series of thirteen short scenes that dramatized this difficult period in his life. Sharp and concisely written, these poems seem thin compared to Kooser's previous work. The final twist, with the kind of unexpected image that enlivened so many of his poems, often struck a flat or overly sentimental note here, as in "Driving to Work":

> Once in a while, when I'm driving to work
> in the morning, I see a schoolgirl
> walking slowly along, and something about her
> is you, and the way you must have been
> when you were a girl, still young
> and full of dreams; and seeing you there, oblivious
> to me, I feel as if
> a bird had darted out and struck the windshield.

This poem does not reveal a failure of technique but of sensibility. The final image is too embarrassingly obvious in its appeal to the emotions. One can understand Kooser's pain but cannot share it. *Old Marriage and New* was perhaps a necessary experiment for Kooser, but this chapbook ranks as the weakest of his mature collections.

Kooser remained little known outside the Midwest and undervalued even there until the publication of *Sure Signs: New and Selected Poems* from the University of Pittsburgh Press in 1980. His early career had been sustained by small regional presses and reviews that praised his work but did not distinguish it from that of dozens of other young Plains poets. *Sure Signs* not only brought Kooser national attention for the first time, it also established him as one of the few openly regional young poets whose work had broad appeal beyond the Midwest.

Sure Signs showed Kooser as a shrewd judge of his own poetry. He ruthlessly cut away his weaker work and presented the reader with only eighty-nine short poems from all of his earlier books. The careful editing gave *Sure Signs* a consistent quality that put most contemporary collections to shame. It also ensured that readers who came upon Kooser's work there for the first time were left impressed with the quality of his achievement. *Sure Signs* confirmed the poet's peculiar organization of his own work. Kooser has always resisted chronological arrangement of his poems. Instead he has done his best to disguise his own development as a poet by organizing his work in sequences that presumably heighten the particular strengths and variety of his poetry. One can assume from this choice that Kooser, with his characteristic modesty, finds the subjects and moods of his poems more interesting than their evidence of his personal development as a poet. One cannot dispute that decision, but it is important to note here how difficult it makes understanding his development, a difficulty intensified by his insistence on dropping unsuccessful poems from his canon. Only two poems in his confessional book, *Old Marriage and New*, for example, survive in *Sure Signs*.

Based on his first seven books and the considerable number of poems he has published in periodicals since *Sure Signs*, however, it seems appropriate now to attempt some overall conclusions about Kooser's development as a poet. In one way the achronological arrangement of *Sure Signs* testifies to Kooser's lack of dramatic growth. Once he discovered a mature personal voice in *Grass County*, Kooser has demonstrated little substantial change. Although he has experimented with other styles such as the confessional or surreal, these experiments have not generally been successful, and he has returned to a few characteristic kinds of poems. On the other hand, while Kooser's poetry has not greatly changed since *Grass County*, it has deepened. In poem after poem he has gradually populated a region of the imagination, a loving recreation of the Great Plains. As he has become increasingly conscious of his role in chronicling this region, so much of which is disappearing into history, his work has developed an intensity and integrity few of his contemporaries can match. He has slowly created a larger structure in which his short poems have acquired a new resonance. This regional allegiance has also helped unify his work, focusing the isolated brilliance of his individual poems into one overall vision. Therefore, without abandoning the short forms he has so carefully mastered, Kooser, through the consistency and authenticity of his concerns, has forged them into an ambitious larger work, a unified *oeuvre* that like an epic encompasses his world.

If Kooser's poetry has grown deeper with each book, it has also grown stronger. Unlike the writing of so many established poets entering middle age, his verse has suffered no drop-off in intensity or workmanship. Experience has only sharpened his skills. Moreover, in developing the overall vision of his work he has never sacrificed the quality and integrity of individual poems to the demands of the larger design. He has not sought refuge in grandiose imaginative schemes but has remained committed to realizing each poem fully in itself, for instinctively he knows that it is not the size of a poet's intentions that ensures survival but the quality of his individual poems. Whatever his other limitations, Kooser has succeeded in the poet's main task—bringing all the forces of language to bear in perfectly achieved poems. Few of his contemporaries have succeeded as often, and none of them in so accessible and engagingly humane a manner. Kooser is unsurpassed in articulating the subtle and complex sensibility of the common American.

Therefore, while one would not claim that Kooser is a major poet, one could well make the case that he will be an enduring one. His work is the genuine article—poetry concerned with themes of permanent value, written flawlessly in an original and distinctive way. However tightly one may draw the boundaries of his accomplishments, once one crosses the border into the territory of his imagination, one finds an unforgettable world of illumination and delight.

Words and Raincoats:
Verbal and Nonverbal Communication

Victor Contoski

In "Selecting a Reader," the work Kooser chose to open *Sure Signs: New and Selected Poems,* he presents us with a curious fable. He imagines a beautiful woman walking up to his book. We see her damp hair, her dirty raincoat and her glasses. She impresses us with her physical presence, and even when she goes over the book, she does so in physical terms—she *thumbs* it. Far from overwhelmed by the poetry, she considers the money she would have to spend on the book; then decides to get her raincoat cleaned instead.

Is not such a poem rather slight to introduce a volume of selected poems? What is the point of this little joke the poet tells on himself? That life is more important than art? Surely life and poetry should interact, both becoming richer by doing so. Yet this reader appears to reject Kooser's poetry outright. Should we not also go out and live—get our raincoats cleaned instead of devoting time to such poetry?

The answers to these questions may reveal a deeper poem than we had first suspected. Just as the woman moves toward the book and then away, so the poet moves towards pretty poetic diction in the first three lines ("beautiful," "poetry," "loneliest moment") and then away toward the real world. (There is not one "beautiful" word in the last ten lines.) We begin with the poet's dream. We finish with the woman walking away—and the focus remains on her, as if the poet were walking away with her into the real world. And in a sense he is.

Thus the title becomes ironic. The "reader" merely browses through the book instead of reading it intently. And while the poet is selecting her, she is rejecting him. The bond between the two, which we have been led to expect from the title, never really seems to develop.

But perhaps we have been expecting the wrong kind of bond with the wrong reader. There are, after all, two readers here, the woman in the poem and the actual reader outside the poem. Kooser uses one, the woman, to show the priorities in his work: that action is often more important than verbal communication, that everyday things such as rain-coats are more important than "the poetic." If Kooser loses the first reader, he may gain the more important second.

Yet even the first reader may not be entirely lost. She reads rather superficially, I take it, but nevertheless contemplates buying the book. In the very act of physically touching the book and going over it lightly, she may have gotten something of the poet's message. Indeed, Kooser's concern with just such things as raincoats may have led her back to real-ity and the cleaners.

I should like in the pages that follow to trace some similar levels of verbal and nonverbal communication in Kooser's work.

Kooser's characters act rather than talk. They radiate a stubborn silence, perhaps because of the broad prairie on which they live. This silence shows on the one hand a kind of pioneer hardiness in the peo-ple. They know from their own lives the relative brutality—as if they almost do not know how to speak, particularity to each other. In "An Old Photograph" we see a husband and wife who emphasize their psychic distance from each other by the physical distance between them in the photograph.

> How far apart
>
> they sit: not touching at shoulder
> or knee, hands clasped in their laps
> as if under each pair was a key
> to a trunk hidden somewhere,
> full of those lessons one keeps
> to himself.

As the poet imagines what their day must have been like as they prepared for the photograph, he does not imagine them in conversation.

When people do speak in Kooser poems, they often do not speak directly *to each other*. In "Shooting a Farmhouse" one of the hunters, knowing the farmhouse to be abandoned, asks the empty air, "Is anyone home?" But his words are really a form of oblique communication to the other hunters, who understand, and laugh. They communicate with each other by blowing out windows, shooting beer cans, and pissing on the floor.

Other examples abound. In "Carrie" the main character complains as she dusts, "There's never an end to dust and dusting." But she has no audience in the poem; she speaks into a void. In "The Blind Always Come as Such a Surprise," the blind seem to be dumb as well. We do not hear their words but the tapping of their canes. In "Tom Ball's Barn" we are told what the barber says, but once again Kooser presents a speaker without presenting the speaker's audience. In "Boarding House" the deaf man and the blind man communicate through a light left burning and squeaky shoes. The doctor in "A Hot Night in Wheat Country" communicates with everybody in North Dakota by the sound of his airplane. And in "Central" the operator speaks at the end of the poem to darkness: "This is Central. / Hello? Is anyone there?"

This absence of words can bestow upon people a kind of dumb eloquence, as when the poet's grandfather waits silently to attend the funeral of the woman who had shared his life.

> Beyond the window, his eighty-eighth winter
> lay white in its furrows. The little creek
> which cut through his cornfield was frozen.
> Past the creek and the broken, brown stubble,
> on a hill which thirty years before
> he'd given the town, a green tent flapped
> under the cedars.

A man works in the distance, and the poet imagines that his grandfather can feel that work in his hands—

> those hard old hands which lay curled and still
> near the soft gray felt hat on the table.

But people who do not speak to each other can also become trapped in a mute cycle of animal life. "The Widow Lester" shows a woman who married because nobody told her she was too old. She repeats the pattern by not telling her husband to wash his feet so that she can hold the smell against him. Even when she speaks to the reader, she does so tersely, grudgingly. Such a cycle can trap even the president, usually a man of glib rhetoric and easy half-truths. He haunts us in "A Presidential Poem" precisely because he says nothing. He communicates by the sound of the refrigerator door opening and closing, and ultimately—wonderful strangeness!—by the lack of any sound at all: the absence of the small noise of breathing when we know he is standing at the foot of the bed.

Yet although people in Kooser's poetry are taciturn, things are not. They speak eloquently, particularly of the past, as if they have absorbed somehow the people with whom they have come in contact. We have already noted how a photograph speaks for Nils and Lydia, how the landscape expresses the feelings of the poet's grandfather. In "Abandoned Farmhouse" the people have long since left, but their things talk to the reader through the poet—shoes, bed, Bible, fields, bedroom wall, sandbox, jar of preserves, a rubber cow, and a doll in overalls.

Sounds, so vitally important to Kooser's characters, also play an important role in Kooser's own communications to his readers. In "Red Wing Church," for example, we see the house of God in apparent disarray. Only about a third of the way into the poem do we realize that the outward disorder really covers a change in a new order.

> They've taken it down to change the house of God
> to Homer Johnson's barn, but it's still a church,
> with clumps of tiger lilies in the grass
> and one of those boxlike, glassed-in signs
> that give the sermon's topic (reading now
> a bird's nest and a little broken glass).
> The good works of the Lord are all around:
> the steeple top is standing in a garden
> just up the alley; it's a hen house now:
> fat leghorns gossip at its crowded door.
> Pews stretch on porches up and down the street,
> the stained-glass windows style the mayor's house,
> and the bell's atop the firehouse in the square.
> The cross in only God knows where.

And in keeping with this sense of a new order, rimes and off-rimes begin to appear. Note *grass* and *glass*, *now* and *around.* This repetition of certain words and sounds, particularly the *ow* sound in *now, around, house, crowded, down, house,* and *firehouse,* gives the poem a more ordered music as it approaches the end. The final line by itself might seem to be the climax of the disorder with which the poem began, but the sentence cannot be taken by itself because it is part of a final couplet. The *square-where* rime and the iambic rhythm emphasize the new order, perhaps a more natural one, that replaces the old. And the stark sense of the final line is mitigated by the poem's orderly music.

In "The Giant Slide" we have another typical Kooser scene, an artifice of civilization abandoned. The poem concludes:

> Call it a passing fancy,
> this slide that nobody slides down now.
> Those screams have all gone east
> on a wind that will never stop blowing
> down from the Rockies and over the plains,
> where things catch on for a little while,
> bright leaves in a fence, and then are gone.

The children have become ghosts—like so many other Kooser characters—though we can still hear their shouts in the long *e*'s of "Those screams have all gone east." And in the line just before, the eerie quality of the alternating long *i*'s and *o*'s emphasizes the sense as the rhythm of the poem slows. Two lines farther down the long *o*'s echo again in *those* and *blowing.* And the end of the poem Kooser masterly dampens the long sounds with the subtle rimes and *n* sounds in *on, fence, then,* and *gone.*

Perhaps Kooser's most subtle manipulation of sound occurs in "Spring Plowing," a serious and delightful poem about dislocation.

> West of Omaha the freshly plowed fields
> steam in the night like lakes.
> The smell of the earth floods over the roads.
> The field mice are moving their nests
> to the higher ground of fence rows,

the old among them crying out to the owls
to take them all. The paths in the grass
are loud with the squeak of their carts.
They keep their lanterns covered.

The long *o* in *Omaha* echoes throughout the poem in *roads, ground, rows, old, out,* and *owls.* We can actually hear the old mice groaning in these sounds, so that when we come to *loud* in the penultimate line, it bears the weight of all those previous long *o*'s—it shouts. We can hear the carts really squeaking in *squeak* and *keep,* but note that the paths, not the carts have become loud—as if the sound has gotten entirely out of control. At the same time we get a sense of hushed silence in the *ths* of *paths* and the *ss* of *grass.* Thus the contrary directions of the sound reinforce the actions of the field mice, who are trying to keep quiet and not succeeding. But at the very end of the poem, as if both mice and poet realize they are getting too loud, sense and sound turn back toward silence. Mindful of their enemies, the mice "keep their lanterns covered"—and note how the silent *p* in *keep* hushes the long *e* sound. The dampening *n*'s in *lantern* quiet the noise, as does the final *d* in *covered*—though we can still hear the rumble of wagons in the *r*'s of the last three words.

Since Kooser's characters speak only minimally for themselves, the poet bears an added responsibility to make his poems eloquent, a task made even more difficult because his subjects often demand simple sentences and straightforward diction. But if Kooser's characters communicate with each other through nonverbal sounds, Kooser often communicates with the reader in a similar way, reinforcing the sense of his poems by the subtle music of his words.

On Restraint

David Baker

I am not concerned here with artistic timidity, moral constraint, or polite decorum—that is, restraint as puritanic virtue—but rather with tactics of restraint which allow us to gauge a poem's opposite pole, its power and passion. Even Walt Whitman is at his most persuasive when his enthusiasms are informed by subdued counter-pressures. In "Crossing Brooklyn Ferry," those ominous, looming "dark patches," which accompany his confessions of secular guilt, temper his later transcendental encouragements to "flow on...with the floodtide." The poem's polar forces—obliteration and regeneration, liability and acceptance—are held in a system of checks-and-balances. The result is precarious and powerful. Other poets use different methods of restraint: Dickinson with her severe, compact technique ("After great pain, a formal feeling comes—"); Bishop in her very stance, what Meredith Merrin calls an "enabling humility." Restraint can ironize, enable, even sustain a poet's great passions and wildness.

Ted Kooser is the most restrained of the five poets I consider here, if restraint also nominates characteristics like compassion and control. A critically undervalued poet, Kooser is a joy to read, even if, every now and then, he may be a little *too* restrained. His touch is so light and his poems generally so compact that occasionally there doesn't seem to be enough passion or material at hand. But after all, much of the power of Kooser's work is accretive, since for decades he has been constructing out of individual poems a long, sustained, and important life work in the manner of E.A. Robinson's *Tilbury Town*, Edgar Lee Master's *Spoon River*, or Richard Hugo's *Great Northwest*. Throughout his new *Weather Central* Kooser's individual poems are evocative, often perfectly realized, even as they also become part and parcel of his larger project, the creation in poetry of a distinctly Midwestern social text, as in "Lincoln, Nebraska," where

...there
is something beautiful

> about a dirty town in rain,
> where tin cans, rails,
> and toppled shopping carts
> are the sutures of silver
> holding the guts in,
>
> keeping the blue wound closed,
> while over a pawnshop, the plain
> wet flag of a yellow window
> holds out the cautious welcome
> of an embassy.

Kooser is highly selective in the amount and type of material he includes in a poem. Only seven of the fifty-eight poems in *Weather Central* are longer than a page; the longest, "City Limits," runs to forty lines. He is a devoted chronicler of the Midwest, but so careful, so meticulous, that even his most modest poems ring with pleasing recognitions:

> It is morning. My father
> in shirtsleeves is sweeping
> the sidewalk in front of his store,
> standing up straight in the bow
> of his gondola, paddling
> the endless gray streets of his life
> with an old yellow oar—
> happy there, hailing his friends.

Here in "The Sweeper," and throughout this book, recognition and connection are Kooser's recurrent longings—the connective goodwill of neighbors and families, the connections of the images themselves. Notice how he activates the poem's only metaphor exactly halfway through this poem with "in the bow / of his gondola, paddling," where a plain description of the father's movement turns into the stroke of a gondolier, the absolutely familiar touched with a wistful exotica. He is uncanny in selecting such right-seeming metaphors, but he is also a realist, an Imagist writing haiku-like verse, whose tropes are rarely dramatically transformative but rather clarifying. He wants us to see things more sharply.

He connects his deliberate images with a kind of restrained, respectful sanity, like "Aunt Mildred" who "picked up a pencil stub and pinched it hard, / straightened her spine, and wrote a small / but generous letter to the world."

Kooser rarely refers to himself in his work, and then hardly ever in first person. This kind of restraint is particularly striking in a period when so much poetry is, to parrot Hawthorne's *Zenobia*, so much "Self, self, self!" The closest Kooser comes to self-portraiture may be the image of the blue heron in the book's first poem, "Etude," where the first-person speaker watches "a Great Blue Heron / fish in the cattails, easing ahead / with the stealth of a lover composing a letter." He sees in the bird's actions and its "blue suit" the reflection of a businessman who "holds down an everyday job / in an office" (like Kooser's own occupation as an insurance executive):

> Long days swim beneath the glass top
> of his desk, each one alike. On the lip
> of each morning, a bubble trembles.
> No one has seen him there, writing a letter
> to a woman he loves. His pencil is poised
> in the air like the beak of a bird.
> He would spear the whole world if he could,
> toss it and swallow it live.

The letter is a figure for the kind of lifelike text Kooser seems to strive for in his poems. The final sentence with its sudden, dramatic feat is even more effective given this love poem's delicate restraint. Midway into *Weather Central* we encounter the image of the heron again, in "A Poetry Reading," though by now he's "an old blue heron with yellow eyes," a poet opening his "book on its spine, a split fish." These mere hints are among the most directly self-revealing moments in the book. Kooser reserves his more emotional involvements for his characters, as in the tender "Four Secretaries," where all day, like ordinary sirens, they "call back and forth, / singing their troubled marriage ballads, / their day-care, car-park, landlord songs." Again like a poet, the speaker here is separated from the cohabitants of his office because of his position. His distance seems to sharpen his sympathy:

And their sadness—how deep and full of love
is their sadness when one among them
is hurt, and they hear her calling
and gather about her to cry.

Kooser is a poet of deep passion for the daily, workaday world, but he
is more interested in human behavior than in the buried motivations for
such. He is a reporter, not an editorialist.

With their chiseled lines, perfectly balanced stanzas, unfanciful im-
agery, and cleanest of syntax, virtually every poem in *Weather Central* is a
model of the plain style. But here's a paradox: some of the traits of this
style (its transparent inflections and dialect, its invisible craft) may be im-
pediments to appreciating the unique gifts of this plain-spoken Midwest-
ern poet. Yet I think Kooser's a central poet. Poems like "Weather Cen-
tral," "Another Ghost Story," "Fireflies," "In Late Spring," "Snakeskin,"
and any number of other splendid poems here ought to find their place
in the representative anthologies of our time. Kooser documents the
dignities, habits, and small griefs of daily life, our hunger for connection,
our struggle to find balance in natural and unnaturally human worlds.

A far more acclaimed and much-awarded poet, Charles Simic plays
the Romantic to Kooser's Realist. They were born in 1938 and 1939,
respectively, and have published a dozen volumes apiece. Each is master-
ful at plain-spoken rhetoric and impeccably tight free-verse techniques.
Each is skilled at creating memorable individual images as well as coher-
ent patterns of metaphor. Miniaturists, each exploits the short poem to
great advantage; only two of the seventy poems in *A Wedding in Hell* are
longer than a page, thirty lines being the longest. Simic employs many of
the same strategies of restraint that distinguish Kooser's poems.

But Simic's metaphors transform where Kooser's clarify:

In the frying pan
On the stove
I found my love
And me naked.

Chopped onions

Fell on our heads
And made us cry.
It's like a parade,
I told her, confetti
When some guy
Reaches the moon.

"Means of transport,"
She replied obscurely
While we fried.
"Means of transport!"

Simic likes to wink at us "obscurely," as here in a poem that opens with the most restrained of rhetorics but the oddest of metaphors. Lovers as potatoes, or cuts of liver? "Transport" takes us into the surreal, as many of his poems ferry us from the familiar to the entirely alien, from the mundane to the holy, or from the dim to the philosophical (or vice versa). As he professes in another poem, "'I'm crazy about her shrimp!' / I shout to the gods above." Simic is a Postmodern Romantic, a mystic grinding his forehead into the stones though he knows that God is dead and buried, a believer who asserts the transcendent moment but who also perceives the transcendence is likely to send us to the kind of place he describes in "Pascal's Idea": "It was terrifying / And I suppose a bit like / What your heaven and hell combined must be." Poem after poem insists on these kinds of metamorphic changes. I like to amass Kooser's poems, letting them gather in larger social scene, but I prefer Simic's a few at a time. Too much similar magic at once exposes its tricks.

To American audiences part of Simic's charm derives from his Continental-sounding images and cosmopolitan sensibilities. If he has a riddler's sense of humor, he can also don the Romantic's blackest cape. He recalls Kafka's great European absurdist masterpiece "The Hunger Artist" in the prose poem "Voice from the Cage," where caged animals act out their existential agony: "Sorrow, sickness, and fleabites are our lot.... Even the lion doesn't believe the fables anymore. 'Pray to the Lord,' the monkeys shriek." Even the freakish speaker has "dyed [his] hair green like Baudelaire." This contorted display of grotesqueries, like a "circus of quick, terrified glances," is repeated in many poems. Toothless monkeys, "chickens living in a rusty old hearse," a gorilla suit with "silly angel wings," a white cat "picking at the bloody head of a fish"—such often feral malformities are the shadow-images of the faceless soldiers and anonymous "refugees crowding the roads" who also populate Simic's poems. Expatriation, the brutal repetitions of history, the chaos of broken walls, of failed faiths, drive the speaker in "Explaining a Few Things" underground, like Dostoevsky's "sick man." Once again, armies and animals are Simic's companions:

> Every worm is a martyr,
> Every sparrow subject to injustice,
> I said to my cat,
> Since there was no one else around.
>
> It's raining. In spite of their huge armies
> What can the ants do?
> And the roach on the wall
> like a waiter in an empty restaurant?
>
> I'm going to the cellar
> To stroke the rat caught in a trap.
> You watch the sky.
> If it clears, scratch on the door.

As crisp and plainly spoken as Kooser's documents to the commonplace, still this poem is a world and an age away from Lincoln, Nebraska.

Charles Simic has been writing like this for a long time, sharply, seriously, with a rhetoric of restraint but with a vision of haunted strangeness. Still, I think his talent is growing, as his poems continue to deepen, subtly but surely. The poems of *A Wedding in Hell* are more commonly absorbing than the work of his famous books of the seventies, such as *Dismantling the Silence* or *Classic Ballroom Dances*. "O dreams like evening shadows on a windy meadow," he sings in "A Wedding in Hell," "And your hands, Mother, like white mice." His plainness makes these surprises, these pointed and surreal mutations, all the more powerful.

Galway Kinnell is another brand of Romantic altogether, as broadly sweeping and declarative as Simic is furrowed and allegorical. He's Whitman to Simic's Baudelaire. And like Whitman's, his tactics of restraint are far fewer and more subtle than either Kooser's or Simic's. I don't think *Imperfect Thirst* is Kinnell's best book, but this poet has such command that his average poems are often better than most other poets' best; and to be sure, there are gems in this book to more than compensate for the disappointments.

Kinnell's gift has always been to mediate between the visible, substantial world and the inutterably spiritual or mystical, and the approach he takes in his greatest poems, like "The Bear," "The Last River," or any section of *The Book of Nightmares*, requires giving over the body's self to the regions of mystery and otherness he identifies in "There Are Things I Tell to No One": "I believe, / rather, in a music of grace / that we hear, sometimes, playing to us / from the other side of happiness." It's an all-or-nothing poetic, Romanticism at its purest, whose procedures are dramatic and self-obliterating and whose tactics are typically the opposite of restraint. Some of this passion still resides in Kinnell's new poems, though the presiding aesthetic of our age is anything but transcendental-friendly. (Is the end of *every* century marked by Victorian-like decoration, cultural prudery and resentment, a foregrounding of the historical, the rational, the scientific?) Frequent critical discouragement with the later work of James Dickey, James Wright, W.S. Merwin, even Kinnell, may be only partly the poets' culpability and partly because of the bearing of criticism away from the Romantic. Even Kinnell seems sometimes skeptical of his Romantic leanings.

Imperfect Thirst is a well-balanced book, with five poems in each of the five sections and an introductory "proem." Kinnell has always counted carefully, shaping his wildness with that particular form of order. It is uncanny, for instance, how many of his superb poems have seven sections: "The Porcupine," "The Bear," "Memories of My Father," "Another Night in the Ruins," all ten of the *Nightmares*, many more. But then, fine music is also mathematical. And music is the condition to which Kinnell's aesthetic aspires in *Imperfect Thirst*. One of the best works in this volume, "'The Music of Poetry,'" is at once a love poem and a catalogue of the values of Romanticism. We find the speaker in the middle of his own lecture "at a podium...on Bleeker Street," trying to come up with a "unified theory" of poetry:

that the music resulting from any of the methods
of organizing English into rhythmic surges
can sound like the music resulting from any other,
being the music not of a method but of the language;
and after proposing that free verse is a variant
of formal verse, using unpredictably the acoustic
repetitions which formal verse employs regularly....

Begun with pseudo-scientific detachment, his explanation soon finds more satisfying answers in "the humpback whale's gasp-cries," tribal rituals, and the songs of "clasped lovers." Where Kooser's and Simic's love poems are models of compression, Kinnell's poetry is additive, an accumulating prescription of virtues. Its eventual goal is "to let the audience hear that our poems are of the same order as those of the other animals / and are composed, like theirs, when we find ourselves / synchronized with the rhythms of the earth." Kinnell's other, more hidden model is Whitman's "When I Heard the Learn'd Astronomer." (Whitman's hermit thrush also adds its song to Kinnell's here.) In both poems the speaker rejects the jargon of the academic in favor of a solitary, direct connection with nature. So the praiseworthy traits of Romanticism—seclusion, animal knowledge, primitive practice, disengagement with the scholarly and public, erotic naturalism—provide Kinnell with the components of this *ars poetica*. The poem ends as the details of his talk fade, as his social discourse decays, as his mind drifts into a reverie "causing me to garble a few words / and tangle my syntax," all at the thought of his "beloved [who] may have / put down her book and drawn up her eider-down" before sleep. She is another example of the natural, Romantic hero: "I imagine I can hear / her say my name into the slow waves / of the night and, faintly, being alone, sing."

Other poems in *Imperfect Thirst* search for similar articulations: "bleats," cries, "excruciated singsong," gasps, "wolf's howls," and all other manner of natural, alogical communication. It's part of Kinnell's argument with the structures of culture and sense. Usually his critiques are effective, but sometimes, as in "Holy Shit," they just don't work. A deconstruction of the oxymoronic interjection "holy shit," this seventy-nine line poem begins with more than three pages of epigraphs, in historical order, drawn from religious sources, and all about defecation,

Plato, Saint Bernard, Chaucer's Pardoner, the *Shacharit*, Whitman again, and Jung are among the conjured voices. But Kinnell is not always an effective satirist, and the poem, which consists of examples proving that living things (as opposed to "the gods") shit, seems merely too witty and self-satisfied to succeed as a brash acceptance of a simple, natural function: "The white-tailed deer stops and solfs her / quarter-notes the size and color / of nicoise olives onto the snow." It wants to be the kind of radical, audacious, ultimately political confrontation that Allen Ginsberg can sometimes bring off, but it remains oddly constructed.

Other poems in *Imperfect Thirst* suffer differently. "Parkinson's Disease" attempts to answer the impossible question, "Could heaven be a time, after we are dead, / of remembering the knowledge / flesh had from flesh?" But it strains with philosophizing and with its many rhetorical gestures of connection to Sharon Olds's poems in *The Father*. Readers will find poems to love and poems to flip. "The Deconstruction of Emily Dickinson" shows Kinnell's satiric humor at its most topical and flexible, an anthologist's dream, and the restrained tenderness of "The Cellist" and "Neverland" suitably balance the fabular grace of "The Striped Snake and the Goldfinch" and the "wild fiery" joy of "Flies."

A bird flies through almost every poem in Brigit Pegeen Kelly's new *Song*. The relative newcomer of this group, Kelly won the 1994 Lamont Prize for this superlative second book of poems, which follows by seven years her Yale winner, *To the Place of Trumpets*. She's a deliberate writer, though like Kinnell she is also a Romantic of the more transcendental flavor, and so her birds like "flame-flung arrows," her swans and finches, even her crow like a "lord of highness," provide not only the models of song for a human voice aspiring to otherness' but also seems to bear communications from beyond. Jonathan Edwards, in his tract of Puritan typology, *Images or Shadows of Divine Things*, declares that "Ravens are birds of the air that are expressly used by Christ as types of the Devil.... The raven by its blackness represents the prince of darkness." While Kelly's birds are not so conclusively symbolic, still they seem to indicate types of providential suggestion, like accompaniments or spiritual equivalents. They are a language to be interpreted, a celestial music to be learned. Kelly's title poem is a good example of her method in the twenty-seven poems of *Song*. About a group of boys who have stolen and killed a girl's pet goat, hanging its severed head in a tree and leaving its body beside some railroad tracks, "Song" is a clear narrative with a denser, fabular mystique:

> It was harder work than they had imagined.
> The goat cried like a man and struggled hard. But they
> Finished the job. They hung the bleeding head by the school
> And then ran off into the darkness that seems to hide every
>   thing.
> The head hung in the tree. The body lay by the tracks.
> The head called to the body. The body to the head.
> They missed each other. The missing grew large between them,
> Until it pulled the heart right out of the body, until
> The drawn heart flew toward the head, flew as a bird flies
> Back to its cage and the familiar perch from which it trills.
> Then the heart sang in the head, softly at first and then louder...

The grief of separation articulated in the goat's bird-like song finds itself repeated by the girl, who looks everywhere for her lost companion, as well as by the boys, whose guilt ultimately will manifest itself in song, again embodied by a bird: "They would / Wake in the night thinking they heard the wind in the trees / Or a night bird, but their hearts beating harder." Kelly suggests a number of tragic falls from grace—the destruction of youthful innocence, a parable of brutal rape, the forced cleaving of "head" from "heart." She severs the word *tragedy* itself, whose Greek origin *tragos* literally means "goat-song," after the type of masks worn by actors at the feasts of Dionysus. Like Kinnell, Kelly proposes that the song may be the most revealing and instructive source for understanding an event that might otherwise remain both an enigma and a secret:

>   There
> Would be a whistle, a hum, a high murmur, and, at last, a song,
> Not a cruel song, no, no, not cruel at all. This song
> Is sweet. It is sweet. The heart dies of this sweetness.

Throughout *Song*, Kelly pushes for these kinds of resonant moments of direct contact with mystery and passion. Her style conveys a similar, grave tension. In these passages from "Song," the dense allusion and the riddling nature of things seem balanced by Kelly's restrained voice and brief, direct sentences. In turn, her short sentences are contained within very long lines—typically between twelve and eighteen syllables—which are also heavily stressed by as many as eight or nine accents. This slow, thick movement is never burdensome, due in part to Kelly's voice, under-spoken, whispered, amazed.

In "Song" meaning unfolds by association and music. "Dead Doe" is even less linear, a shattered narrative revising its own progress and vision. More than in any other poem in *Song*, here Kelly opens up her dense lines and stanzas, her tight syntax, in a kind of wide-eyed horror. Even the po-em's first line conveys a give-and-take rhetorical hesitation: "The doe lay dead on her back in a field of asters: no." The poem's ostensible mission is instructive, as the speaker tries to explain to her son what they have seen. She is guide and explicator, but she is also protector, and her hesitant, revis-ing rhetoric seems designed to shield the child's innocent eyes, only slowly revealing the figure of death, both shocking and transfiguring:

> The doe lay dead on her back beside the school bus stop: yes.
> Where we waited.
> Her belly white as a cut pear. Where we waited: no: off
> from where we waited: yes
> at a distance: making a distance
> we kept,
> as we kept her dead run in sight, that we might see if she chose
> to go skyward...

In her effort to explain the presence of death to her son, that their "waiting might...be upheld by significance," the speaker measures her own maternal role against that of the dead doe: "The doe lay dead: she could / do nothing: // the dead can mother nothing...nothing / but our sight." But sight, of course, leads to vision and revelation. Again Kelly deploys her figure of birds as a signal of spiritual or providential import:

> The doe lay dead: yes: and at a distance, with her legs up and frozen,
> she trickled
>
> our vision: at a distance she was

for a moment no deer

at all
but two swans: we saw two swans
and they were fighting
or they were coupling
or they were stabbing the ground for some prize
worth nothing....
And this is the soul: like it or not. Yes: the soul comes down: yes: comes into
the deer: yes: who dies: yes: and in her death twins herself into swans....

The astonishing double transfiguration—the doe into swans, the swans into the soul—is Kelly at her finest, her most adventurous. The poem's shifting centers, its alternating "yes" and "no," its modulations between fact and figure, the body and soul, all set up the final metamorphosis of the poem. As the soulful swans were "mothered" by the single figure of the doe, so does the speaker mother two souls, hers and her son's: "and we are not afraid as we watch her soul fly on: paired / as the soul always is: with itself: / with others."

There is not a weak poem among the twenty-seven poems in *Song*, and not one sounds like anybody else's. Her talent is great and her embrace is large, from the singular determinations of familial belonging to the most metaphysical explorations of history, faith, and language. She is not an ecstatic poet, but one for whom mystery and adventure are best approached in humble, if certain, song. Her power hums and broods rather than bursts. Kinnell catalogued his bold Romantic *ars poetica* in "The Music of Poetry"; Kelly reveals the graceful restraint of hers in "The Music Lesson": "the lesson's /Passion is patience."

Charles Wright uses large, summary abstractions the way most poets use images. His images alone sustain the oblique storylines of his poems. These tactics are the reverse of most other poets. *Chickamagua* is an essential collection of poetry from one of our most original poets, a lyric master who continues to adjust and refine his complex poetic. Like most of the other poets here considered, Wright is a Romantic, but he is more expansive than Simic, more speculative than Kinnell, and more lavish than Kelly. Readers of Wright's work will here rediscover his wide range of influences and allusions: Southern idiom and landscape; Italian art and culture; Continental surrealism; Oriental detail and clarity; as well as jaunts into Vorticism, Imagism, and Futurism (as he quips in one poem addressed to Charles Simic, those "who don't remember the Futurists are condemned to repeat them").

Almost nothing ever happens in a Charles Wright poem. This is his central act of restraint, a spiritualist's abstinence, where meditation is not absence but an alternative to action and to linear, dramatic finality:

> Unlike a disease, whatever I've learned
> Is not communicable.
>   A single organism,
> It does its work in the dark.
> Anything that we think we've learned,
>   we've learned in the dark.
> If there is one secret to this life, it is this life.

And here in "Mid-winter Snowfall in the Piazza Dante," Wright's speaker is nearly always physically static and rhetorically circular. He sits in his backyard "rubbing this tiny snail shell," he watches "the hills empurple and sky [go] nectarine," he eats "*gnocchi* and roast veal" at a *caffe* in Florence, and he ponders. We might understand something more of Wright's aesthetic by noticing that "sitting" and "reading" are the primary participles in the titles of the first sections of this book, while "waiting," "watching," and "looking" come at the end. In the middle (and all the way through) he is talking and talking. The eye becomes a voice. Even given his bounty of allusions and references, I think Wright's truest forebear is Emerson, whom he never mentions. In "Circles," perhaps his most difficult and lovely essay, Emerson could be prescribing Wright's revolving imagery and rhetorical stance: "Conversation is a game of circles. In conversation we pluck up the *termini* which bound the common silence on every side." Wright's voice throughout *Chickamauga* is conversational—never lax, never dull, but also never spoken in the larger oratorical tone of Kinnell. If Wright seems continually to muse to an intimate friend, he also knows that the winding destination of language is also its extinction, that the real meanings—personal as well as historical—are ultimately "not communicable." Emerson in "Circles" concurs: "And yet here again see the swift circumscription! Good as is discourse, silence is better, and shames it."

There are precious few contemporary poets in whose work I find as much sheer wisdom as Wright's. He is fearless in his use of grand generalities, as comfortable with "O we were abstract and true. / How could we know that grace would fall from us like shed skin, / that reality, our piebald dog, would hunt us down?" as with "Snip, snip goes wind through the autumn trees" ("Waiting for Tu Fu"). "Blaise Pascal Lip-syncs the Void" *begins* with the kind of summary realization at which most other poets' work strains to arrive: "It's not good to be complete. / It's not good to be concupiscent, / caught as we are / Between a the and a the, / neither of which we know and neither of which knows us." Like Wallace Stevens, echoed in these lines, Wright treats the general (an "a") as a type of distinct particularity (a "the"). The abstract is as tangible and stimulating as any concrete detail. Emerson once more in "Circles": "Generalization is always a new influx of the divinity into the mind. Hence the thrill that attends it." Still, however thrilling, the operations of language ultimately persist in baffling Wright's desire for transcendence, as he says in "Looking Outside the Cabin Window, I remember a Line by Li Po": "We who would see beyond seeing / see only language, that burning field."

Wright's affinity with Emerson is also apparent in his rhetoric. Emerson is invariably effective at the level of the sentence, but his paragraphs are often monuments to circular structure or to impressionistic meandering. That can be pretty damning for any essayist attempting philosophical stratagems, less troublesome for a poet of Wright's skill and orientation. Wright is a master of the sentence, and his own circular movement in both the stanza and the section seems well-tuned to his thematic faith that "I remember the word and forget the word / although the word / Hovers in flame around me." Both Emerson and Wright glean considerable rhetorical power by varying the structure of their sentences, migrating with ease from the elongated compound-complex sentence to the clipped aphoristic kicker. I hear Emerson and also Franklin in pronouncements like these: "Ambition is such a small thing"; "This text is a shadow text." His diverse syntactic arrangements reinforce Wright's doubled persona, both ambitious and humble, and his very long lines are suited to contain his sentence variety. If Wright's language can seem too opulent or his line too thickened on occasion, veering toward the over-lavish, this quality is more frequent in *Zone Journals* than in *Chickamauga*. More often, the rich, flexible syntax is an apt partner for Wright's questing imagination.

I can, in fact, think of no other recent poet who can successfully deploy very long lines in such utterly non-narrative poems. In "Sprung Narratives," the book's longest poem at nine pages, Wright again refers to one of his masters as he alternately reveals and conceals his own strategy for story. Gerard Manley Hopkins's sprung rhythm, that endlessly strange and accurate self-description of Hopkins's metric idiosyncrasies, of course provides the trope for Wright's more extended application. Where Hopkins says that "the stresses come together," making a dense, nearly overlapping rhythmic pressure, Wright also suggests that memory is much less a narrative line than a series of bumping, elliptical shards, merging into and abandoning each other. The poem shifts through many possible plots and settings—Wright's childhood, Italy in the 1960s, his seventeen years in Laguna Beach, his return "home" in Virginia—and yet, all along, Wright extinguishes story in favor of image, image in favor of abstraction: "Who knows what the story line / became…. The world is a language we never quite understand, / But think we catch the drift of." He urges himself toward a continued temperance, his deepest act of restraint: "Returned to the dwarf orchard, / Pilgrim, / Sit still and lengthen your lines, / Shorten your poems and listen to what the darkness says / With its mouthful of cold air." Wright's ascetic discipline is an instruction and an aesthetic. The whole world seems to orbit in a kind of meditative, slow circle around Wright's grave influence. That's the brilliant paradox throughout this big, powerful book. In a poetry where nothing ever happens, everything is possible.

Ted Kooser:
The Chekhov of American Poetry

Jonathan Holden

In his latest poetry collection, *Weather Central,* Ted Kooser continues to turn out the kind of short lyric of which he is the undisputed master; but here as in his previous collections with Pitt Press, *Sure Signs* (1980) and *One World at a Time* (1985), Kooser produces far more than a collection of beautiful little poems. His writing is reminiscent of the short stories of Anton Chekhov. Chekhov, we remember, was (amid his several lives) a country doctor. In fact (as is well known), the tuberculosis which Chekhov eventually died from was the result of his making constant treks to the Russian hinterland to treat the rural poor, long before the invention of antibiotics. Chekhov was a man attentive to his people, and there is a similar nurturing attentiveness to "local" people in Kooser's poetry—a humanitarian vision. Indeed, Kooser might well be regarded as a kind of country doctor to his community—there to help them recognize the beauty around them, to record the seasons for them, to keep a sort of quiet almanac of their lives and deaths; for, like Chekhov's writing, Kooser's writing is the result of a coherent vision not only of people dwelling together in a particular place but of the place itself. Like Chekhov's stories, the human relevance of Kooser's poems extends far beyond his "village." It is universal.

In art, the proof of the pudding is always in the tasting. Great art has many properties: structural beauty, memorability, enticing surfaces. But if, as with Kooser, the art is realist art, a *sine qua non* is that it be accurate. Consider the following passage for its accuracy:

IN LATE SPRING

One of the National Guard's F-4 fighters,
making a long approach to the Lincoln airfield,
comes howling in over the treetops, its shadow
flapping along behind it like the skin of a sheep,
setting the coyotes crying back in the woods,

and then the dogs, and then there is a sudden quiet
that rings a little, the way an empty pan
rings when you wipe it dry, and then it is
Sunday again, a summer Sunday afternoon,
and beyond my window, the Russian olives
sigh foolishly into the air through the throats of their flowers,
and bluegills nibble the clouds afloat on the pond.

Under the windmill, a cluster of peonies huddles,
bald-headed now....

Always Kooser is recording the events of an entire community. Like Chekhov, Kooser notices people, too. Indeed, it is perhaps Kooser's interest in people other than himself which sets his poems both apart from and above the poems of virtually all of his contemporaries. Here is an example, "Four Secretaries":

All through the day I hear or overhear
their clear, light voices calling
from desk to desk, young women whose fingers
play casually over their documents,

setting the incoming checks to one side,
the thick computer reports to the other,
tapping the correspondence into stacks
while they sing to each other, not intending

to sing nor knowing how beautiful
their voices are as they call back and forth,
singing their troubled marriage ballads,
their day-care, car-park, landlord songs.

Even their anger with one another
is lovely: the color rising in their throats,
their white fists clenched in their laps,
the quiet between them that follows.

And their sadness—how deep and full of love
is their sadness when one among them
is hurt, and they hear her calling
and gather about her to cry.

The clarity of Kooser's vision in this poem reminds me of an anthropologist marveling at the collective behavior of a tribe. The poem is dangerously close to being sentimental; but, as Richard Hugo wrote in *The Triggering Town*, "If you don't risk sentimentality, you're not in the ballpark." The word *beautiful* as used here by Kooser has approximately the same meaning as it does in the poems of William Carlos Williams, where *beautiful* is a metaphor for that which is so startlingly real that, in its blemishes, it borders on ugliness. *Beautiful* for both Kooser and Williams means something like "authentic." Kooser is endlessly fascinated with the epistemological conditions of authenticity.

Great poetry, like Kooser's, like Chekhov's stories, is not sentimental, but it is characterized by a kind of tender wisdom communicated with absolute precision; for example, Kooser's poem "In Passing," which describes passing somebody who seems vaguely familiar on the street and not being able to decide whether or not to acknowledge them:

From half a block off I see you coming,
walking briskly along, carrying parcels,
furtively glancing up into faces
of people approaching, looking for someone
you know, holding your smile in your mouth
like a pebble, keeping it moist and ready,
being careful not to swallow.
. . .
From a few feet away, you recognize me,
or think you do. I see you preparing your face,
getting your greeting ready. Do I know you?
Both of us wonder. Swiftly we meet and pass,
averting our eyes, close enough to touch,
but not touching. I could not let you know
that I've forgotten, and yet you know.

Thank heavens not all the poems in *Weather Central* are this good; a few indulge, almost by reflex and a bit too mechanically, in the personifications that are the signature of Kooser's style. But a few of the poems here, though short are truly major poems. Poems like "Some Kinds of Love" and "Another Story" transcend all the usual categories. In them, as in all of Kooser's work, we view people going about their lives in landscape; but these poems have a quiet weight that is truly unusual, because it is unforced. It is not rhetorical. Such poems are equal to the best poems of Thomas Hardy, poems like Hardy's "In Time of 'The Breaking of Nations,'" with its famous ending: "Yonder a maid and her wight / Come whispering by; / War's annals will cloud into night / Ere their story die."

In "Another Story," the landscape and its figures could be in Hardy's "Wessex," in Nebraska, or in the Ukraine. The poem is in the past tense, giving it a kind of monumentality, viewing its figures *sub specie aeternitatis*:

In a country churchyard, two workmen
were digging a grave. It was summer,
but cool in the cedar-blue shade
of the white clapboard church where they labored.

Their picks did all of the talking.
Beyond them, a field of tall corn
glittered with heat, and above, a lone bird
rose on the air like ash.

The grave grew slowly down
and out of the world, and the world rolled
under the work. Then the men stopped.
One stooped to scrape in the clay.

When he stood, light-headed,
swaying a little, he held in his hand
an old cowbell, covered with dirt
and packed with darkness.

He scraped out the earth with his knife.
The bell had no clapper. He shook it.
A meadowlark piped on a fence post.
In the distance, a feeder thunked.

He handed it across the grave
to the younger man, who held it in his hands
like a baby bird, then rang it tenderly.
A crow cawed in a cedar top.

He rang it again. On the highway,
a mile away, a semi trumpeted.
In the cornfield, an irrigation pump
thumped with a regular heartbeat.

He handed it back to the older man,
who set it aside. All afternoon,
they worked without a word between them.
At intervals each touched the empty bell.

"At intervals." Though the poem doesn't mention music, the men's lives *are* music. And the poem is music transcribed—the symphony of the community—in which Kooser's final line is a note of genius.

Ted Kooser is, like Anton Chekhov, a kind of healer. The character of the persona of his poetry is the man himself, and the community knows it. This character is, without asserting himself, exemplary. He simply demonstrates, in poem after poem, the possibilities of moral authority in poetry. But there are as many different kinds of character as there are people in the world. Let us examine some more "types"—the first a kind of scapegoat; the second a poet as clown; the third an intellectual living guardedly in a half-savage country; the fourth is horrified by her own knowingness; the last a famous poet/editor grappling with breast cancer.

The "In Between" Landscapes of Transformation in Ted Kooser's *Weather Central*

Mary K. Stillwell

ETUDE

I have been watching a Great Blue Heron
fish in the cattails, easing ahead
with the stealth of a lover composing a letter,
the hungry words looping and blue
as they coil and uncoil, as they kiss and sting.

Let's say that he holds down an everyday job
in an office. His blue suit blends in.
Long days swim beneath the glass top
of his desk, each one alike. On the lip
of each morning, a bubble trembles.

No one has seen him there, writing a letter
to a woman he loves. His pencil is poised
in the air like the beak of a bird.
He would speak the whole world if he could,
toss it and swallow it live.[1]

"Etude," which launches *Weather Central*, Ted Kooser's most recent full-length collection of poems, is in many ways typical of the poet's work. The poem is what it professes to be: an etude, a study, a preview of all the poems that are to follow. It also defines the major poetic devices or characteristics that will be important throughout the 1994 volume: direct, plain-spoken language; use of interior and exterior landscape(s); and explicit metaphor that particularizes the poet's life.

Many of us who make our home on the plains recognize the Great Blue Heron in the cattails, the bubbles along the water's surface, the blue suit of the everyday job. The poet's guiding metaphor, Great Blue

Heron/lover-artist, is one we can appreciate, perhaps even participate in, as the bird eases ahead in our memory as well as on the printed page before us.

That Kooser's poetry is frequently classified as regional comes as no surprise.[2] Critics throughout the poet's career have pointed to his phenomenology of the plains in and around Lincoln, Nebraska, where he has lived since 1963.[3] Kooser's work, according to Peter Stitt, "grows directly out of the life he leads as a more or less average citizen of a more or less average small city set nearly at the center of the United States."[4] David Baker, reviewing for *Poetry*, sees *Weather Central* as part of Kooser's "larger project, the creation in poetry of a distinctly Midwestern social text."[5]

Born in Ames, Iowa, in 1939, Kooser's roots are in the Midwest. He received his B.S. in English education from Iowa State University and then moved to the Lincoln area to work on his M.A. in English, which he received from the University of Nebraska in 1968. Although he has taught poetry writing from time to time and has managed his own press for many years, Kooser has earned his living in a nonacademic, nonliterary environment. Only this year has Kooser retired from Lincoln Benefit Life Company, where he was vice president of marketing.[6]

In his close attention to plains life, Kooser can be placed within the tradition of William Carlos Williams. However, Kooser, like Williams before him, suggests that although art is rooted in the local, it need not remain only there. Indeed, Kooser's preoccupation is with mutuality: both the particular and the universal are among his central poetic concerns. As we shall see, an understanding of the way Kooser makes mutuality manifest is crucial to the explication of his poetry. This in turn will lead us to a fuller appreciation of the scope of Kooser's work and to a reassessment of his place among contemporary American writers.

THE SPACE BETWEEN

Although our discussion here will focus on the poems in *Weather Central*, metaphor and Kooser's interest in mutuality can be seen as fundamental to much of his earlier work as well. Kooser has been extensively published. His eight full-length collections include *Official Entry Blank* (Lincoln: University of Nebraska Press, 1969); *A Local Habitation*

& *A Name* (San Luis Obispo: Solo Press, 1974); *Not Coming to Be Barked At* (Milwaukee: Pentagram Press, 1976); *Sure Signs: New and Selected Poems* (Pittsburgh: University of Pittsburgh Press, 1980); *One World at a Time* (Pittsburgh: University of Pittsburgh Press, 1985); *The Blizzard Voices* (St. Paul: Bieler Press, 1986); and *A Book of Things* (Lincoln: Lyra Press, 1995).[7]

The metaphoric form that Kooser employs in "Etude" can be found in a number of poems that comprise *Weather Central*. Tom Hansen, writing in the *North Dakota Quarterly*, describes it as the "three-stanza or tripartite poem which loosely parallels the ABA sonata form."[8] Heron, as we have seen, becomes lover becomes the heron. What Hansen makes clear is that Kooser "doesn't merely compare the stalking of the heron to the letter-writing lover and then turn away from the one, A, to focus on the other, B" (224). The letter-writer, Hansen continues, "still displays qualities that are heronesque. Derived from A, this B retains vestiges of its original A-ness" (224). In the final stanza, in a similar way, "B leads back into A" (224). In other words, a "clearing" or "space" has been created *between* the lover and the heron so that each can participate or share by means of metaphor in the other's essential qualities or being.

Metaphor works because of the space between the thing and that with which it is compared and because of the ability of the thing and that with which it is compared to cross over this space, each to the other. The word "metaphor" comes to English from the Greek *metapherein*, to transfer.[9] Within that space between, or landscape of transformation, one thing is at the same time separate from another and becomes it. Metaphor enables, or forces, the reader to look more closely, to see the thing more clearly, to meditate on identity and difference. It is here in this "in between" that Kooser makes the universal manifest.

In a more abstract manner and in different terms, Martin Heidegger, in *Poetry, Language, Thought*, expresses more fully what the "in between" allows:

> In the midst of beings as a whole an open place occurs. There is a clearing, a lighting. Thought of in reference to what is, to beings this clearing is in a greater degree than are beings. This open center is therefore not surrounded by what is; rather, the

lighting center itself encircles all that is, like the Nothing which we scarcely know.... Only this clearing grants and guarantees to us humans a passage to those beings that we ourselves are not, and access to the being we ourselves are.[10]

The *auseinandersetzen*, known to the German existentialists as the "in between," is where being comes into the world. It is a time-ful place where the summer and spring meet and converse, where presence and absence rub shoulders, past and present commiserate, where one species transforms into another, one sense informs another. It is, according to Kooser, that place Robert Bly describes, where great leaps are made "from the conscious to the unconscious and back again" and transformation occurs.[11] And, as Kooser has pointed out, "the more daring the metaphor, the more resonate and powerful are its effects."[12]

Although Kooser's form is often raised, the particular form and structure he chooses have not been considered as ways of meaning. That the "in between" can be articulated as form and *means* is, in a fact, a point Robert Bly stresses. "Rapid association is a form of content," Bly writes in *Leaping Poetry*, and although he is writing about Wallace Stevens, the same can be said of Kooser's work: the content of a poem lies in the "*distance* between" what is given in the world and what is imagined by the poet. "The farther a poem gets from its initial worldly circumstance without breaking the thread," Bly asserts, "the more content it has" (14).

THE ROLE OF THE POET

Kooser immediately establishes the role of the poet as seer, as one who makes meaning in *Weather Central*. In "Etude," the reader is introduced to the poet meditating on the heron in a manner that suggests biblical creation, the Maker meditating on his new world, and a point of view not unlike Ralph Waldo Emerson's. Through metaphor, as we have seen, heron then becomes the lover composing the letter (3). The words are the hungry words of the lover but they continue to include the hunger of the heron for fish. The searching movements of the heron, "coil and uncoil," are writing movements.

In the shift to the second stanza, the heron more boldly asserts human dimension. Kooser moves further into this transformative space with the ease of his heron in water. By using the colloquial "Let's say," rapid though the association may be, mutuality is accepted with ease (6). The heron is now the blue-suited office worker, preparing the way for the reader to accept the "long days," in line 8, as fish. The glass top of the desk also exists as water's surface where bubbles tremble (8-10).

In lines 11 and 12, the poet meditates on the lover (recently heron) with whom he is conflated—all three lead solitary lives, all three are concerned with "hungry words"—from a perspective close to that of his initial position, the "I" of line 1. Kooser, in describing the office worker with "His pencil is poised / in the air like the beak of a bird," suggests that Genesis-like moment when the poet stands "On the lip / of each morning" ready to begin his attempt to create order from the apparent chaos of daily life (12-15).

By poem's end, poet and lover participate in the motion and action of the heron. Within the act of writing, the poet grasps for the poem (meaning in the world), the lover reaches for his love, and the heron spears the fish he was looking for in stanza one. At this moment, the hungry heron/lover/poet is engaged in a sort of creative ecstasy. "Etude," from this perspective, describes the artistic discipline, and the reader in the reading of the poem participates in the creative act itself.

In the seven sections of *Weather Central* that follow (again, echoes of Genesis), the poet's world—the microcosm *and* macrocosm—is revealed as he creates and interacts with the landscape around and within him. The metaphors and images in one poem often provide foundation stones for those following. When the heron shows up again in "The Poetry Reading," in section 2, for example, he carries with him to the podium all the qualities of A and B—if we continue to use Hansen's analogy—lover, letter-writer, poet, heron easing ahead through the water found in "Etude"—providing added poignancy and pathos to the short poem (35).

We know, by the poem's title, just where we are and what we are witnessing. The poet/ heron has caught the fish he was stalking once when he was young in "Etude." By the second stanza, however, the poet is all too aware of nature's (and his own) transience and he articulates his own aging in heronesque terms—"gray neck," "yellow eye," for example. The tilt of the poet's head over the page, the book open "on its spine, a split fish," for the benefit of the good eye recalls the heron's familiar head movement as it searches the cattails (35).

The space between one human being and another, between human being and other creatures, nature, and inanimate objects, is frequently mediated in Kooser's poems. The "in between" foregrounds relationship and provides a place for the exchange of and participation in the various characteristics of one with other. This is Kooser's text, sacred if you will, by which he reads himself, his life, his history.

In "An Epiphany," for example, Kooser subtly juxtaposes the worlds of the Brown Recluse Spider and Kooser's wife, bringing them closer and closer until they seem to collapse and merge.

> …The hair was my wife's,
> long and dark, a few loose strands, a curl
> she might idly have turned on a finger,
> she might idly have twisted, speaking to me,
> and the legs of the beetle were broken. (67)

Bly, writing about what he terms "wild association," might well be writing about "An Epiphany" when he suggests that "powerful feeling makes the mind associate faster, and evidently the presence of swift association makes the emotions still more alive; it increases the adrenalin flow."[13] The association of the "she" of the spider and the "she" of the wife intensifies quickly, dramatically heightening the poem's emotional impact—precipitated by the danger and vulnerability of which the poet becomes suddenly aware.

We see the mutuality found in the metaphor intensified by Kooser time and time again in poems such as "Ditchburning in February," "For Jeff," "In Passing," and "Old Dog in March," to name only a few.

MUTUALITY: POET AND READER

No less important to the effectiveness of the poems that comprise *Weather Central* is the distance that Kooser is able to bridge, to cross, perhaps to close, between himself (his persona) and the reader. Kooser accomplishes this crossing or mediation, another kind of leap, in three distinct, often interrelated, ways: first, by his use of distinct, recognizable sensual detail; second, by his portrayal of his poetic persona as familiar; and third, by the ways he employs direct address of the reader to form relationship.

Kooser brings the reader to experience the apparent subject matter through the use of rich and evocative detail for which his work is so well known. Kooser is, to quote David Baker, "a devoted chronicler of the Midwest, but so careful, so meticulous, that even his most modest poems ring with pleasing recognitions" (34).

"In Late Spring," for example, rings with rich, evocative description beginning with the flight of an F-4 jet fighter as it crosses the line of vision.

> One of the National Guard's F-4 jet fighters,
> making a long approach to the Lincoln airfield,
> comes howling in over the treetops, its shadow
> flapping along behind it like the skin of a sheep,
> setting the coyotes crying back in the woods,
> and then the dogs, and then there is a sudden quiet (7).

The visual depiction, detailed in line 2 as the F-4 is making "a long approach," includes the plane's rate of speed and its angle of descent. By line 3, the reader hears the sound of the jet "howling in over the treetops." Once Kooser has introduced the reader to physical qualities of the image, he amplifies and colors our knowledge of it through the use of metaphor and simile.

As Kooser begins his description of the jet, its howl, the poet is already looking ahead to coyotes and dogs. The jet's shadow, "like the skin of a sheep," suggests an undercurrent of violence as soon as Kooser places it in the close proximity of coyotes and dogs. Through the use of interrelated senses and metaphor, Kooser, working like a sorcerer, invites us into the text of the poem.

Kooser does not rely on sight alone for graphic detailing of place, event, or person. "In Late Spring" is vivid to the reader because Kooser appeals to the other senses as well in his descriptions. Energized sound—"howling," "crying," and "flapping"—in the early lines of the poem give way to the "ring" of quiet which joins that of the empty pan. The Russian Olives "sigh" and Kooser, engaging in a pun, joins his own subvocal reading to "bee-song."

Description is tactile as well: "perfect porcelain bells," bald-headed peonies, the wet pan is wiped dry. The mutuality of simile and person-ification underscore the familiarity of detail: ferns have "shy ears," the horsefly "twirls his mustache" and brushes dust from his sleeves, the tu-lip wears lipstick, spring dashes by on her "run-down broken toe shoes."

Kooser also uses his persona effectively to engage the reader rather than to set himself apart, an egocentrism that could stress or even shat-ter the poet-reader relationship as well as the meaning of the poem as a whole. By carefully choosing the precise moment of his own introduc-tion into the poem, Kooser often forges alliances with the reader that suggest intimacy or complicity. The fourth stanza begins:

I have been reading for hours, or intending to read,
but over the bee-song of the book I could faintly hear
my neighbor up the road a quarter mile
calling out to his daughter, and hear her calling back,
not in words but in musical notes... (7)

This builds on the relationship that the poet has already established with his phenomenological precision and involvement. The reader is commit-ted to a journey with the "I" before the formal introduction occurs.

This journey, established here in the initial poem of section 1 of the collection, will continue throughout *Weather Central*. When the speaker of "In Late Spring" announces that "the world knows my place and stands and holds a chair / for me," the reader is poised to listen to what the balance of the collection has to say about that world (25-26). In learning about Kooser's world, we learn about the one we share with him.

Once again, Kooser has drawn the reader into the "in between" with him. When the poet announces "I have forgotten my place in the world," the reader, similarly engaged by the rich and evocative physical world that has been being described, recognizes the feeling. And, in fact, it is a feeling the reader never entirely shakes as the poem moves to conclusion. The world knows our place, too, and reveals itself to us as it does to Kooser. We continue our journey with Kooser as he enters the mutual space shared between him and the horsefly. Our connection, as reader, to other, to the natural world, is intimate. When Kooser participates with the horsefly in the twirling of his mustache, we, in a sense, twirl our own. We, too, brush the pollen from our sleeves.

Kooser also uses direct address, often with the pronouns "you" and/or "your," in such a way as to invite the reader into the poem and sometimes to fuse speaker with reader. Take "A Heart of Gold," for example, one of Kooser's widely-anthologized shorter poems that opens:

> It's an old beer bottle
> with a heart of gold. There's a lot
> of defeat in those shoulders,
> sprinkled with dandruff, battered
> by years of huddling up
> with good buddies, out of the wind. (21)

Once again, through detail, Kooser makes what he sees so vivid that it is as though the reader is looking at, picking up, and peeling the label from the beer bottle. The reader knows that old familiar bottle beside the road so well that she is not surprised when Kooser refers to it in line 9 (more than halfway through the poem) as "your." The writer and reader are joined in such a way as to suggest that the experience of one is that of the other, what is true for one holds true for the other.

In "Snakeskin," though the "you" is introduced early on in the poem, the rhythm of the poem, echoing the sound of the poem's primary metaphor, that of the train, assists in drawing the reader into the motion of the poem, into travel with the writer into the adventure of the future (*WC*, 11). Kooser frequently employs "us" to similar effect. "Let us leave our scene / there," he whispers deep into "Oceans of Fun" (*WC*, 22,16-17). While leaving a family in their own moment, enjoying the water slide at a local theme park, we (poet and reader) are called to examine our own vulnerable position on a planet that is hurling "more than a thousand miles an hour" (24).

LIFE IN THE MIDLANDS

The geographic "in between," intimately associated with the historical, as well as the personal, also provides a place and space for transformation to occur—not only within the poem but also within the reader's understanding of her/his own life. Whether alongside the road, as in "A Heart of Gold," or at his desk in Garland, Nebraska, Kooser has involved the reader in the geography of being in the world (*Dasein* to the existentialists). The titles of many of the poems of the early part of the collection provide a geographical and historical triptych: "City Limits," "Lincoln, Nebraska," "Site," "A Statue of the Unknown Soldier," and "The Gilbert Stuart Portrait of Washington."

As Yi-Fu Tuan has observed, "Place is security, space is freedom: we are attached to the one and long for the others."[14] Kooser uses the security of a well-articulated place to allow for a flight into the unknown of the future. In other words, by the poet's close detailing of location, Kooser makes it knowable. The reader feels safe, safe enough to free herself from her own identity enough so that she might follow the writer into unknown territory, into the other, into new ways of thinking and of seeing the world.

This place/space called "in-between," "clearing," and so forth, is, as already noted, time-ful. While father is caught mid-slide in "Oceans of Fun," anchoring us there at that frozen moment, we can dare to look, and leap, elsewhere, to literally and figuratively view time in the movement of our planet.

TIME AND THE BETWEEN

The river of time comes to surface from time to time throughout the collection from its more mythic beginnings in "Etude" through to the weather report at precisely six-fifteen. Temporal and mythic time, in some ways the "stuff of transformation" in many Kooser poems, are profoundly interrelated. The poet's father with his broom, in "The Sweeper," can be read as both literal as archetypal as the father/gondola paddler moves along the river of his/all life/Life (*WC*, 84).

The circle of life, both in human terms and in the seasonal imagery, occur and reoccur throughout *Weather Central*. Past and present and future merge, separate, and join again in "For Jeff" (*WC*, 78). Considerations of time and mortality become more insistent in sections 4, 5, and 6 when we meet the people significant to Kooser's life. But perhaps nowhere is the theme of time more clearly or directly stated by Kooser than in "An Abandoned Stone Schoolhouse in the Nebraska Sandhills," which stands at the midpoint of the collection.

Time, in Kooser's hands, is not at all an abstract concept, which is perhaps why literary critics have often overlooked the "ideas" or "intellectual constructs" in the poet's work. "Touch the wall," Kooser invites, "and a hundred thousand years brush away, // just like that" (9,10,11). Substance transforms within the poem: stone encompasses water, is time. Not only is our time here limited, our voices, even the poet's voice, will soon fade, finally disappear altogether.

"The poem 'Surveyors' also addresses temporal and mythic time, don't you think?" Kooser asks.[15] The question is, of course, rhetorical.

SURVEYORS

They have come from the past,
wearing their orange doublets
like medieval pages.

Seeing through time, they see
nothing of us. For them
the world is rock upon rock.

There is always the one
on one side of the highway,
holding his yellow staff,

and one on the other,
his one eye boring through
cars and trucks. It is as if

we were all invisible,

> streaming between them
> like ghosts, not snapping
>
> the tightened string of light
> they hold between them, not
> catching it across the bumper
>
> and dragging them bouncing
> behind us into our lives.
> We mean nothing to them
>
> in our waxed sedans, in our
> business suits and fresh spring
> dresses. They stand by the road
>
> in the leaning grass, lifting
> their heavy gloves of gold
> to wave across the traffic,
>
> and though they cannot see us,
> helpfully we wave back. (49-50)

The workers themselves, the men doing the surveying (looking onto the contemporary highway before them), "have come from the past," the reader is advised in line 1. Further, in the two following lines, they are described as wearing "doublets," albeit orange ones, "like medieval pages." These workers, we are told, are "seeing through time." In some senses, these workmen are mythic, archetypal, hardly ordinary men at all. At the same time, however, Kooser suggests they are ubiquitous.

The cyclopes on the highway before us, poet and reader alike, exhibit powers that even Kryptonite cannot stop. At the same time they do not seem to be able to see mere mortals: "We were all invisible." We want their attention as though they were gods—"we helpfully wave back"—even as we know "they cannot see us." It is not surprising that Kooser, who has made his career in life insurance, should write so movingly about the seen and unseen, the mortal and the immortal, ghosts and mythic beings each of whom seems to change places several times during the course of the poem.

Frederico Garcia Lorca's essay, "Theory of Function of Duende," described by Bly in *Leaping Poetry*, comes to mind (28-30). Bly writes that "Duende involves a kind of elation when death is present in the room, it is associated with 'dark' sounds, and when a poet has duende inside him, he brushes past death with each step, and in that presence associates fast" (29). When Kooser drives by death out surveying life, we shudder along with him, hurry on by, and wave back, grateful that it is not our time to be pulled aside.

KOOSER'S MIDCONTINENT WEATHER REPORT

"Weather Central," grounded in both temporal and mythic time, ends the collection in a way parallel to "Etude," the poem from which the series evolved. From the chaos of the beginning, an order, subsequently written by the poet's hand poised midair in "Etude," we have arrived at a map, designed, above all else, to proffer at least momentary order.

WEATHER CENTRAL

Each evening at six-fifteen, the weatherman
turns a shoulder to us, extends his hand,
and talking softly as a groom, cautiously
smooths and strokes the massive, dappled flank
of the continent, touching the cloudy whorls
that drift like galaxies across the hide,
tracing the loops of harness with their barbs
and bells and penants; then, with a horsefly's touch,
he brushes a mountain range and sets a shudder
running just under the skin. His bearing
is cavalier from years of success and he laughs
at the science, yet makes no sudden moves
that might startle that splendid order
or loosen the physics. One would not want to wake
the enormous Appaloosa mare of weather,
asleep in her stall on a peaceful moonlit night. (87)

The time is as precise and as regular as clockwork when the weatherman takes his place, midcountry, at "six-fifteen" on the TV screen. He is, for the moment, in control, though he is cautious enough. The poet's ability to order and fix, it is suggested, is as precarious as the weatherman's ability to map and present weather conditions. What both do, through a variety of meaningful signs and symbols, is to show the reader/viewer how things look to be at this moment. Projections and predictions here on the plains, despite Doppler, are risky business.

So sensitive is the object—horse, weatherman, life itself—that "with a horsefly's touch/ he [weatherman literally but also poet] brushes a mountain range and sets a shudder / running just under the skin" (8-10).

Once again, through the use of the familiar (And what could be more mundane and recognizable than the evening weather report?), Kooser leads the reader into the mysterious, into the "in between," that place we can look at for some short period of time, say from six-fifteen to six-twenty at the very least, in order to obtain a fresh perspective on our lives and on life in general. Despite its fragility, it is a powerful perspective, one that connects us to our world and to all time.

Jeannie Thompson writes that with the Appaloosa mare of weather that closes the poem and the collection, Kooser is "cautious of this powerful creature" and that he suggests that we "*Do not disturb, go on with your life.*"[16] David Baker sees this poem, along with others, as "splendid poems" that should find their way into "representative anthologies," because Kooser is able to document "the dignities, habits, and small griefs of daily life, our hunger for connection, our struggle to find balance in natural and unnaturally-human worlds" (36). While this documentation is no small feat, Baker's statement, and Thompson's, too, draw attention away from what is uniquely and profoundly Kooser.

What the poet offers in this final poem—and throughout the collection that bears its name—is, I believe, both landscape and possibility. Mutuality—and the *auseinandersetzen*, "seem," "clearing," whatever that it affords—provides the means of transcending the confines of our own skins, our own section of the continent, our own continent, to make a leap for ourselves beyond past, present, and future into the dead center of the richness of life. This is Kooser's gift to readers no matter where they live.

Notes

1. Ted Kooser, *Weather Central* (Pittsburgh: University of Pittsburgh Press, 1994), p. 3. All poems and excerpts reprinted with permission of publisher. Subsequent citations appear in parentheses in the text, along with line designation, if necessary.

2. In addition to the works quoted within this text, several others are particularly noteworthy in their treatment of Kooser's work. They include Gilbert Allen, "Measuring the Mainstream-A Review Essay," *Southern Humanities Review* 17 (1983): 171-7 8; Dana Gioia, "Explaining Ted Kooser," *Can Poetry Matter: Essays on Poetry and American Culture* (St. Paul, Minn.: Graywolf, 1992), pp. 92-112; Jean H.Johnson, "Two Visions," review of *Weather Central*, by Ted Kooser, and *The October Palace*, by Jane Hirshfield, *Poet Lore* 90 (1995): 52-55; and James R. Saucerman, "Poems of Popular Common Ground: Four Voices of the Midwest," *Midwest Miscellany* 22 (1994): 9-17.

3. Matthew C. Brennan, "Ted Kooser," in *Dictionary of Literary Biography* 105 (Detroit: Gale, 1991), p. 144. Subsequent citations appear in parentheses in the text. Unless otherwise noted, biographical data comes from this source.

4. Peter Stitt, "The World at Hand," *The Georgia Review* 34 (fall 1980): 662. Subsequent citations appear in parentheses in the text.

5. David Baker, "On Restraint," *Poetry* 168, no.1 (1996): 34. Subsequent citations appear in parentheses in the text.

6. Ted Kooser, letter to author, 18 November 1998.

7. Kooser's chapbooks and special collections include *Grass Country* (privately printed, 1971); *Twenty Poems* (Crete, Nebr.: Best Cellar Press, 1973); *Shooting a Farmhouse / So This is Nebraska* (St. Paul, Minn.: Ally Press, 1975); *Voyages to the Island Sea*, with Harley Elliott (LaCrosse, Wisc.: Center for Contemporary Poetry, 1976); *Old Marriage and New* (Austin: Cold Mountain Press, 1978*); Cottonwood County*, with William Kloefkorn (Lincoln: Windflower Press, 1979); *Etudes* (Cleveland, Ohio: Bits Press, Case Western Reserve University, 1992); and *A Decade of Ted Kooser: Valentines* (Omaha: Penumbra Press, 1996).

8. Tom Hansen, review of *Etudes*, by Ted Kooser, *North Dakota Quarterly* 62, no. 3 (1993): 224, hereafter cited in parentheses in the text.

9. *Webster's Collegiate Dictionary*, 9th ed., s.v. "metaphor."

10. Martin Heidegger, *Poetry, Language, Thought*, trans. Albert Hofstadter (New York: Harper & Row, 1971), p. 53.

11. Ted Kooser, letter to author, 22 November 1997. Robert Bly, *Leaping Poetry: An Idea with Poems and Translations* (Boston: Beacon Press, 1975), p. 2; hereafter cited in parentheses in the text.

12. Ted Kooser, letter to author, 31 December 1997.

13. *Leaping Poetry* (see note 11 above), p. 8.

14. Tuan, Yi-Fu, *Space and Place: The Perspective of Experience* (Minneapolis: University of Minnesota Press, 1977), p. 3.

15. Kooser, letter to author, 22 November 1997.

16. Jeannie Thompson, review of *Weather Central*, by Ted Kooser, *Southern Humanities Review* 30 (1996): 407.

Introducing Ted Kooser

David Mason

When Ted Kooser was named Poet Laureate of the United States in the fall of 2004, Britain's *Times Literary Supplement* responded by asking just who he was. As it happens, they asked an American poet, August Kleinzahler, who also claimed not to know. The fact that Kleinzahler was in the dark may say more about his own narrow reading, or about the fractious world of American poetry, than it does about Kooser, who has had a loyal following in America for thirty years. Now that he has won the Pulitzer Prize for *Delights & Shadows* (Copper Canyon Press, 2004), arbiters of taste like Kleinzahler may continue to scratch their heads in bewilderment, but Kooser's audience will only continue to grow. It's an audience appreciative of his short, accessible poems, his concern for the "common reader" rather than the professional critic.

As it happens, this audience is not as unsophisticated as some critics might believe. They understand that Kooser is a poet of visual acuity, an observer of the physical world as adept as William Carlos Williams and Elizabeth Bishop at their best.

So why have critics too seldom noticed him until now? I would suggest two reasons. First, Kooser is a poet of the American Midwest — its cities, towns and farms—and the power brokers of American poetry are generally inclined to overlook that part of the country. Second, Kooser worked in the business world for thirty years as an insurance executive. Never mind that a career path in business has also been taken by Wallace Stevens, Robert Philips, Dana Gioia and others. The fact is that American poets do most of their schmoozing in academic circles and are very slow to admit writers who come from outside those circles. Kooser's *Sure Signs: New and Selected Poems* (1980) contains this little ditty with which anyone who has ever held down a job, especially an office job, can identify:

> They had torn off my face at the office.
> The night that I finally noticed

that it was not growing back, I decided
to slit my wrists. Nothing ran out;
I was empty. Both of my hands fell off
shortly thereafter. Now at my job
they allow me to type with the stumps.
It pleases them to have helped me,
and I gain in speed and confidence.

It's possible that some academic poets are unfamiliar with this experience, but many of us know it intimately. In the business years Kooser trained himself to rise early and write before he went to work. When at sixty he was hit with oral cancer, he underwent surgery and radiation therapy, which made him temporarily sensitive to sunlight. So the ritual of getting up before dawn and taking long rambles in the Nebraska countryside became therapeutic as well, leading to a very good collection of short poems, *Winter Morning Walks: 100 Postcards to Jim Harrison*. Cancer also helped him decide to take early retirement from business, and two more collections have followed: *Braided Creek* (with Jim Harrison) and *Delights & Shadows*. The first of these is striking because neither Kooser nor Harrison labels which poems he authored, so the book puts poem and world ahead of ego. The second and most recent volume is notable for many things, in particular one poem I shall discuss in detail.

Before that, however, I have several more observations to make, some of them based on my friendship with the poet.

First, Ted is a writer who gives me faith that writing well *matters*. He has written many more poems than he has published in magazines, and has published many more poems than he has collected in books. That winnowing process over the years becomes as important as the morning's alertness to one page, one metaphor, one close observation offering surprise and recognition.

Second, the faith in doing the work and doing it well is the only way to survive the permutations of a career in poetry. Ted would no doubt object to the use of that word *career*, since like Frost he unites vocation and avocation in a spirit of play. But *career* implies the whole arc of effort over a lifetime and the public recognition of that effort, so I find myself stuck with the word for now. Over the last decade I have too often been caught up in literary controversy—the teapot tempests of the poetry world. I know what it means to suffer identification with a vociferous literary movement. The drawback of this is that my poems are too often read as reflections of this movement rather than the work of an individual trying to write poetry as best he can. Ted saw it coming and gently warned me about it, and has never been stuck in the same tar baby, or anything like it. His example has sustained me as I've tried to extricate myself and cut my own path.

Over the years, Ted has formulated his aesthetic stance so he can present it to students. Of course, it's not the only model other writers can follow, nor would he want it to be. Elements of this aesthetic are clearly outlined in his new treatise, *The Poetry Home Repair Manual.* I call it a treatise and not a textbook because it has more in common with Horace's *Ars Poetica* and Lu Chi's *Wen Fu.* It contains simple, sound advice in the context of a life of faith, and by faith I mean the quiet rigor and devotion to the work itself without expectation of reward. Ted would never pretend to a Buddhist context, but there's a nobility in his selflessness, his patience, his willingness to wait and watch when the poem or the life isn't going his way. He believes in lucidity. A certain kind of opacity might elevate the poet over the reader or interpreter, and Ted is generally not interested in that separating aspect. He believes poetry is a gift for which both giver and receiver can be grateful, if it is done well. The reader has rights, he reminds us, and poets have no right to wear out their welcome in the reader's home.

The poet, then, is a citizen, no more or less important than any other skilled laborer in the country. The poet is not a high priest, a shaman, or any of a dozen other high-falutin titles that have been expropriated over the years. This is not merely a materialistic definition of what the poet makes because metaphorical language is always open to multiple dimensions of experience.

But the poet's job is in part to keep his or her ego in perspective, as Kooser jokingly suggests in a well-known poem called "Selecting a Reader":

> First, I would have her be beautiful,
> and walking carefully up to my poetry

at the loneliest moment of an afternoon,
her hair still damp at the neck
from washing it. She would be wearing
a raincoat, an old one, dirty
from not having money enough for the cleaners.
She will take out her glasses, and there
in the bookstore, she will thumb
over my poems, then put the book back
up on its shelf. She will say to herself,
"For that kind of money, I can get
my raincoat cleaned." And she will.

So far, I've been talking about a deliberate modesty by which Ted Kooser exalts world over ego. I hope I have made it clear that his artistry is sophisticated, though devoid of pretence. I should also be clear that Kooser's is not the only sort of poetry I can enjoy; I love many poets who employ their resources with more showy self-consciousness, just as I enjoy opera as well as the best songs by Bob Dylan or Hank Williams. On a "high art / low art" continuum, Kooser is somewhere in the middle. He's not Henry James and he's not Lenny Bruce. This "middle way," coupled with his Midwestern identity, causes a few people to dismiss him as if he were poetry's Grandma Moses, an untutored country bumpkin, master of a crude style.

Of course, it's a misreading. Kooser is the sort of regional writer who transcends region by virtue of his stance and his technique. He has urban poems and office poems as well as poems observing nature. He has a strong narrative undercurrent, a civilizing interest in other people's lives. And he has that fabulous visual alertness critics keep noticing, a way of waking us up to small things, which always turn out to be large things.

This brings me around, finally, to one of my favorite poems from the new book, *Delights & Shadows*. I remember first reading it in *The Georgia Review* and Xeroxing it for friends. The poem is called "That Was I." Though only thirty-six lines long, it has sweep and rhetorical power:

I was that older man you saw sitting

in a confetti of yellow light and falling leaves
on a bench at the empty horseshoe courts
in Thayer, Nebraska—brown jacket, soft cap,
wiping my glasses. I had noticed, of course,
that the rows of sunken horseshoe pits
with their rusty stakes, grown over with grass,
were like old graves, but I was not letting
my thoughts go there. Instead I was looking
with hope to a grapevine draped over
a fence in a neighboring yard, and knowing
that I could hold on. Yes, that was I.

And that was I, the round-shouldered man
you saw that afternoon in Rising City
as you drove past the abandoned Mini Golf,
fists deep in my pockets, nose dripping,
my cap pulled down against the wind
as I walked the miniature Main Street
peering into the child-size plywood store,
the poor red school, the faded barn, thinking
that not even in such an abbreviated world
with no more than its little events—the snap
of a grasshopper's wing against a paper cup—
could a person control this life. Yes, that was I.

And that was I you spotted that evening
just before dark, in a weedy cemetery
west of Staplehurst, down on one knee
as if trying to make out the name on a stone,
some lonely old man, you thought, come there
to pity himself in the reliable sadness
of grass among graves, but that was not so.
Instead I had found in its perfect web
a handsome black and yellow spider
pumping its legs to try to shake my footing
as if I were a gift, an enormous moth
that it could snare and eat. Yes, that was I.

There are all sorts of literary connections here, the obvious ones to Emily Dickinson and Walt Whitman, but what I really want to notice is the poem's forms of address. There is an "I," but an unstable one. It either identifies with other people—as artists or other empathetic souls might do—or actually becomes them, depending on how you read it. There's a sort of metamorphosis here, a transformational sense of identity akin to Ovid. At the end, the "I" even becomes, from the spider's point of view, a moth. So this floating "I," this fluid and compassionate speaker, is noticed and sometimes misinterpreted by a "you." Now, one of the effects of the second person in poetry is to form an immediate bond with the reader or auditor. Whatever the experience being conveyed, the poem insists that you are having it. Or you and I are having it together, engaged in this integration of points of view that we call reading or listening. Kooser has written that "Poetry's purpose is to reach other people and to touch their hearts. If a poem doesn't make sense to anybody but its author, nobody but its author will care a whit about it."

"That Was I" is precisely about this process, then: reading and writing as part of that civilizing empathy we all need to experience as human beings. It's the reason good writing exists. The very enigma of identification in this poem is part of its universality. The poem demonstrates that we are not quite so separate from each other as we sometimes believe.

Two sets of images underline this point: games and graves. We are creatures of play, and we are creatures who will die. No denying that. In the first stanza we have the old man "on a bench at the empty horseshoe courts / in Thayer, Nebraska . . . ." I get the impression of one of those shrinking Midwest towns—too few of the old man's friends are left to play horseshoes, and "the rows of sunken horseshoe pits / with their rusty stakes, grown over with grass, / were like old graves . . . ." (This last image is much like the grave becoming earth again in Emily Dickinson's "Because I Could Not Stop for Death"). Located just north of Highway 34 some distance west of Kooser's home, Thayer appears on paper to be just that sort of shrinking town, and Kooser has often pointed out to us the tenuous signs of human habitation in a vast, open landscape. Still, it was a place of games once (and might still be). Now the old man, wiping his glasses so he can see better, focuses on a vine taking possession of a neighboring fence. He is holding on, rather like that vine—or holding on like the fence as the rapacious vine slowly takes over.

The second stanza's setting, Rising City, is a bit north and east of Thayer. It's also closer to a main road, Highway 92, which if taken west combines with Highway 2 and takes you through the Sandhills. I Googled Rising City and found a somewhat unhelpful website declaring, "Check us out . . . . we're closer than you think!" There does seem to be more going on here than in Thayer, though the Mini Golf location is abandoned. Kooser's round-shouldered man tours the empty buildings of the golf course, a little imaginary world as depleted as the larger one, and meditates on our inability to "control this life." Games, like poems, are efforts to make a tentative order in the world, and here we see that order called into question.

In the last stanza Kooser comes closer to home. We're not actually in a town this time (Staplehurst is roughly ten miles west of Garland) but outside of it. Here we find the "I" in a cemetery and assume he's "some lonely old man . . . come there / to pity himself in the reliable sadness / of grass among graves . . . . At this point the surprise takes place. First, it's crucial to notice that we're wrong about this guy. He's not a grieving old man. Rather, like that first figure we encountered, he's focused on an image of tenacity and survival. Second, he's rather enjoying himself, or enjoying the "handsome black and yellow spider." To this spider, his looming presence might be dinner, so the spider is fooled too, as we all are, by what is seen and judged. There's something matter-of-factly ominous in the spider's intent, of course, just as in Frost's sonnet, "Design." But Kooser's skillful rhetoric finds its own way of implicating all of us in these processes of survival and understanding.

Ultimately, Kooser is a poet out of the Transcendentalist tradition in American letters. He knows well what Emerson told us: "Small and mean things serve as well as great symbols. The meaner the type by which a law is expressed, the more pungent it is, and the more lasting in the memories of men . . . ." That's why Kooser has this figure kneeling and looking closely at something small. That's also why he sets us up to recognize it slowly, to misread the scene before we can read it properly, so the poem is about awakening consciousness rather than a closing down.

It's a great poem without making any big gestures at greatness. It has all of Ted's wisdom in it, his compassion and skepticism and respect

If you open yourself to what this poetry offers, you have to admit that much of what seems so simple is deceptively so. For this reason, Ted is commonly compared to Frost, and while his vision is not quite Frost's and his technique is less inclined to the sort of formal mastery Frost espoused, he is indeed a writer who repays re-reading even while he speaks to us directly on a first hearing. Critics who bypass Kooser, thinking him insufficiently complex, are missing a rigorous, original American voice.

From "Further Views"
in *The Midwestern Pastoral*

William Barillas

Born in Ames, Iowa, and now retired from a career as an insurance executive, Kooser has spent most of his life in Nebraska, where he is often referred to as the unofficial state poet laureate. (The Library of Congress named him U.S. Poet Laureate in August 2004.) Like Harrison and Wright, Kooser writes poetry on rural themes in a manner reflecting long study of world literature, especially Asian and Latin American poetry. In *Official Entry Blank* (1969) and ten subsequent books of poetry, Kooser has elevated unassuming subjects, both people and places, usually by means of startling metaphors that heighten the sensual and associative power of his images. Among many typical passages is the first stanza of "So This Is Nebraska," which effortlessly transforms a highway into a horse and the plumage of birds into combustible flashes of color:

> The gravel road rides with a slow gallop
> over the fields, the telephone lines
> streaming behind, its billow of dust
> full of the sparks of redwing blackbirds.

The poem continues with the driver proceeding down the road, noting barns, the thickness of air on a July afternoon, and an abandoned truck surrounded by a lush growth of hollyhock. "You feel like that," Kooser writes, establishing a greater intimacy by addressing the reader: "you feel like letting / your tires go flat, like letting the mice / build a nest in your muffler, like being no more than a truck in the weeds" (*Sure Signs*, 39). Kooser's use of the second-person voice in "So This Is Nebraska" is consistent with his fundamentally communitarian outlook. Even more than Roethke, Wright, and Harrison in their poems, Kooser hews closely to human associations, whether friends, family, neighbors, or even strangers, whom he treats not as separate and unknowable others, but as kindred beings whose concerns impinge on his consciousness. "It's never made much sense to me to set poetry apart from its social context," he admits in a short statement titled "Some of the Things I Think about When Working on a Poem." He speaks of a desire to "honor my reader's patience and generosity by presenting what I have to say as clearly and succinctly as possible." Disdaining modernist elitism and alienation, Kooser embraces Nebraska and its people, finding poignancy in the personal effects of people long dead, in animal signs like the shed skin of a snake, or elements of local landscape like "an empty stone house alone in a wheatfield" (*Sure Signs*, 78).

Kooser views landscape with an eye for social history, writing, for example, about small farms that failed, or were failed by the industrial economy. In "Abandoned Farmhouse" he approaches an old homestead in the manner of Leopold, interpreting visible signs of its former inhabitants much as one reads a written text.

> He was a big man, says the size of his shoes
> on a pile of broken dishes by the house . . .
> but not a man for farming, say the fields
> cluttered with boulders and the leaky barn.

A "bedroom wall / papered with lilacs" testifies to a woman's presence, and a "sandbox made from a tractor tire" tells of a child. A litany of absence and loss, the poem develops its sad cadence by the repetition of the verb "say" or "says," as in the line "It was lonely here, says the narrow country road." Every aspect of the place, whether stones in the field or jars of fruit, speaks of poverty, isolation, and failure. "Something went wrong, they say" (*Sure Signs*, 64). Kooser does not attribute that failure to the family that once lived in the house, blaming them in some hard utilitarian manner for their plight. Instead he leaves it to the reader to speculate about social trends that led to their difficulties. Whatever "went wrong" may have had as much to do with government agricultural policy and, more broadly, attitudes about land, as with the abilities of the farming couple. Something went wrong with pastoral ideology; the failure here is not merely personal but also cultural and political.

Like other Midwestern pastoralists, Kooser is drawn to places of significance in what Harrison calls the "soul history" of the nation. In "Fort Robinson," he recalls a visit to the former military outpost in western Nebraska, where Lakota holy man and war leader Crazy Horse was assassinated in 1877 and where, as Kooser notes, "Dull Knife and his

Northern Cheyenne / were held captive that terrible winter" of 1878-1879. Typically, it is through personal narrative that Kooser evokes the site's significance. He and his young son never leave the car because "the grounds crew" at the historical site is "killing the magpies . . . going from tree to tree / with sticks and ladders" to knock down the nestlings and kill them on the ground. This violence by representatives of the state recalls Fort Robinson's mission as a staging platform for the subjugation of the Cheyenne, Lakota, and other western tribes during the Plains War. Rather than being didactic, Kooser simply and clearly describes the scene, letting the historical comparison form itself in the reader's mind. As his son weeps in the back seat, the speaker drives off "into those ragged buttes / the Cheyenne climbed that winter, fleeing" (*Sure Signs*, 40). The participle "fleeing" may refer either to the speaker and his son or to the Cheyenne, a grammatical ambiguity that implies rather than states the poet's empathy with Dull Knife's band. He creates a parallel rather than merging his identity with that of conquered people, as did Roethke in declaring "I'll be an Indian." However well meaning and multivalent, Roethke's assertion contains a certain arrogance. Like Harrison, who writes in *Just before Dark* that he "would not dream of trying to 'become'" an Indian (314), Kooser does not presume to speak for those who are capable of speaking for themselves. He exercises the same restraint in his unpublished long poem "Pursuing Black Hawk," a narrative of the Black Hawk War told not from a Sauk point of view, but in the voice of a young white militiaman. Like his Romantic predecessors, Kooser looks to midwestern landscape for a usable past. But he avoids Whitmanian panhumanism—famously phrased in "Song of Myself" in the line "I am the man. . . . I suffered. . . . I was there" (64)—in favor of narrative that reflects his own cultural background.

In addition to his empathy for rural midwesterners, Kooser's grounding in regional landscape, history, and ecology gives his collaboration with Harrison an air of inevitability. The two writers have corresponded for many years, their letters often taking the form of poems. Two books have resulted from this exchange: Kooser's *Winter Morning Walks: One Hundred Postcards to Jim Harrison* (2002) and *Braided Creek: A Conversation in Poetry* (2003), a collection of epigrammatic poems by Harrison and Kooser, addressed to one another. The poems in both books meditate on friendship, aging, and the consolation of beloved local land-

scapes, renewing these traditional pastoral themes by use of the episto-
lary mode. Reading the poems gives one the sense of having joined the
writers' fellowship of outdoor words and walks.

Although published in book form a year later, the poems in *Braided
Creek* predate those in *Winter Morning Walks*. For several years, Kooser
and Harrison sent each other poems resembling haiku in their brevity,
vivid imagery, and philosophical implications. Before Kooser edited the
volume, he and Harrison agreed not to attribute particular poems to
either writer, a decision that creates two distinct effects. First, readers
familiar with the authors' earlier writings may take pleasure in discerning
one poet's voice from the other's, according to a poem's diction, tone,
figures of speech, and allusions. The last line, for example, of the fol-
lowing poem reveals it with near certainty to be Harrison's, since he used
the phrase as the title of his first book of nonfiction: "At 62 I've out-
lived 95 percent / of the world. I'll be home / just before dark (33). In
many cases, however, it is impossible to ascribe a poem with any degree
of likelihood to either Harrison or Kooser. Far from being a source of
frustration, the suspension of authorial credit creates a harmonic effect,
a layering of two voices that emphasizes sounds, images, and ideas rath-
er than the poets as individuals. It ultimately does not matter whether
Harrison or Kooser wrote the following couplet: "On every topographic
map, / the fingerprints of God" (7). What *is* important is that either
poet *could* have written it, and that both believe the statement to be true.
Taking pleasure in the poems' ambiguity of provenance requires of the
reader the Romantic virtue of "negative capability," which John Keats
famously defined in a letter to his brothers as the ability of "being in
uncertainties, Mysteries, Doubts, without any irritable reaching after fact
& reason" (I, 209).

At the same time, however, Harrison's and Kooser's coauthorship
challenges the Romantic emphasis on the individual artist, the "Roman-
tic 'I'" that Harrison has said he wishes not to be confined by. "When
asked about attributions for the individual poems," the book's dust jacket
copy reads, "one of them replied 'Everyone gets tired of this continued
cult of the personality. . . . This book is an assertion in favor of poetry
and against credentials.'" The poetic creed asserted in *Braided Creek* is one
of spirituality and place, a quiet wisdom conveyed in earthy, self-effacing
humor and images of domestic life and rural midwestern landscape. The

book's final poem illustrates the ecological principle of forest succession, while contrasting nature's mutability with its persistence—pastoral literature's perennial consolation for our mortality: "The pastures grow up / with red cedars / once the horses are gone" (85)

Images of midwestern landscape reflecting the theme of mortality also provide *Winter Morning Walks*, the other book resulting from Kooser's correspondence with Harrison, with its central motif. *Winter Morning Walks*, as Mary K. Stillwell notes in her study of the book, combines "the story of a middle-aged poet facing the aftermath of cancer surgery with the archetypal journey of Everyman summoned by Death" (399). In the summer of 1998, doctors removed a tumor from Kooser's tongue and discovered cancer in his lymph nodes. They prescribed radiation treatment, which along with the cancer itself sapped the poet's spirit and energy. He did not feel up to reading or writing until November, when his health had improved enough that he could take regular exercise. Under a doctor's orders to avoid sunlight for a year (as Kooser recounts in the book's preface), he "began taking a two-mile walk each morning . . . before dawn, hiking the isolated country roads near [Garland, Nebraska] where I live, sometimes with my wife but most often alone" (5). Following one such walk, he felt up to writing a poem. Before long he had made a ritual of writing every day, shaping what he had seen and thought about during or immediately after his walk into short poems. He decided to paste them on postcards to send to Harrison, who is never specifically addressed but is always present by implication as a sympathetic audience of one.

Following the same pastoral convention as *Walden* and *A Sand County Almanac*, the poems in *Winter Morning Walks* form a cycle structured on the changing seasons. From November 9 to March 20, Kooser notes the date and the weather, then describes one moment, one thought emerging from the discipline of his daily walk. On December 31 ("Cold and snowing") he speaks of the year that is ending as a book whose "opening pages" he cannot remember, followed by his "mother's death / in the cold, wet chapters of spring." Complicating the metaphor of nature as a book, earlier employed by Leopold, Kooser speaks of the year, rather than the landscape, as the figurative volume. Elements of landscape become the imagery, theme, and textual apparatus of this year-as-volume. Thus the initial chapters of spring give way to a "featureless text of summer / burning with illness" and "a conclusion" (by implication, the poems in

Winter Morning Walks to date) narrating the year's "first hard frosts." The last of three stanzas concludes the extended metaphor with images summing up autumn, early winter, and that day's walk, the last of the year:

> A bibliography of falling leaves,
> an index of bare trees,
> and finally, a crow flying like a signature
> over the soft white endpapers of the year.
>
> (54)

The crow enters the poem as it did the poet's day, black against the snow and overcast sky, black as ink running across the whiteness of paper. The simile of the crow as a signature—an author's personalization of a book—implies a unity of identity and consciousness between place and person. By such figures of speech Kooser connects seasons of the year with the stages and transitions in human life.

Stillwell is exactly right when she describes these poems as "unified by time, threaded along the regularity of the month and date, repeated like a mantra—*I am here, I am here*" (409). Mantras, phrases repeated in the practice of Eastern meditation, help one focus on the moment and thereby transcend fear and desire. The poems in *Winter Morning Walks*, like those in *Braided Creek* and in fact like so much pastoral writing from Emerson to Kooser, constitute a kind of American Buddhist scripture, a spiritual literature in which human selfhood is characterized as one with place, inseparable from the characteristic seasons, plants, and animals of local landscape. Roethke writes that his "true self runs toward a Hill" (*Collected Poems*, 243). While the poet of *Winter Morning Walks* cannot run, he walks, if at times shakily, from sickness to health and from autumn to the spring equinox. By patterning his book on the seasons of the year, Kooser implies that health and happiness require that one walk—that is, live—as much as possible according to the rhythms of nature.

Kooser's recent writing is marked by the same understated virtuosity and attentiveness to people and place. *Delights & Shadows* (2004), for which Kooser received the Pulitzer Prize in poetry, features homely still lifes ("Casting Reels"), portraits of rural midwesterners ("Pearl"), and evocations of neglected landscapes ("Old Cemetery"). Kooser's facility with metaphor remains undiminished, as in "On the Road," in which "a pebble of quartz" picked up during a walk figures as "one drop of the earth's milk / dirty and cold" (77). He has also made his debut as a prose writer with two recent books. *The Poetry Home Repair Manual* (2005), a writing guide for beginning poets, champions intelligibility as a poetic virtue. Its humorous title subtly invokes the midwestern tinkerer archetype, emphasizing poetry as the result of work rather than of inspiration alone. *Local Wonders: Seasons in the Bohemian Alps* (2002) is a book of nature writing arranged in four sections about spring, summer, autumn, and winter in the countryside around Garland, where Kooser has lived since the early 1980s. The Bohemian Alps of the title are glacial hills "which in the late 1870s began to be settled by Czech and German immigrants from that region of central Europe once known as Bohemia" (xi). Kooser focuses as much on the area's social dimensions—its history and the character of the living descendants of those original settlers—as on its physical landscape. One unifying motif in the book is Kooser's repeated citation of Bohemian proverbs, used to conclude passages of narration or description. An example appears after he laments the subdivision of previously open land into smaller lots for the construction of large, expensive homes. In building on hilltops (a placement that Frank Lloyd Wright warned against) the wealthy of Lincoln demonstrate an arrogant pastoralism that is ultimately self-defeating. The owners of a new hilltop house just north of Kooser's old farmstead may have anticipated "sunsets and sunrises, but soon their view to the east will be interrupted, because another family has bought a hilltop about a hundred yards away and will be building their own house there within the year." The families have urbanized the country to which they retreated; they "will have to draw their blinds at night and listen to each other's screen doors slam just as they did in the city." Kooser ends the passage with the homespun wisdom of the area's pioneers: "I trust in the Bohemian saying, 'He who places his ladder too steeply will easily fall backward'" (11).

Kooser's *Local Wonders* adds to an established tradition of midwestern nature writing, distinguished of course by Leopold but also by writers like the late Paul Gruchow, whose essays also challenge hidebound myths of progress and modernity while celebrating the particularities of landscape.

Ted Kooser (1939—)

Steven P. Schneider

Ted Kooser has emerged over the last several decades as a major American poet. For those familiar with Kooser's work, this may come as no surprise. When the sixty-six-year-old Midwesterner was appointed poet laureate of the United States in 2004, however, many East and West Coast critics and poets knew little about Ted Kooser or his work. He had spent his entire life in the states of Iowa and Nebraska, much of it working in the insurance business, and developed his poetry with strong ties to that region. Indeed, the term "regional" has become something of a blessing and a curse for Ted Kooser: he has been both praised and dismissed for his regionalism. Like other American writers, such as Willa Cather, William Faulkner, and Robert Frost, Kooser draws inspiration from places some do not consider prime real estate. Like these other writers, Kooser has discovered an authentic American voice, and his best poetry expresses a depth of emotion and connection to both the natural world and human community that makes his work universal.

Kooser's appointment as poet laureate of the United States recognized a lifetime of achievement. He served in that position for twenty months. Meanwhile, his tenth collection of poems, *Delights & Shadows*, was also published in 2004. It won the Pulitzer Prize for Poetry in 2005, along with the Society of Midland Authors Award for Poetry. In addition to his many books of poetry, Kooser wrote a prize-winning nonfiction book titled *Local Wonders: Seasons in the Bohemian Alps* (2002).

Kooser's poetry matters to readers because it speaks to their experience of everyday life, illuminating matters of the heart and of the world around them. He explains in an online 2008 interview with David Baker, poetry editor of the *Kenyon Review*, and Tim Hofmeister, professor of classics at Denison University, that in his job working for an insurance company, "I worked every day with people who didn't read poetry, who hadn't read it since they were in high school, and I wanted to write for them." He values simplicity and clarity in his work and is best known for short, lyrical poems with startling metaphors. In a world of violence and disorder, Kooser expresses a quiet and calm voice, one that grounds readers in the world around them. He says: "I think a big part of making art of any kind is an attempt to secure order, and there can be a lot of pleasure in making something small and orderly."

Ted Kooser's poetry also matters because of the ways it demonstrates the creative process as something magical. His strong associative powers of imagination allow readers to discover in his poetry surprising and often pleasurable connections. In his poem "Etude," for example, Kooser makes the imaginative connection between a great blue heron and a man in a blue suit sitting at his desk. He notes in the *Kenyon Review* interview: "I do believe that a lot of this material or connection comes forth by dictation—something deep in me, something that I'm not really in control of." Later in the same interview, when commenting upon another poem with startling metaphors, "A Washing of Hands," he notes that "when those metaphors come to me, unbidden, it feels magical."

His dedication to his craft is an inspiration to aspiring artists and writers and to anyone who has struggled with the creative process. To make time to write he got into the habit of getting up at 4:30 a.m. every day and would write until around 7 a.m. before heading off to the insurance company in Lincoln, Nebraska, where he worked. He continues this habit of writing early each day, even though he is now retired from the insurance business. "I get up every morning," Kooser says, "and I sit in the same chair every morning, with my coffee pot at hand, and write in a notebook" (*Kenyon Review*). Although not every morning results in a memorable poem, he has learned "that unless I'm sitting there with my notebook, on the day when the good one comes, I'm never going to get it at all."

Kooser's career as a writer can be divided into three major phases. In the first phase, he experimented with different poetic forms and often published chapbooks in which he tested out his explorations of poetry style and voice. The University of Nebraska Press published his first collection of poems, *Official Entry Blank* (1969), which was followed by two chapbooks and then two book-length collections of poetry, *A Local Habitation & A Name* (1974) and *Not Coming to Be Barked At* (1976).

Many of Kooser's earliest poems were first published by *Prairie Schooner*, a literary journal also published by the University of Nebraska Press. The relationship with *Prairie Schooner* has been important to Kooser throughout his writing career. He noted that "Bernice Slote was the first editor of a distinguished literary journal to publish my poems. Several appeared in *Prairie Schooner* when I was in my twenties. That publication meant a lot to me and I remember sending copies to just about everybody I could think of . . . . I have since published a number of poems in *Prairie Schooner* and have always been able to trust the successive editors to show me which of my poems were worth publishing and which not" (e-mail message to contributor, October 23, 2000).

With the publication of his fourth book, *Sure Signs: New and Selected Poems* (1980), many readers began to recognize Kooser as an important voice on the American poetic landscape. The publication of this volume signaled the end of his apprenticeship—the first major phase of his career as a poet. During the second phase of his career, beginning with the publication of *One World at a Time* (1985), Kooser published five more books of poetry. These include *Weather Central* (1994) and *Winter Morning Walks: One Hundred Postcards to Jim Harrison* (2000), a collection of poems written during the poet's recovery from oral cancer. During the years 1980 to 2004 the poet solidified his reputation as a master of the use of metaphor and the short lyric. He also wrote and published a number of poems that are considered contemporary classics.

In the third phase of his career, Kooser has embarked upon a career as a public figure. Although he is reserved and prefers to spend his time on his farm in Garland, Nebraska, with his wife Kathleen and their two dogs, Kooser has become a frequently invited guest and reader of his poetry at universities, colleges, book clubs, and community organizations as well as an ambassador of the art form. During his tenure as poet laureate of the United States, he launched the Web site and national newspaper column, "American Life in Poetry," which is Kooser's pet project to make poetry accessible to the American reading public through newspapers. In this third phase of his career, Kooser continued to publish major collections of his poetry, including *Delights & Shadows* (2004) and *Valentines* (2008). He also wrote two books on writing, *The Poetry Home Repair Manual* (2005) and, with Steve Cox, *Writing Brave and Free: Encouraging Words for People Who Want to Start Writing* (2006). He has won numerous awards for his work, including two NEA fellowships in poetry, the Pushcart Prize, the Stanley Kunitz Prize, the James Boatwright Prize, and a Merit Award from the Nebraska Arts Council.

FORMATIVE YEARS

Ted Kooser was born in Ames, Iowa, on April 25, 1939. His father, Theodore Briggs Kooser, began his career in retail as the drapery manager in a small family-owned department store, Tilden's, where he met his future wife, Vera Moser. In 1943, he moved down Ames's Main Street and became manager of the Younker's Store. Vera Moser Kooser stayed home to raise Ted and his sister, Judy. His parents had a lasting influence upon the poet. He inherited a strong work ethic from his father and an appreciation of natural wonders from his mother. In his book, *Delights & Shadows*, he pays tribute to each of them in poems that are titled respectively "Mother" and "Father."

Kooser attended Iowa State University, where he earned a bachelor of science degree in 1962. He took a position teaching high school in Madrid, Iowa, for the 1962-1963 school year but then moved to Lincoln, Nebraska, where he enrolled as a graduate student in the creative writing program at the University of Nebraska at Lincoln. Kooser had been writing poetry since his late teens and moved to Lincoln in order to study with the poet Karl Shapiro, whom he admired greatly.

Kooser, however, did not immediately complete his graduate studies. He dropped out of school and answered an ad in a Lincoln newspaper for an entry-level job with an insurance company. He ended up working many years in the insurance field, and when he retired he was a vice president for Lincoln Benefit Life.

From the very beginning of his career in the insurance industry, Kooser viewed his job as a way to support his writing poetry. Like William Carlos Williams and Wallace Stevens, Ted Kooser supported himself financially outside the academic or publishing world and managed to develop an enduring body of creative work.

Kooser finished his graduate studies and earned a master's degree from the University of Nebraska at Lincoln in 1968. Kooser's Midwestern roots and foothold in the nonacademic world influenced his poetry greatly. Although he does not consider himself a regional writer, he does acknowledge that "most of my work reflects my interest in my surroundings here on the Great Plains" (*Contemporary Authors*, p. 257). The introduction to the *Kenyon Review* interview suggests that Kooser's poetry is "regional and realistic" and "akin to the paintings of Grant Wood." (Best known for his painting *American Gothic*, Grant Wood was part of a Midwestern regionalist movement that included Paul Engle, Hamlin Garland, and the Iowa poet James Hearst.)

Kooser himself has noted an affinity for the work of the painters Edward Hopper and Andrew Wyeth. Both artists bucked the modernist trend toward abstraction in favor of a realistic art rooted in place. Moreover, each painter discovers the poetic in the everyday and leads us see it new ways. Kooser has said that "there's a melancholy in the Hoppers that I have in my poems. Of course, that melancholy is also present in Wyeth" (e-mail message to contributor, August 18, 2008).

The populist appeal of his poetry depends upon its simplicity of language, clarity of perception, and affinity for human life and community. His work, then, can be considered part of what the critic Dana Gioia has described as a "broader shift in sensibility in the arts" that has returned "tonality in serious music, representation in painting" and the "reaffirmation of song and story" in poetry (p. 39).

EARLY POETRY

Kooser's first collection of poems, *Official Entry Blank* (1969), published by the University of Nebraska Press, served well as his "official entry" into the poetry world. The collection is distinctive in its willingness to embrace and experiment in different forms. There are haikus, a sonnet, and a number of poems that employ a variety of rhyme schemes. Nevertheless, the predominant mode is free verse, a style that would prevail in his subsequent collections.

The first poem of the collection, "Official Entry Form," is based upon poetry contest entry forms. Written in a tongue-in-check tone, it pokes fun at the submission process to such contests. The final two lines of the poem serve as a reminder of the dominant poetic form at the time: "And please remember that we all / Prefer free verse to the traditional" (p. 3).

The most memorable poems in Kooser's first volume are in free verse. These include "Beer Bottle," "Abandoned Farmhouse," and "A Letter from Aunt Belle," each of which the poet republished in his 1980 book *Sure Signs: New and Selected Poems.* The tone and subject matter of "Beer Bottle," with its fierce enjambment and attention to everyday objects, were clearly influenced by William Carlos Williams.

One of the more surprising poems in *Official Entry Blank* is titled "Walt Whitman." It is difficult to think of two poets more unlike one another. Whitman writes long, billowing lines in poems that sometimes go on for many pages; Kooser writes terse lines in poems that rarely exceed a single page. Whitman not only speaks for himself but also develops a persona in his poems that is "representative" of democracy. Kooser's voice and persona are much more subdued, understated, and modest. Nevertheless, Kooser pays a curious kind of homage to the nineteenth-century bard while at the same time underscoring the differences between them.

WALT WHITMAN

Whose tongue's erection lapped America—
Whose beard and hers were interwoven, coarse
As Kansas bushels pumpkined with his chants—

Who wiped his boots on fat Poor Richard's kite,
Undid his hoary fly and started west—

Who shouldered Lincoln's coffin like a bale,
And seeded orchards as he puffed along—

Who kissed a soldier's amputated leg—

May he become our country's tallest tale:
A giant in a checkered mackinaw,
Astride the blue ox of his insolence.

(p. 43)

This portrait of Whitman paints him as larger than life and satirizes the poet who boasted of his "barbaric yawp" and sang the body electric. Kooser's choice of words "erection" and "fly" in his poem evoke the sexual Whitman who wrote, in "Song of Myself," "Urge and urge and urge / Always the procreant urge of the world." Yet Kooser also presents the empathetic bard whose elegy of Lincoln "When Lilacs Last in the Dooryard Bloom'd" is one of the enduring memorials in American poetry. Kooser also alludes to the Whitman who attended to wounded Civil War soldiers and wrote the great antiwar poem "The Wound-Dresser."

In his poem Kooser joins a long list of American poets compelled to wrestle with Whitman, who cast a long shadow over all the American poets that came after him. Ezra Pound, Langston Hughes, Muriel Rukeyser, Louis Simpson, and William Stafford, for example, have all written Walt Whitman poems. A poet of understatement and lyric compression, Kooser expresses antipathy for the epic stature of Walt Whitman. Yet one hears in this poem an admiration for the poet who was not all bravura but was also the champion of the underdog.

In contrast to "Walt Whitman," "For Karl Shapiro, Having Gone Back to the Sonnet" is written not in free verse but as a sonnet. Kooser, as a graduate student at the University of Nebraska at Lincoln in the early 1960s, studied with Karl Shapiro, who was then on the faculty of the Department of English. Kooser says of this time, "I really came to Nebraska to go to grad school because Karl was there, and I liked his poems. We became good friends in short order, and spent a good deal of time together, talking about books and literature and enjoying ourselves" (e-mail message to contributor, July 18, 2008).

Shapiro encouraged the young poet and wrote a short introduction to his second full-length collection, *A Local Habitation & A Name*. In the above-mentioned poem Kooser reflects on Shapiro's decision to return to the sonnet and likens writing one to playing a spinet. While he is happy for his mentor to be "playing a tune on limited keys" (p. 50), to Kooser a sonnet feels like a straitjacket and he cannot wait to escape. He writes:

> In the closing six bars on this Spinet,
> With my fingers too fat for the keys,
> And my necktie already caught in it—
> Make it let go of me please!

Although Kooser would continue to experiment with formal verse, he rarely wrote or published sonnets after his first book. On the topic of formal verse, he has said that "deciding to use a fixed metrical form before a poem begins to shape itself is putting the cart before the horse. If during its genesis a poem begins to lean toward a fixed form, fine. Then it might make sense to let it fill out a kind of container that it seems bent on filling. But the error comes when writers sit down to write sonnets and don't have the right poetry to fill them with" (e-mail message to contributor, October 24, 2000).

After the publication of his first book, Kooser founded and operated a small press, Windflower. In the beginning he published single monthly sheets with one poem per sheet. This evolved to a stapled quarterly journal, called the *Salt Creek Reader*, which he published for several years. During the early 1970s he also published books by two of his close friends, fellow Nebraskans Bill Kloefkorn and Don Welch, as well as a chapbook of his own work titled *Grass County* (1971). In addition, he published several anthologies of poetry through Windflower Press. One of these, *The Windflower Home Almanac of Poetry*, was listed by *Library Journal* as one of the best books from small presses for 1980.

In the introduction to Kooser's second book of poetry, *A Local Habitation & A Name* (1974), Karl Shapiro suggests that William Carlos Williams provides an important context for reading Kooser. "For all its guff," Shapiro writes, "William Carlos Williams' dogma of the Local remains the touchstone of what authentic American poetry we have." For Shapiro, Kooser is a poet of the local, and his place is the Midwest. "Few poets have captured the spirit of the place as well as he," writes Shapiro. Later, in an interview in *On Common Ground* (1983), edited by Mark Sanders and J. V. Brummels, Kooser would confirm this approach to poetry: "People have known for years that the best way to involve a reader in what he's reading is to introduce concrete imagery, and when you live in a place you draw your imagery from what's around you" (Sanders, p. 102).

The stronger work in his second book of poetry is reflected in the poems that engage the landscape, its churches and barns and coffee shops and the people who inhabit them. The first poem, "The Red Wing Church," concerns itself with the dismantling of the church and the dispersal of its steeple, stained-glass windows, pews, and church bell. Kooser writes:

> The good works of the Lord are all around:
> the steeple-top is standing in a garden
> just up the alley; it's a hen-house now:
>
> .   .   .
>
> Pews stretch on porches up and down the street,
> the stained-glass windows style the mayor's house,
> and the bell's atop the firehouse in the square.

The reader does not learn in this little, enigmatic poem what happened that led to the church being disassembled. The breakup of this house of worship into disparate parts is a gesture that gets repeated elsewhere in this volume and throughout Kooser's poetry. Farmhouses are abandoned, barns fall apart, bridges and roads disappear in snowstorms. The harsh landscape and economy of small towns and rural Midwestern life take their toll upon the structures and lives built there.

In "Abandoned Farmhouse," Kooser describes a farmhouse abandoned by its family, the surrounding fields "cluttered with boulders." He writes: "Something went wrong, says the empty house / in the weed-choked yard" (p. 27). Details in the poem suggest that the family who lived there was not up to the task of maintaining their farm and came upon hard financial times that led to their abandonment of it. No dates are given or historical context provided; it could as well be the time of the Great Depression or more recent times when small family farmers have been pressed to give up their livelihoods because of competition and encroachment from agribusiness. *A Local Habitation & A Name* includes several other poems where barns and the lives that maintain them fall apart. The best of these, "Tom Ball's Barn," accounts for the hard luck of Tom Ball, whose mortgage went unpaid and who has diabetes and falls to his death from a silo.

Although most poems in this collection focus on the landscape and its inhabitants, in several of the poems the reader will discover the poet, characteristically an unobtrusive and somewhat vulnerable figure. In "Selecting a Reader," the poet reflects on a reader who approaches one of his books in a bookstore. Although she is tempted to buy it, she puts the book back on the shelf. She says to herself, "For that kind of money, I can get / my raincoat cleaned.' And she will" (p. 59). The gesture here is self-deprecating and frugal, learned through the poet's residence in two farm states.

A Local Habitation & A Name is also revealing for what Kooser shares about his first marriage in poems such as "For My Former Wife, Watching TV, in the Past," "Plain Song," and "Airmail from Mother." These poems speak to the pain of divorce and to the separation from his son, Jeffrey Charles. Kooser's first wife, Diana Tressler, was a schoolteacher whom he had married in 1962. Their marriage ended in a divorce in 1969. Nevertheless, he dedicated this second volume of poems to her with the inscription "for Diana, anyway." His affection for their son shines through in the poems "I Put My Hand on My Son's Head" and "The Constellation Orion."

Kooser's third book-length collection, *Not Coming to Be Barked At* (1976), followed quickly on the heels of his second collection and was dedicated to the author William Cole, who had been one of the poet's early supporters and admirers. A slim volume of forty-nine pages, it contains several poems that have become contemporary classics, including "Uncle Adler" and "So This Is Nebraska." In these poems, Kooser displays his mastery of metaphor and simile.

In "Uncle Adler," Kooser begins the poem with a striking metaphor, comparing the old uncle to a barn or house with "cardboard / in all of its windows" (p. 18). He extends the metaphor in the next several lines:

> The oil in his eyes was so old
> it would barely light,
> and his chest was a chimney
> full of bees.
>
> (p. 18)

In his book *Why Poetry Matters* (2008), Jay Parini notes that poetry is very much the language of metaphor and that "metaphor is the fiber of language itself. As such, analogical thinking is central to the human enterprise of making sense. It actually organizes our experience in subtle ways. Without metaphor, there is no thinking at all" (p. 69). We can feel Kooser thinking about old age in this poem through his use of metaphors. They help the poet to make sense of what is happening to the aging uncle.

In the second half of "Uncle Adler," Kooser employs simile to account for Uncle Adler's demise:

his Adam's-apple hung like a ham
in a stairwell. Lawyers
encircled the farm like a fence, . . .

(p. 18)

By the end of the poem, he has presented a masterful profile of a man whose life is collapsing on him: "He suddenly sucked in his breath so hard / the whole estate fell in on him" (p. 18).

The same pattern of metaphoric language followed by a series of similes is employed by Kooser in his popular "So This Is Nebraska." In this poem he expresses a palpable love for a place that to many seems desolate and unwelcoming. Kooser has embraced Nebraska like the other great writers who have made it their home, including Willa Cather, John Neihardt, Weldon Kees, Mari Sandoz, and Wright Morris. Although he resists any comparison of himself or his generation of Nebraska poets to these previous literary giants, he does admit that "some of the poets living and working in Nebraska today have written, and will write, strong and enduring poems, and that these may become a part of the literary culture" (Sanders, p. 102).

In *Not Coming to Be Barked At,* a good number of the poems are situated in either Nebraska or Iowa and employ titles that tie them to those landscapes: "In a Country Cemetery," "Farmlights in Iowa," "Fort Robinson," "Late September in Nebraska." This third collection reflects the work of a maturing poet, one who has discovered his voice through experimentation and who displays here the mastery of craft and distinctiveness of style that would characterize his future work.

Kooser published a chapbook of poems titled *Old Marriage and New* (1978) about his divorce from Diana Tressler and his subsequent marriage to Kathleen Rutledge, a journalist who worked her way up the ranks and eventually served, from 2001 until her retirement in 2007, as the first woman editor of the *Lincoln Journal Star. Old Marriage and New* is notable for its autobiographical revelations but lacks the intensity of confessional poetry addressing marital breakups. Dana Gioia, in his essay "Explaining Ted Kooser," first published in *On Common Ground,* faults these poems for being overly sentimental. Gioia writes: "Writing about the failure of his first marriage and the promise of his second, Kooser carefully established a series of thirteen short scenes which dramatized this difficult period in his life. Sharp and concisely written, these poems still seem thin compared to Kooser's previous work" (p. 98).

The publication of *Sure Signs* in 1980 marked the end of the first major phase of Kooser's poetic career. One finds in these poems the influence of Edgar Lee Masters' *Spoon River Anthology*. Kooser's poems share with Masters' work an attentiveness to the quirkiness and tragedies of small town life. One also sees in these poems the influence of William Carlos Williams in their attention to ordinary objects and buildings—beer bottles, old photographs, furnaces, caps, abandoned farmhouses, leaky faucets, and country cemeteries. In his interview with Mark Sanders, Kooser notes: "I detest poems of self-pity, though, and poems of self-absorption. I love poems which celebrate things—telephones, pigs, rocks, you name it" (p. 104). In *Sure Signs* there are few if any signs of self-absorption and lots of "things" that trigger Kooser's imagination.

One of the previously unpublished poems in *Sure Signs* is titled "An Old Photograph." Kooser wrote this poem based upon the actual photograph of his great-aunt Lavinia and great-uncle Rob Hansel. It introduces into his work the "ecphrastic" impulse, whereby a poet comments upon or interprets a work of art, or as in this case, a photograph. Later in his career, in his Pulitzer Prize-winning collection *Delights & Shadows* (2004), Kooser would include a group of poems entitled "Four Civil War Paintings by Winslow Homer." His eye for the precise visual detail is evident in "An Old Photograph," and he sees in the space between the couple the distance that has come between them from enduring a long life of hardship. He writes:

> How far apart
> they sit; not touching at shoulder
> or knee, hands clasped in their laps
> as if under each pair was a key
> to a trunk hidden somewhere,
> full of those lessons one keeps
> to himself.
>
> (p. 5)

John Hollander, in his book *The Gazer's Spirit* (2005), notes that "most poems on photographs are still directed to portraits, and that, indeed, photography is the most contemporary form of portraiture. The documented trace of a past personal presence is always compelling" (p. 67). Kooser's poem does not pose epistemological questions about the relationship between photographic subject and the camera. Rather he focuses his attention on what is both seen and unseen and traces a personal history of this couple that accounts for their "stern statement."

The critical reception of *Sure Signs* was mostly favorable. Peter Stitt, writing in the *Georgia Review*, concluded that "Kooser is a good poet, a skilled and cunning writer, and ought to be recognized as an authentic 'poet of the American people'" (p. 662). In an essay in the *Dictionary of Literary Biography*, Matthew C. Brennan wrote that "*Sure Signs* shows an accomplished poet employing distinctive, expressive metaphors" (p. 144). Dana Gioia, one of the poet's earliest and most important critical supporters, had great praise for *Sure Signs*. In his essay "Explaining Ted Kooser," Gioia wrote, "*Sure Signs* showed Kooser as a shrewd judge of his own poetry. He ruthlessly cut away his weaker work, and presented the reader with only eighty-nine short poems from all his earlier books. This careful editing gave *Sure Signs* a consistent quality that put most contemporary collections to shame. It also ensured that readers, who came upon Kooser's work there for the first time, left impressed with the quality of his achievement" (*On Common Ground*, p. 98).

One reviewer, however, was not uniformly impressed. In his review, "Fondled Memories," of several collections of contemporary poetry in the *New York Times Book Review* (October 12, 1980), Charles Molesworth expressed his reservations about *Sure Signs*. Molesworth noted that "Kooser works inside the imagist tradition, tying his feelings rather loosely to a homespun symbolism. Sometimes this is fresh and keen, but it can also be humdrum or clumsy." It is hard to tell from Molesworth's review which poems he found "fresh and keen" and which ones loose and "homespun." Molesworth also complained that there was little breathing space in the collection: "Seldom allowing themselves much room—there are about 88 poems in 90 pages—these poems' brevity fights a rearguard action against becoming quaint." He concluded his review with the observation that "the 'sure signs' of the title hint at a great mystery, but the simplicity of diction and structure prevents it from ever being revealed" (p. 36). Kooser has described this review as "sneering in nature" and observed that Molesworth "was as hard on Charles Simic and Louise Glück and the others as he was on me, so I was getting kicked in good company" (Sanders, p. 105).

Molesworth's review of *Sure Signs*, with its grudging praise and its references to Kooser's "quaintness," did signal, nevertheless, that his work had gained the attention of readers outside the Midwest. Moreover, his work had been discussed in the same critical breath as several other important contemporary poets. As a marker of the trajectory of his career as a poet, the review is important for these reasons. It is also important in that it reflects an Eastern or urban bias against Kooser that has occasionally been expressed, either directly or indirectly, in interviews or reviews of the poet's work.

MATURE PHASE OF THE POET'S CAREER

In *One World at a Time* (1985), the volume following *Sure Signs*, Kooser continued to write with the confidence reflected in his selected poems. He had established himself as a poet who extended his readership beyond the Midwest but who continued to focus his own gaze upon the people and region he knows best. In an elegy to his father, Theodore Briggs Kooser, the poet reflects upon his father's life as a shopkeeper in Midwestern towns "walking the hard floors / of the retail business" (p. 13). The poem is a touching tribute to his father and describes the palpable joy he experienced in his dry goods store.

Kooser, like his father, has a good eye for people, especially as he registers them in the poem "Walking at Noon Near the Burlington Depot in Lincoln, Nebraska," a poem dedicated to the memory of the poet James Wright. In this poem the reader sees factory workers on break from their jobs who "smoke / in the warm spring sunlight / thick with butterscotch," and a girl who sits in her car, "broken down over its tires," and listens to the radio (p. 31). Through a series of arresting images, Kooser portrays the beauty and sadness of Midwestern life, a subject that Wright wrote about in poems such as "Autumn Begins in Martins Ferry, Ohio."

The poem "At Nightfall" begins, as do so many others, with a precisely rendered description of a natural occurrence, in this case a swallow weaving "one bright white feather into her nest / to guide her flight home in the darkness" (p. 37). The poet reflects that this is a sign of the world's "innocent progress." The moment of wonder, or happiness in this discovery, is transformed, however, in the last five lines of the poem, where the poet reflects on the dismal state of the world.

> But to what
> safe place shall any of us return
> in the last smoky nightfall,
> when we in our madness have put the torch
> to the hope in every nest and feather?
>
> (p. 37)

One hears in these final melancholy lines an echo of "Fire and Ice" by Robert Frost, a poem that reflects upon how the world will end. When asked about whether his poetry is political, Kooser responded: "I think that all poems are subversive when set against our American culture, and for that reason they have political significance. I also believe that poems are instruments of persuasion, and that might be seen to be political" (e-mail message to contributor, July 18, 2008). "At Nightfall" registers a quiet protest against those who destroy the environment and persuades the reader to appreciate an intimate connection to the natural world and to the human community, underscoring our fragile existence.

One World at a Time consolidated the gains that Kooser had established for his work in *Sure Signs*. The poems are similar in length to those in the previous volume. Moreover, the Midwestern landscape and its people continue to be the focus of his work. There are fine poems about cleaning a bass, a hearty woman named Myrtle who delivers the daily newspaper, and an old porch swing.

In his next book, *The Blizzard Voices* (1986), Kooser experimented by writing a sequence of dramatic monologues about the historic blizzard of 1888. The volume was republished in 2006 with a new introduction by the poet. Kooser explains, "I snagged these poems from actual reminiscences, recorded in old age, of people who survived the most talked about storm in American history, the Blizzard of 1888, also known as the Schoolchildren's Blizzard because of the many children and their teachers who were trapped in rural schools on the bitterly cold days of

January 12 and 13 of that year" (Introduction, 2006 edition). The book has a historical thrust, distinguishing it from much of Kooser's other poetry, which is derived from the poet's firsthand observation of people and places. Rather, in *The Blizzard Voices*, the poet spent time researching the dramatic snowstorm and based his monologues upon strands of information he culled from secondary sources. "Preparing to write these poems," he noted in his introduction, "I read town and county histories that mention the blizzard."

In *The Blizzard Voices*, recollection of the snowstorm is made up of thirty-six separate poems in first-person dramatic monologues. We hear from schoolteachers, children, and farmers about what they were doing when the blizzard hit and how they managed to survive it. The poems, several of which are illustrated with drawings by Tom Pohrt, are well-sculpted pieces of poetic lore and history. The collection was performed as a play by the Lincoln Community Playhouse in the late 1980s. The Pulitzer-Prize winning composer Paul Moravec also turned *The Blizzard Voices* into an evening-long dramatic oratorio, which was premiered by Opera Omaha on September 12, 2008.

In one of the poems a woman who taught in a country school recalls leading her students through the storm to safety.

> When the blizzard hit, it blew
> some of the shutters closed
> with a bang, breaking some panes,
> and the snow came pouring in.
> Toward evening, our fuel was gone,
> so we set out walking,
> holding each other's hands.
> It was impossible to see,
> but we followed a row
> of dead sunflower stalks
> all the way to a nearby farm.
> I never see a sunflower now
> that I don't count my lucky stars.
>
> ("A Woman's Voice")

Reminiscent of Edwin Arlington Robinson, Kooser presents charac-
ters who are affected adversely by natural forces larger than themselves.
He acknowledged in an interview for *Contemporary Authors* that Edwin
Arlington Robinson, along with Robert Frost, May Swenson, and John
Crowe Ransom were among the first poets he read and who remained a
strong influence upon him (p. 257).

The slender group of dramatic monologues that make up *The Bliz-
zard Voices* was followed by the much longer collection *Weather Central* in
1994. In this volume a number of the poems concern themselves with
natural life: fireflies, barn owls, a snakeskin, and spider eggs. In "Barn
Owl," Kooser playfully describes a barn owl inviting a mouse into its lair.
The poem became one of those selected for his later collection *Valentines*
and relies upon the conceit of the owl as a lover to seduce its prey. In
"Snakeskin," the poet reflects on picking up a cast-off snakeskin and the
speed with which it once moved across the ground. He writes: "you can
feel / the speed along it, feel / in your bones the tick of wheels" (p. 11).
Kooser shows his familiarity with natural life in these poems and demon-
strates an adroit ability to bring them to life through figurative language.

The description of natural phenomena comes naturally to Kooser.
His familiarity with them stems from his boyhood years in Iowa and
from living most of his adult life in a farm state. In *Weather Central*, Koos-
er gazes at the unfinished Gilbert Stuart painting of George Washington
that hung in his boyhood classroom.

The Gilbert Stuart portrait of Washington was begun in 1796 and is
often referred to as "The Athenaeum." The narrator in the poem "The
Gilbert Stuart Portrait of Washington" begins by addressing the reader,
familiar with the portrait from its appearance on the U.S. one-dollar bill:

> You know it as well as the back of your hand,
> that face like a blushing bouquet
> of pink peonies set in the shadows of war,
> the father of our country, patient,
> sucking the past from his wooden teeth.
>
> (p. 38)

In the poem, a reproduction of the painting hangs in a boyhood classroom that Kooser attended. His attention is on the man in the portrait, who "had little time / for the likes of Gilbert Stuart, that son / of a snuff-grinding Tory" (p. 38). Stuart was one of the most famous portrait artists of his era. He painted over one thousand portraits, including six U.S. presidents, yet this portrait of George Washington went unfinished. Kooser reflects on the circumstances of Washington's posing for the famous portraitist.

> Perched on a chair in a cold stone barn,
> according to Stuart, he smiled only once,
> when a stallion ran past. He cared more
> for thoroughbred horses and farming
> than he did for the presidency.
>
> (p. 38)

Kooser reflects not only on the preoccupied former general in this poem but also on the passage of time, represented by the passing of the seasons and the black octagonal clock next to which the painting hangs. He writes: "We learned our lessons while the big clock / clacked, its Roman numerals arranged / in a wreath and sealed under glass" (p. 39). In this poem, Kooser displays knowledge of art history and instructs the reader not only about this portrait but also about how it loomed large in his education. It is a marvelous poetic response to a silent work of art and at the same time a reminiscence of the slow passage of time in his boyhood classroom.

In another poem about a work of art, "The Statue of an Unknown Soldier," the poet casts a critical eye upon the proportions of a statue of a soldier in the courthouse square in Seward, Nebraska. The poet notes: "he looks like a child, his head too large / for the care-broken, delicate shoulders." The poet also brings the statue to life, noting how weary he must be "from walking so far / from the quarry." In his ragged uniform and rifle by his side, this sad-looking soldier is subjected to the "smoke of blizzards" and the "grapeshot of hail" (p. 71) as well as the town's high school majorettes who stride proudly past him every Fourth of July.

Kooser includes in *Weather Central* his wry reflections of a poetry reading given by the Russian poet Yevgeny Yevtushenko in Lincoln, an account of a visit to an abandoned schoolhouse in the Nebraska Sand-hills, and a moving poem written on the morning of his son Jeff's wedding. In "Yevtushenko," he relies upon simile and metaphor to describe the reading by the great Russian poet: "You read your windy poems, Yevtushenko, / like a tree in the wind." When the reading is over, the Russian writer scoops up his "leaves" and sits down. Afterward, at a party at the state governor's mansion, Kooser and then Governor Bob Kerrey sit through a long movie Yevtushenko had made of his life and listen to him recite a list of the people he has known: Henry Kissinger, Richard Nixon, and Robert Kennedy. The concluding two stanzas of the poem, however, leave the impression that the Russian poet is much too full of himself for Nebraska standards. "The Governor's eyes were as hollow as Lincoln's" (p. 33), observes Kooser, and ends the poem by describing the reception given the literary giant as a perfunctory obligation hosted by an elected official.

In "An Abandoned Stone Schoolhouse in the Nebraska Sandhills," Kooser ponders the stone walls of an old, deserted schoolhouse. In his poem Kooser reflects: "Touch the wall with your fingertips, / and a hundred thousand years brush away . . . ." He ends the poem by imagining a river trickling inside the sandstone, "cleaning itself / as it eases along through the sand, / rubbing away at our names and our voices" (p. 45).

The passage of time occupies the poet's attention increasingly in his work as he grows older. *Weather Central* is a book published in the richness of maturity and toward the end of the second phase of the poet's career. Several of the poems are wistful, nostalgic for an earlier time in the poet's life. His poems "For Jeff" and "The Sweeper" reflect on ties that bind the generations. In the former poem, the poet recalls times he spent with both his son and his father in a park, the identical park he walks in on the morning of his son's wedding. In "The Sweeper," he recalls his father in shirtsleeves "sweeping / the sidewalk in front of his store." The poem hinges on a wonderful metaphor, in which the broom is likened to "an old yellow oar," the father happy to be "in the bow / of his gondola" (p. 84) greeting friends outside his store.

Kooser's next book, *Winter Morning Walks* (2000), was important to the poet in many ways. First, the writing of these poems was therapeutic for him while he was recovering from radiation therapy for cancer. Sec-

ond, they extend and deepen his longtime correspondence and friend-
ship with the writer Jim Harrison, to whom these poems were typed on
postcards and mailed. Third, unlike his other books of poetry that took
years to compile, the poems in this collection were written over a few
short months.

In the preface to the collection Kooser explains the context for writ-
ing these poems:

> In the autumn of 1998, during my recovery from surgery and
> radiation for cancer, I began taking a two-mile walk each morn-
> ing. I'd been told by my radiation oncologist to stay out of the
> sun for a year because of my skin sensitivity, so I exercised
> before dawn, hiking the isolated country roads near where I
> live, sometimes with my wife but most often alone.
>
> (Preface)

Depressed by his illness the previous summer, he almost gave up on
reading and writing. Kooser found the walks salutary and began to write
again. He remarks in the preface: "One morning in November, follow-
ing my walk, I surprised myself by trying my hand at a poem. Soon I was
writing every day." Years before he had "carried on a correspondence in
haiku" with his friend Jim Harrison, and he decided to paste on a post-
card the poems he was now writing and sent them to Harrison. *Winter
Morning Walks* is a collection of one hundred of these poems and is
subtitled "One Hundred Postcards to Jim Harrison."

All of the poems in the collection indicate the date of their writing,
beginning on November 9 and ending on March 20. Most of them be-
gin with a brief line set off from the rest of the poem, which describes
the weather on that particular morning. These terse "weather reports"
function in a way as the title of each poem, although the collection reads
like a journal with the date at the top of each entry. The longest poem
in the collection, "Foggy and dripping," is nineteen lines; the shortest
poem, "Quiet and clear," dated February 18, is a mere two lines. Most of
the poems average between eight and twelve lines. The sparseness of the
poems, their attention to natural detail, and the ways in which they open
up vistas of experience are reminiscent of the haiku.

In one of the more moving poems, dated November 14, Kooser asks for more time to share his life with his wife Kathleen:

> My wife and I walk the cold road
> in silence, asking for thirty more years.
>
> There's a pink and blue sunrise
> with an accent of red:
> a hunter's cap burns like a coal
> in the yellow-gray eye of the woods.
>
> (p. 15)

This poem begins with a direct statement and then moves to a description of nature, ending with the use of metaphor that brings the sunrise to life. The poem makes its leap from the first stanza to the next and leaves the reader with an image of longing and hope. The poems in this collection move through observations of the pre-dawn Nebraska landscape, with its chickadees, bare trees, and wind gusts. By focusing his attention on the present moment and upon the natural world, the poet gains strength through his writing. There is a kind of Zen meditation at work here, in which the self surrenders to the world and becomes enlarged. Moreover, in the routine of writing these poems, Kooser draws inspiration from the creative process. By the entry dated February 21 he feels fully revived:

> Fate, here I stand, hat in hand,
> in my fifty-ninth year,
> a man of able body and a merry spirit.
> I'll take whatever work you have.
>
> (p. 98)

In this short poem the poet sounds an optimistic note, declaring himself fit and looking forward to whatever the future brings. He ends the collection on the vernal equinox, March 20, declaring "How important it must be . . . that I have written these poems" (p. 120).

After more than thirty years of publishing poetry, Kooser published his first book of nonfiction, *Local Wonders*, in 2002. The "Bohemian

Alps" he refers to is a north-south range of low hills about seventy miles from the eastern edge of Nebraska. It is here that Kooser lives, and in this collection of four essays, each named for a different season, he writes of his experiences and observations of the very changeable Nebraska weather, the local flora and fauna, and the comings and goings of his country neighbors. In "Spring," for example, the opening essay of the collection, Kooser reflects on how "wild plums grow everywhere along the roadsides in our part of the country, each thicket originally started by some bird pausing on a fence wire just long enough to deposit a plum pit coated with a dollop of rich lime" (p. 14).

These same wild plums turn up in his poem "Mother" in the collection *Delights & Shadows,* and in the "Spring" essay he laments that they are sprayed routinely with herbicides. In *Local Wonders,* Kooser complains about how the countryside is being divided up into parcels of land. He notes: "One recently approved residential development in our area was vigorously opposed by the county planning and zoning commission, local landowners, and the state Game and Parks Commission, but it was approved." He concludes this short anecdote about the finagling of developers with one of the many Bohemian proverbs in the book: "Money is a master everywhere" (p. 22).

While Kooser shares many wry observations about life in the "Bohemian Alps," he clings to his sense of pleasure and delight in ordinary things. He writes: "I delight in the things I discover right within reach. At sixty-one years of age, I have seen, within a short distance from my house, my first moondog and my first bobcat." Happiness, for this writer, is to discover a natural wonder he has never seen before. He comments in "Spring" that "the first syllable of happiness, hap—with its luckiness, its chanciness, its sudden surprises—is a source of much delight in my life" (p. 13). In this regard, *Local Wonders* calls to mind previous first-person nonfiction accounts of nature, such as Henry David Thoreau's *Walden* and Annie Dillard's *Pilgrim at Tinker Creek.*

His next book, *Braided Creek* (2003), is a collection of short, epigrammatic poems that Kooser coauthored with his friend Jim Harrison. None of the poems is attributed to either writer. Together they explore and celebrate the natural world. The poems have a haiku-like feeling to them: concise, quiet, lucid, wise, and humorous. The collection is testimony to the abiding value of friendship and manifests a true spirit of collaboration.

THE POET LAUREATE

With his selection as U.S. poet laureate in August 2004, Ted Kooser embarked on the third major phase of his literary career. The announcement was made by James H. Billington, Librarian of Congress, who described Kooser as "a major poetic voice for rural and small-town America and the first poet laureate chosen from the Great Plains. His verse reaches beyond his native region to touch on universal themes in accessible ways" ("UNL Professor Ted Kooser Appointed U.S. Poet Laureate," press release, August 12, 2004).

When asked in an interview about whether he was shocked upon receiving the appointment, he responded that "the honor overrode the shock. I was at first terrified, but I decided if the Library of Congress was willing to take a chance on a poet from the Great Plains, I'd better do the best job I could" (*Kenyon Review*). In the twenty months that he served as poet laureate, Kooser estimates that he made around two hundred appearances and gave one hundred interviews, speaking to book clubs, community groups, high schools, colleges, and universities.

Perhaps his most lasting legacy as poet laureate will be the "American Life in Poetry" project that he started and which is sponsored by the Poetry Foundation. It consists of a weekly newspaper column that features a poem selected by Ted Kooser. The column is issued at no cost to newspapers, reaches nearly 4 million readers, and includes a brief introduction by Kooser to the selected poem. The mission of this ongoing project is to promote poetry. In the project description on the "American Life in Poetry" Web site, where the chosen poem also appears each week, Kooser notes that "newspapers are close to my heart and my family. As Poet Laureate I want to show the people who read newspapers that poetry can be for them, can give them a chuckle or an insight."

The same year that he was selected poet laureate, Kooser published *Delights & Shadows* (2004). In his tenth collection of poems, the poet reflects on mortality, aging, and the loss of family and friends.

In its first section, "Walking on Tiptoe," more than half of the poems concern themselves with old age, the infirmities of illness, and the dead or dying. In "At the Cancer Clinic" the poet expresses his admiration for the grace of a sick woman being helped toward the examining room by her two sisters: "how patient she is in the crisp white sails / of her clothes" (p. 7). In "Mourners," the poet is struck by the community of mourners who gather after the funeral "under the rustling churchyard maples / and talk softly, like clusters of leaves" (p. 16). They had been drawn there to say good-bye to someone but afterward bond closely together: "they keep saying hello and hello" (p. 16). Given his own bout with cancer and his retirement from the insurance business in 2000, it seems fitting for Kooser to cast his eye upon the fragile nature of human life and the frailties of the elderly in these poems. He does so with grace and aplomb, drawing upon sharp observation and surprising metaphors, just as he has done so skillfully throughout his career.

The poet peoples the second section of *Delights & Shadows* with members of his own family, including moving elegies entitled "Mother" and "Father" and a long narrative poem about a visit to his cousin Pearl. In "Mother," the poet contrasts the mid-April landscape and its wild plums blooming at the roadside with the fact that his mother has been dead one month. In that time she has "missed three rains and one nightlong / watch for tornadoes" (p. 25). The poem hinges on the poet's reflection upon the powers of observation that he has inherited from his mother. He concludes the poem with this tribute:

> Were it not for the way you taught me to look
> at the world, to see the life at play in everything,
> I would have to be lonely forever.
>
> (p. 26)

In the companion poem "Father," written on what would have been his father's ninety-seventh birthday, May 19, 1999, the poet reflects on what it would have been like if his father were still alive, "driving from clinic to clinic, / an ancient, fearful hypochondriac." The poem recalls a favorite anecdote of his father about the poet's grandmother looking out the window at the moment of his father's birth and seeing lilacs in bloom. The poem ends with a message for his deceased father: "lilacs are blooming in side yards / all over Iowa, still welcoming you" (p. 36).

In each of these poems there is an abiding sense of strength, optimism, and renewal that Kooser attributes to his parents. Moreover, the endings of each poem affirm the poet's connection to the natural world and his sense of wonder even in the face of loss.

The narrative poem "Pearl" runs for four pages, making it one of the very longest poems in Kooser's opus. In it he describes his visit to inform his aging cousin Pearl about the death of the poet's mother, Vera, who had been a childhood playmate of Pearl's. Pearl, who at ninety was a year older than Vera, had lived alone for nearly twenty years. Kooser discovers that she is seeing and talking to ghosts, whom she claims survey everything she owns. Pearl and the poet carry on a dialogue in which Kooser suggests that she get medical care for this problem. This long narrative poem is an affectionate portrait of his aging cousin which ends with the tongue-in-cheek observation that after he leaves, the "others stepped out of the stripes of light / and resumed their inventory" (p. 40).

Delights & Shadows moves between the memory and observation, light and darkness, including the four ecphrastic poems based upon Civil War paintings by Winslow Homer. Kooser presents a careful reading of the visual choreography in each painting, both describing the work and reflecting upon its execution. He demonstrates his uncanny ability to enter a visual work of art and transform it into a poem, whose verbal textures unveil a narrative through which we see the painting more richly.

In "A Box of Pastels," the poet recalls holding on his knees "a simple wooden box" that contained a set of pastels once used by the Impressionist artist Mary Cassatt. He notes that the peach- and pink-colored pastels "were worn down to stubs, / while the cool colors—violet, ultramarine— / had been set, scarcely touched, to one side." The poet reflects that Cassatt "had little patience with darkness, and her heart / held only a measure of shadow" (p. 63). In this poem he is contemplating the subject of his book, the balance between light and darkness. Even when he wades into the shadows to confront death, old age, and illness, Kooser emerges from the experience with some transformative discovery, revealing the indomitable nature of the human spirit.

Delights & Shadows was followed by *Flying at Night: Poems 1965-1985* (2005), a selection of poems from *Sure Signs* and *One World at a Time*.

Kooser has also published two books on the craft of writing since his becoming U.S. poet laureate. The first of these, *The Poetry Home Repair Manual* (2005), provides practical advice for beginning poets. The cover of the book features a toolbox, indicative of the poet's penchant to view his craft in ways similar to a carpenter. In a preface, "About This Book," Kooser suggests "the craft of careful writing and meticulous revision *can* be taught" (p. xi). He also acknowledges that his book is for those writers who want to communicate with their readers, a premise not universally shared in contemporary poetry.

In writing *The Poetry Home Repair Manual*, Kooser found it important to share what he has learned over the course of his career. "My writing philosophy owes much to an idea that Lewis Hyde expresses in his book *The Gift: Imagination and the Erotic Life of Property*. He suggests that those who are gifted should give something back" (p. xii). In this fine book on poetic craft, Kooser "gives back" by sharing his favorite "tools" with those starting out, including excellent advice on fine-tuning metaphors and similes, writing from memory, and working with detail.

The second of the two books Kooser has published on writing, *Writing Brave and Free* (2006), is coauthored with Steve Cox, a lifelong editor and publisher and director emeritus of the University of Arizona Press. Written for a more general audience, *Writing Brave and Free* also provides helpful tools for the beginning writer as well as inspiration and encouragement.

Ted Kooser's next book, *Valentines* (2008), is a collection of valentine poems written over the course of twenty years. In his introduction he explains that the custom of sending out annual valentine poems was inspired by that of a family friend, Dace Burdic. The first of the Kooser "valentines," "Pocket Poem," was sent in 1986 to about fifty women, many of them wives of the poet's friends. By the time he stopped the annual tradition of having them mailed from Valentine, Nebraska, he had around twenty-six hundred names on the mailing list. The very last poem in the collection, "The Hog-Nosed Snake," is for Kathleen, the poet's wife.

Kooser explains that many of the poems "refer to hearts, or suggest them, or would drop in the color red somewhere, but not all of them are that way. My favorite in the valentine book is 'Splitting an Order,' which is about love, but does it without the heart or the color" (e-mail message to contributor, July 26, 2008). In this poem, Kooser describes "an old man cutting a sandwich in half" (p. 37) to share with his wife. It is a touching poem about the way an old couple takes care of one another, sharing just about everything. The husband's kind gesture is met with appreciation by his wife, who "smooths the starched white napkin over her knees / and meets his eyes and holds out both old hands to him" (p. 37). The poem clicks shut with the image of her extending her hands to her husband, in a gesture both loving and grateful. This couple comes to represent for Kooser the abiding power of love in a lifelong marriage.

CONCLUSION

Ted Kooser's career as a poet, now in its fifth decade, represents a fierce independence, a loyalty to the place he has made his home, and a commitment to both the craft of writing and to making poetry accessible to his readers. By all measures he has succeeded, offering us a poetic world rich in sensory images, startling metaphors, and human empathy.

In the preface to his book *Why Poetry Matters,* Jay Parini writes that "the language of poetry can, I believe, save us. It can ground us in spiritual and moral realities, offering the consolations of philosophy, teaching us how to speak about our lives, and how—indeed—to live them" (p. xiv).

The poetry of Ted Kooser grounds readers in these realities, helping them to live their lives more consciously. Through the use of metaphor, he illustrates the associative power of the imagination to make connections, reminding us of the magic in our lives and in the creative process. Because of his willingness to write directly from the heart, he has developed a personal style harmonious with who he is and that speaks to a broad, reading public. His commitment to craft over the course of a long career provides a lighthouse of hope to all artists who labor in the dark, uncertain of their efforts but determined to express their voice.

SELECTED BIBLIOGRAPHY

WORKS OF TED KOOSER

Poetry

Official Entry Blank. Lincoln: University of Nebraska Press, 1969.

A Local Habitation & A Name. San Luis Obispo, Calif: Solo Press, 1974.

Not Coming to Be Barked At. Milwaukee: Pentagram Press, 1976.

Sure Signs. Pittsburgh: University of Pittsburgh Press, 1980.

One World at a Time. Pittsburgh: University of Pittsburgh Press, 1985.

The Blizzard Voices. St. Paul: Bieler Press, 1986; Lincoln: University of Nebraska Press, 2006.

Weather Central. Pittsburgh: University of Pittsburgh Press, 1994.

Winter Morning Walks: One Hundred Postcards to Jim Harrison. Pittsburgh: Carnegie Mellon University Press, 2000.

Braided Creek. With Jim Harrison. Port Townsend, Wash.: Copper Canyon Press, 2003.

Delights & Shadows. Port Townsend, Wash.: Copper Canyon Press, 2004.

Flying at Night: Poems 1965-1985. Pittsburgh: University of Pittsburgh Press, 2005.

Valentines. Lincoln: University of Nebraska Press, 2008.

Nonfiction

Local Wonders: Seasons in the Bohemian Alps. Lincoln: University of Nebraska Press, 2002.

The Poetry Home Repair Manual. Lincoln: University of Nebraska Press, 2005.

Writing Brave and Free. With Steve Cox. Lincoln: University of Nebraska Press, 2006.

Chapbooks and Special Editions

Grass County. Privately printed, 1971.

Twenty Poems. Crete, Neb.: Best Cellar Press, 1973.

Shooting a Farmhouse / So This is Nebraska. St. Paul, Minn.: Ally Press, 1975.

Voyages to the Inland Sea. With Harley Elliott. La Crosse, Wis.: Center for Contemporary Poetry, 1976.

Old Marriage and New. Austin, Tex: Cold Mountain Press, 1978.

Cottonwood County. With William Kloefkorn. Lincoln: Windflower Press, 1979.

Etudes. Cleveland: Bits Press, Case Western Reserve University, 1992.

A Book of Things. Lincoln, Neb.: Lyra Press, 1995.

A Decade of Ted Kooser Valentines. Omaha, Neb.: Penumbra Press, 1996.

Lights on a Ground of Darkness. Lincoln: University of Nebraska Press, 2005.

CRITICAL AND BIOGRAPHICAL STUDIES

Allen, Gilbert. "Measuring the Mainstream: A Review Essay." *Southern Humanities Review* 17: 171-178. (spring 1983).

Brennan, Matthew C. "Ted Kooser." In *Dictionary of Literary Biography.* Vol. 105: *American Poets Since World War II, Second Series.* Edited by R. S. Gwynn. Detroit: Gale Research, 1991. Pp. 143-150.

Gioia, Dana. "Explaining Ted Kooser." In *On Common Ground: The Poetry of William Kloefkorn, Ted Kooser, Greg Kuzma, and Don Welch.* Edited by Mark Sanders and J. V. Brummels. Ord, Neb.: Sandhills Press, 1983. Pp. 88-98.

Mason, David. "Introducing Ted Kooser." *Dark Horse: A Journal of Poetry and Opinion* (Scotland) 17: 10-15. (summer 2005).

Molesworth, Charles. "Fondled Memories." *New York Times Book Review,* October 12, 1980, pp. 14, 36-37.

Riggs, Thomas. *Contemporary Poets, Sixth Edition.* New York: St. James Press, 1996.

Stitt, Peter. "The World at Hand." *Georgia Review* 34: 661-669 (fall 1980).

"Ted Kooser." In Vol. 136: *Contemporary Authors New Revision Series.* Detroit: Gale, 2005. Pp. 255-258.

INTERVIEWS

Baker, David, and Hofmeister, Tim. "A Conversation with Ted Kooser." *Kenyon Review* (http://www.kenyonreview/kro/kooser-interview.php), January 2008.

Clark, Dalli. "Drawn to the Ordinary World: An Interview with Former U. S. Poet Laureate Ted Kooser." *Sojourn: A Journal of the Arts* (University of Texas at Dallas) 19: 94-99 (2006).

Gross, Terry. "Talking with the Nation's Poet Laureate." *Fresh Art from WHYY*, July 4, 2005.

Hatcher, Arnold. "An interview with Ted Kooser." *Voyages to the Inland Sea VI: Essays and Poems by Harley Elliott and Ted Kooser.* Edited by John Judson. La Crosse, Wis.: Center for Contemporary Poetry, 1976. Pp. 37-50.

Meats, Stephen. "An Interview with Ted Kooser." *Midwest Quarterly* 46, no. 4: 335-343 (summer 2005).

Sanders, Mark. "An Interview with Ted Kooser." In *On Common Ground: The Poetry of William Kloefkorn, Ted Kooser, Greg Kuzma, and Don Welch.* Edited by Mark Sanders and J. V. Brummels. Ord, Neb.: Sandhills Press, 1983. Pp. 99-105.

OTHER SOURCES

Gioia, Dana. *Can Poetry Matter?: Essays on Poetry and American Culture.* Minneapolis: Graywolf Press, 1992.

Hollander, John. *The Gazer's Spirit: Poems Speaking to Silent Works of Art.* Chicago: University of Chicago Press, 2005.

Parini, Jay. *Why Poetry Matters.* New Haven, Conn.: Yale University Press, 2008.

Looking Forward

A Small Aid for Kooser Research

Michael A. Istavan, Jr.

With exception to early essays by George von Glahn and Mark Sanders, serious critical scholarship on the writings of Ted Kooser began after the 1980 release of the now-classic *Sure Signs*, Kooser's fifth major collection of poems. Looking back over the thirty-plus years since then, only about a dozen or so significant studies—none of which book-length—currently boulder out against the relative flatscape of secondary materials constituted mostly by quick and dirty reviews. Aside from the essays by Wes Mantooth, Allan Benn, and Mary K. Stillwell in this special issue of *Midwestern Miscellany*, the following works particularly stand out and, in my view, must be consulted by the Kooser scholar: David Baker's "Ted's Box"; William Barillas's Chapter 7 of *The Midwestern Pastoral*; Victor Contoski's "Words and Raincoats"; Dana Gioia's "The Anonymity of the Regional Poet"; Jeff Gundy's "Among the Erratics"; Jonathan Holden's "The Chekov of American Poetry"; Denise Low's "Sight in Motion"; David Mason's "Introducing Ted Kooser"; and both Mary K. Stillwell's "The 'In Between'" and her "When a Walk is a Poem."

Like the blind feeling into the elevator with their porcupine quills (as they do in Kooser's enchanting poem, "The Blind Always Come as Such a Surprise"), such news about the state of Kooser scholarship may come as a surprise—and it especially comes as a surprise that Kooser, published from early on at strong presses (1969, 1980, 1985, 1994, and 2000, as well as 2002, 2005, 2006, and 2008) and in major literary journals (such as *The New Yorker* and *Atlantic Monthly*), does not even have a listing in the first volume of Philip Greasley's 2001 *Dictionary of Midwestern Literature* (which is intended to cover the lives and works of not only established, but also emerging, contemporary Midwestern authors). One wonders how all this can be when Kooser started receiving national attention since the mid-70s (largely due to William Cole's ahead-of-the-curve praises in several issues of *Saturday Review*), and since then has won prestigious honors and awards: two National Endowment for the Arts fellowships (1976 and 1984), the Stanley Kunitz Prize (1984), the Pushcart Prize (1984), the Richard Hugo Prize (1994), the James Boatwright Award (2000), two appointments as the U.S. Poet Laureate (2004-2006), the Pulitzer prize for poetry (2005) (for *Delights & Shadows*), and much more.

Explanations for Kooser's undervaluation have been offered: his work is so transparent that there are no interpretive problems for critics to feel a sense of worth by solving (Gioia ARP 92); the literary establishment is dismissive of writers of the American Midwest especially when they focus on "small towns and agricultural countryside" (92; see Mason ITK 10); Kooser spent thirty years working in insurance instead of schmoozing in academic circles (10); and so on. Whatever the truth may be, I believe the days of worrying why Kooser is not receiving adequate attention are numbered. Before us are sure signs that a storm of critical notice is imminent. Aside from the accolades (and the enduring promotion by the eminent Gioia), consider the following: the 2005 Kooser tribute issue of *Midwest Quarterly*; this very Kooser issue of *Midwestern Miscellany*; the long-looming release (hopefully in Fall 2012) of Stillwell's book-length study *Bright Lights Flying Behind*; and, finally, the research tools created (1) by myself (a labor of love that I will be donating to Love Library at the University of Nebraska-Lincoln), (2) by Steven Schneider (a project that Kooser believes is the best published bio-bibliographical piece on him), and (3) by Daniel Gillane (a purportedly exhaustive bibliography that, despite an unforeseen hiccup with the University of Nebraska Press a few years back, will hopefully appear soon).

Even with the upsetting news that Sanders's proposed book, *The Weight of the Weather*, has been put on indefinite hiatus due to claims by several presses that Kooser is not important enough to merit such extended critical study, I am highly encouraged by these first plump raindrops. My goal in this paper, which is intended as a companion to my bibliographic project, is to provide a small research aid for the looming downpour of researchers. I hope to facilitate Kooser scholarship primarily by way of cataloguing the major preoccupations of commentators over the course of his career. In addition to providing an overview of commonly discussed preoccupations, influences, themes, topics, and so on (a circumscription meant to provide some enabling constraint on the process of developing research projects), I will highlight several specific directions for research that come to mind along the way. Pretty much everything is still open for investigation. But I think it is helpful to be aware, even at this nascent stage of Kooser studies, of what has been largely attended to.

Most commentators have noted Kooser's power to draw unexpected associations between drastically different phenomena, and how such association-making has the effect of showing the familiar to be exotic—and vice versa (see Kooser JMI 17). Flip open one of his books, place your finger at random, and you will find him busy disclosing kinships (see Barillas 211 and 238; Bunge 51; Kooser MQI 336). Open *Sure Signs*, for example. In "The Salesman" we see the kinship between stockings and batwings. In "Christmas Eve" we see the kinship between an old man's heart and the fluttering of an injured bird. Open *Delights & Shadows*. In "A Rainy Morning" we see the kinship between the woman pumping the wheels of her wheelchair and the pianist bending forward to strike the keys. Open *Weather Central*. In "The Sweeper" we see the kinship between the sweeping of Kooser's father and the paddling of a gondolier.

Kooser's most talked about association-making device is metaphor (see Allen 175; Barillas 216; Hansen; Low SM; Mason MRW 190; Stillwell IB 99). The many commentators who highlight Kooser's mastery of metaphor tend to focus on the small instances of kinship: stockings and batwings. What often goes overlooked is that Kooser, like the "metaphysical poet" John Donne, is a master of the sustained metaphor—the conceit: a complex and protracted comparison between apparently drastically different things (see Kooser DBI). A paradigm example of Kooser's mastery of the conceit is "Etude" (from *Weather Central*), a poem that he describes as his strongest and most representative work (MQI; DBI). Over the course of the poem, Kooser highlights shared features between the blue heron fishing in the cattails and the blue-suit at his business desk writing a love letter: both are armed, for example, with sharp tools (pencil or beak) in their stealthy pursuit of the catch. Kooser's facility with conceit is so refined, in fact, that on occasion he will extend a metaphor into other poems. Still apparently possessing its lover features, for example, the heron makes another *Weather Central* appearance in "A Poetry Reading," where it finally catches the fish from "Etude" (see Stillwell IB 100). Study of Kooser's power for conceit, which perhaps should involve the metaphysical poets from the 17th to 20th centuries, is one of the most important topics that I will mention here.

It is crucial to remember that there are many other devices besides metaphor that Kooser uses to make associations. There is simile, for example. In the Thoreau-like collection of essays, *Local Wonders*, Kooser speaks of a "big bullsnake" with "spots like cogs." There is also analogy (comparison of *relationships*). In "Abandoned Farmhouse" (from *Sure Signs*) "toys are strewn in the yard / like branches after a storm." There is also personification (see Gioia ARP 97; Holden). In "Spring Plowing" (from *Sure Signs*) mice flee with their squeaky carts, and in "In Late Spring" (from *Weather Central*) tulips wear lipstick—facts that, as Kooser himself admits, make these poems resemble Disney animated features (MQI 338; see Cryer). There is also metonymy (see Nathan and Nathan 413). At one point in *A Book of Things* Kooser uses song as a metonym for bird: "The nest of some tiny bird, / each blade of dead grass / seemingly spun into its place / on the potter's wheel / of her busy movements, / preparing a vessel for song." Unique verb use is one of the most under-noticed devices that Kooser uses to disclose kinships. "In Houses at the Edge of Town" (from *Sure Signs*) he speaks of gardens *wading* and cucumbers *crawling*. Further investigation of Kooser's use of these more marginal association-devices is worthwhile.

Kooser claims that his association-making power is a natural gift that shows itself spontaneously (DBI). Taking him at his word here, it behooves the biographical researcher to look into possible early nourishment of his unique ability. It has been commonly noted that Kooser's father, despite not being a writer himself, had a fairly strong impact on Kooser's interest in and talent for writing. Not only was he such a talented story-man that people would rather hear him describe a person than see that person themselves, he also had "an interest in the theater" and, along with his wife, "belonged to a group that got together to read plays" in the family living room (Kooser MQI 335). A fact that has not been equally attended to, however, is that Kooser's father also had an important influence on Kooser's particular interest in association-making. In a poignant episode that has never left his mind, Kooser recalls once hearing his father describe a fat but graceful woman as moving "like a piano on castors" (Cryer).

I have mentioned Kooser's father as a general influence, but what about literary influences (past and contemporary)? Kooser has remarked that his childhood home was filled with a unique selection of books:

Shakespeare, Balzac, Alexandre Dumas (père), Ibsen, and John Fox Jr. (MQI 335). Although Kooser pored over every piece in that collection (335), few commentators have worked out the literary connections. Many significant things can be said. Shakespeare, for instance, often employed Kooser's signature device: the conceit (which is largely why he is considered a proto-metaphysical poet). In *As You Like It* he famously makes an extended comparison between the real world of people and the real world of actors ("all the world's a stage"). Balzac, like Kooser, found it important to convey his points through concrete details rather than abstractions. John Fox Jr. kept a detached tone in his novels, typical of the naturalist literary movement to which he belonged. Kooser too takes such a tone in much of his writing (see Mantooth): like a traditional journalist, which Fox in fact was, Kooser often does not directly explore buried motivations behind actions; "a reporter," as Baker says, "not an editorialist," Kooser is more interested in surfaces (OR 36). And so on.

What about more contemporary figures? Kooser's addiction to the "rush" of highlighting kinships (JMI 16-17) that testify to the "impersonal" "universal order" (MQI 336) makes for a major connection with the Ezra Pound of the paradigmatic imagistic poem "In a Station of the Metro": "The apparition of these faces in the crowd; / Petals on a wet, black bough." No doubt Kooser is a proponent of the imagist mission to highlight the repetition of forms, patterns, throughout nature. And it seems clear that both Kooser and Pound endeavor to unlock, bring to attention, overlooked features of items, events, or processes by way of surrounding these items, events, or processes with others that, despite being different (and in the best case scenario *drastically* different), possess the features, too (see Baker TB 345).

This Kooser-Pound connection is not often discussed. Their disagreements take our attention. Kooser complains that with poets like Pound and T. S. Eliot, who use difficult words and exotic allusions, one often needs an encyclopedia nearby to figure out what is being said. Kooser himself does not do such intricate research when writing poems (Low SM 396), and the chief principle of his poetics is to convey ideas in the simplest of terms (Kooser MQI 341; DBI). It is true that these figures, especially due to their elitism, are largely negative influences on Kooser (see Barillas 211). But more thorough work is warranted.

The priority Kooser gives to directness and accessibility has inspired commentators to connect him with William Carlos Williams (see Allen 175; Brummels 348; Dacey 354; Holden; Nathan and Nathan 414; Mason ITK 10; Singer; Stillwell IB 98; WWP 404): both wed literary and colloquial language; both often focus on plain life; both admire the visual arts; both tend to appeal directly to the senses rather than to the intellect with abstract concepts[1]; and the list goes on. To be sure, more needs to be said than that both take serious the mimetic enterprise of bringing into relief everyday objects and happenings, be it a farmhouse or the act of ice skating, with free-verse poetry sparse and accessible. After all, Williams's *Selected Poems* inspired Kooser to stop posing as a poet (which he did in order to impress girls) and become a real one (Kooser MQI 337). Moreover, Kooser says that Williams serves as a model for "local" writing (Stillwell WWP 404). Williams's *In the American Grain* is, in fact, one of Kooser's all-time-favorite books.

Given the stress put on how much these two are alike, it is especially important for the researcher not to forget some key differences. Williams, unlike Pound, was not so much driven to disclosing the repetition of forms in nature—let alone devising sustained comparisons like Kooser and Donne. To be sure, both Kooser and Williams attempted the long poem: Williams with *Paterson* and Kooser with *Winter Morning Walks*. As Mason has pointed out, however, *Paterson* is a loosely-connected mosaic that—due to its obliqueness and obscurity—is closer "in method to T. S. Eliot than [Williams] would have liked to admit." On the other hand, *Winter Morning Walks*, Mason goes on, is "a sequence of well-made miniatures" that can stand alone, that are clear, and that fit tightly together (MRW 188). Some commentators have even been willing to stand by the view that Kooser is more succinct than Williams (Greening RWC 509). The Kooser-Williams relation is complex and warrants major study.

In speaking of Williams's influence, we must not overlook Karl Shapiro's. Several commentators have noted his influence on Kooser and the affinity between them (see Budy 349; Contoski RLH 112; Cryer; Evans 357; Kuzma 374; Sanders PK 418). Much more detailed study is called for, nevertheless. Here are some facts about their relation to get the researcher up and running. Kooser studied Williams in graduate school at the University of Nebraska-Lincoln under the tutelage of Shapiro, who impressed upon Kooser, among other things, a desire to write about the inanimate (Kooser MQI 337; MSI 104). Their intimacy came at a price, however. Spending all of his time working on poetry with Shapiro, in 1964 the English department took away Kooser's teaching assistantship on the grounds of scholastic deficiency (Sanders PK 415). Later, Shapiro helped Kooser get his first collection, *Official Entry Blank*, published in 1969, taking the manuscript to the University of Nebraska Press on Kooser's behalf (Kooser MQI 337). In the introduction for *Local Habitation* (1974) Shapiro says that Kooser's poems are like photographs (Contoski RLH 112)—one of the highest compliments one could receive from Shapiro, who taught that poetry is a way of *seeing* rather than a way of *saying* (Budy 349). As with Kooser, Shapiro's poetry has quick clear lines and subject matter that, although everyday and familiar, can be full of drama and humor (see Evans 357).

It would be beneficial to explore how Kooser was influenced not only by Shapiro's subject matter, economy, take on Williams, and especially humor, but also by—as Kooser himself suggests—Shapiro's pace, timing, syntax, and rhythms (see Kuzma 374). As noticed by Evans, Kooser picked up from Shapiro a "fondness for the prepositional phrase, which gives momentum and rhythm to his lines" (357). In poems like "Shooting a Farmhouse" (from *Sure Signs*) we see these phrases at work: "Back in the house, / the newspapers left over from packing / the old woman's dishes / begin to blow back and forth through the rooms." Any study of Kooser's free verse scansion is going to have to refer back to Shapiro, if only for this reason.[2]

Kooser is seen as close to Frost (see Barbieri; Brummels 348; Contoski RNC 205; Cryer; Greening RWC 508-509; Gustafson 45; Gwynn 685; Jones 280; Kuzma 377; Logan GAD 72; Logan VDM 67; Mason TKH 406; MRW 188 and 192; ITK 15). Their likeness is arguably greater than that between Kooser and Williams. Here are some of the more prominent points of similarity. (1) Even though Frost seems more concerned with meter and direct rhyme than Kooser (ITK 15), both write poems of simplicity and technique that, as Kuzma puts it, "are ever quick to lodge in the ear" (Kuzma 377; compare Gwynn 685). (2) Like Frost, Kooser can be eerily dark at times: playful and yet concerned with nastiness and death (see Mason MRW 188; TKH 406). Take the poem "The Widow Lester," for example: "How his feet stunk in the bed sheets! / I could have told him to wash, / but I wanted to hold that stink against him. / The day he dropped dead in the field, / I was watching. / I was hanging up sheets in the yard, / and I finished." (3) Frost's poems are sometimes didactic ("Carpe Diem"), and the same goes for Kooser (Contoski RNC 205): "A rule of thumb: if you can't use / your gate enough to keep it swinging, / better to leave it standing wide" (from "Gates").[3] (4) Frost's poems invite rumination despite the everydayness of their expression and subject matter ("After Apple Picking"), and the same goes for Kooser. "Old Soldier's Home" (from *Sure Signs*) describes soldiers sitting on a porch and unwrapping "the pale brown packages / of their hands, folding the fingers back / and looking inside, then closing them up again / and gazing off across the grounds, / safe with the secret."[4] (4) In contrast to Pound, Kooser and Frost (like Williams and Thoreau) do not feel the need to travel; sufficiently stimulated by the familiar, they are rooted (Greening RWC 508). Relatedly, both have been called "provincial" (Mason MRW 192). It is important to remember, however, that Frost (see "Acquainted with the Night") and Kooser (see Gwynn 684; Mason TKH 404) are not against using urban settings. More importantly, both try to convey what is universal and of lasting value by way of what is local and particular. In Kooser's case, characteristic Midwestern landscapes, objects, people, and events are used to articulate experiences and feelings that all people—no matter where they live—go through (Link 308; Stillwell WWP 400; Woessner 20). The blind do not just come as a surprise to the Midwesterner.

Three related points of affinity call for study. First, Frost is a master of the conceit like Kooser. "The Silken Tent" develops a protracted comparison between a woman and a tent standing in a summer field. Kooser himself states that he models his own writing after this masterpiece of metaphor and restraint (see "Etude," for example), and he especially appreciates Frost's sensitivity here to the fact that the images described at the beginning of the poem remain on the minds of readers throughout, and thus must harmonize with the end (JMI 17). Second, both authors frequently employ the second person voice. It is one of their strategies for establishing intimacy with the reader, for showing that reader and poet are not as separate as one might believe. In "Good-bye" (from *One World at a Time*) we get: "You lean with one arm out." Indeed, throughout *Not Coming to Be Barked At*, we see a repetition of Frost's "you can" formula: "you can see the old cedars," "you can feel the great joy" (see Gustafson, 45). Third, Frost's aesthetic arguably tends toward communitarianism (see Richardson), and the same goes for Kooser (see Barillas 210-211, 214, and 238; Greening RWC 509). As Barillas notes, Kooser's poem "So This is Nebraska" (from *Sure Signs*) displays its communitarian commitment primarily through its use of the second person voice (210-211 and 238). This commitment is evident in Kooser and Jim Harrison's poetry collection *Braided Creek*, particularly in the fact that they refuse to reveal who wrote what throughout the collection (214). In a poignant show of this commitment, they go so far as to say that even *death* cannot take away our togetherness: "It's nice to think that when / we're fossils we'll all be in the same / thin layer of rock."

In *Official Entry Blank* Kooser has a poem entitled "Walt Whitman," and there are some strong similarities between the two warranting a study. Both are plainspoken (see Manzione) and concern themselves with local affairs. As Evans says, "Kooser understands Whitman's dictum that 'all truths wait in all things.' He writes about anything: driving in the country, a leaky faucet, an abandoned farmhouse" (357), which is perhaps the chief reason he was so liked by Shapiro. Another key resemblance is that Kooser, like Whitman, seems to be writing one massive poem (Gioia ARP 89). Kooser also has several poems that employ Whitman (and Dickinson) style repetition (see Mason TKH 405; ITK 14). In the poem "That Was I" (from *Delights & Shadows*) we get the ritornello of "and that was I" at each stanza.

There are some important differences between Kooser and Whitman to be kept in mind. As Gioia explains, "Kooser (unlike Whitman and his followers) is a truly democratic poet who addresses the reader as an equal. He never assumes the pose of prophet or professor instructing the unenlightened" (ARP 94; see Barillas 213). Moreover, and as Gwynn says, "Whitman tried to capture America by making himself a kosmos, and it is only rarely, as, say in the great catalogue of section 15 of 'Song of Myself' that he can restrain himself from upstaging his fellow citizens." Kooser, on the other hand, "keeps himself in the background and doesn't try to turn everything that he notices into a metaphor for his own sensitivity in noticing it" (684).

A study of the Kooser-Dickinson relation is needed. The epigraph to *Delights & Shadows* is from Dickinson's 1862 letter to the Unitarian minister Thomas W. Higginson: "The Sailor cannot see the North, / but knows the Needle can." Consideration of her poetry also happens to be important when dealing with the crucial task of understanding Kooser's poetics, as I will now explain.[5] One of the fundamental principles of Kooser's poetics—indeed, the ur-principle behind most of the others—is accessibility (Kooser MQI 341, DBI; De Grave 441-442; Stillwell WWP 406; Woessner 23). This mainly involves conveying information with Strunk-and-White clarity (Kooser DBI): eliminating "peculiarities of usage, grammar or punctuation that merely call attention to themselves" and ask the reader "to puzzle over the surface" (Kooser WOP 439). The effect is that a moderately educated non-specialist—Kooser likes to imagine his mother (JMI 11-12)—will have no trouble following. Some commentators have taken Kooser to be saying that poetry should not deal with difficult concepts (Logan VDM 71). This is precisely where Dickinson comes into the picture. According to Kooser, Dickinson writes poetry that, while clear at the level of expression, nevertheless concerns deep matters that require rereading and meditation. Dickinson, in short, is an example of one who writes what Kooser describes as good difficult poetry (DBI).

Much work is to be done on Kooser's relation to the above figures, as well as to several important ones left out—in particular, Thoreau (see Harvey 136), a nature writer like Kooser; Emerson (see Barillas 216; Mason TKH 407; ITK 15), who sees all things as connected like Kooser (see PHR 141; MQI 336); and Stevens (see Brummels 348; Greening RFN 26; RWC 509; Harvey 136; Mason ITK), an insurance executive like Kooser.[6] In discerning Kooser's place in literary history, we must also attend to those figures he claims exert a special influence on him. Besides Frost and Williams, there is Edward Arlington Robinson, May Swenson, John Crowe Ransom, and Randall Jarrell. Kooser also says that he looks to Nancy Willard, Linda Pastan, Tomas Tranströmer, and Rolf Jacobsen for guidance and inspiration (MQI 335; CHI).

Little has been said about Kooser's connection with these figures. Commentators have noted that the model for Kooser's character studies in *Grass County* (1971)—especially in the poem "Tom Ball's Barn"—was E. A. Robinson's Tilbury Town cycle (as well as E. L. Masters's *Spoon River Anthology*) (see Gioia ARP 95). In fact, all of Kooser's poems are accreting into one coherent assemblage, much like this cycle (and this

anthology) (Baker OR 33 and 34; see Contoski RLH 112-113). Kooser
tells us that Swenson's *To Mix with Time* was one of the first poetry col-
lections that compelled him to reread over and over. He also says that her
nature poems are particularly inspiring (MQI 335), and that he is floored
by her apparent ability to "write in any form and about anything" (CHI;
see PHR 4, 28, and 130). In *Writing Brave and Free*, Kooser uses a work by
John Crowe Ransom to demonstrate one of the most important require-
ments of poetry: that it be inviting, engaging, accessible (63-65; see PHR
4). I find several connections between Jarrell and Kooser: affinity with
Frost, interest in children's literature, and both are commended by Sha-
piro (see PHR 4). Kooser admires Willard's ability to make poems rich
in metaphor and at the same time clear as Pastan (DPP). He regards her
as one of the country's most inventive poets (PHR 157). Kooser praises
Tranströmer's ability to cover up dissimilarities between the phenome-
na whose kinship he is attempting to highlight (PHR 3, 142, 165; JMI
16-17). I find that, despite referring to quotidian affairs with language
that is superficially clear, Tranströmer's work is often, like Kooser's, very
mysterious.[7]

The Kooser-Jacobsen relation is worthy of particular attention.
Both figures have a strong concern with memorializing vanishing ways
of life. Throughout his oeuvre, Kooser seems concerned with chroni-
cling the disappearance of rural culture (Baker OR 34; Budy 351; Evans
358; Galbraith 184; Gioia ARP 93; Stillwell WWP). In fact, he finds his
most important work to be the essay "Lights on a Ground of Darkness,"
an overt and careful chronicling effort (CHI). Jacobsen's own chronicling
effort is evident in his collection *The Roads Have Come to an End Now*. The
poem "De store symfoniers tid" ("The Age of the Great Symphonies")
is an elegy for the age of the great symphonies, which is vanishing largely
due to technological development. The elegiac tone here is prevalent in
many of Kooser's works.[8]

Some reviewers have complained that Kooser's work shows no
moral and political concern and that its lack of protest is a function
of obliviousness to the horrors of the world (see Gustafson 45; Jones
280; Link 308). There are grounds, I think, to challenge this (see Bari-
llas 212; Gioia ARP 90; Mason MRW 188 and 191; Stillwell WWP 407).
In "December 7th" Kooser expresses his outrage, although subtly and
without direct mention of himself, at offseason deer hunting (see Mason

MRW 188). In general, when you look at the landscape described here in *Winter Morning Walks*, where humans—like the cancer that Kooser is battling—are portrayed as invasive users ("cutting stone from the land, building roads, turning land into fields"), there is a sense in which Kooser is engaging in political writing (Stillwell WWP 407). This seems true across Kooser's oeuvre. "Creamed Corn" (from *Delights & Shadows*) confronts unintentional racism. *Local Wonders* criticizes, among other things, reckless housing development. "The Blind Come as Such a Surprise" "quietly raises," as Gioia puts it, "certain moral . . . issues" (ARP 90). Indeed, referring back to the Kooser-Jacobsen discussion, I find that many of Kooser's elegiac works have a ring of social criticism to them.[9] Researchers might particularly be interested in studying Kooser's political-oriented writings on Native Americans, and I think doing so will be helpful for his incorporation into Ethnic Literature courses. In *One World at a Time* we get "Geronimo's Mirror." *Flying at Night* contains poems referring to massacres. Barillas points out an excellent example from *Sure Signs* (212). Kooser and his son, here in the poem "Fort Robinson," do not get out of the car to see the historical site of Crazy Horse's 1877 assassination because the grounds crew is going from tree to tree killing magpies. The reader is nudged to draw the parallel here between these state workers and those that subjugated Native American prisoners held at Fort Robinson.

A study of sentiment in Kooser's work is of great importance, especially since several critics have attacked him for being overly sentimental (and nostalgic) (see Galbraith 184; Logan VDM). Logan has pressed the point most forcefully, directing his energies at Kooser's 2008 collection of Valentine's Day poems. Valentine's Day, in Kooser's defense, is a holiday created in the spirit of gushiness, and so the overt sentimentality is okay here—if not in fact purposeful. Kooser agrees, explaining in the preface that his main goal is for readers to have fun (viii)—a goal especially evident in the several bawdy moments and the frequent parodying of sappy love poetry (see Benn). That said, Kooser is frequently on the verge of lapsing into sentimentality throughout his oeuvre (see Cryer; Galbraith 184; Gioia ARP 90; Greening RFN 26; Holden; Low SM 397; Manzione; Welch 435). As Kooser himself says (perhaps having in mind poems like "North of Alliance" and "So This is Nebraska"): "I tend to be someone who writes with a great deal of sentiment. I'm willing to take that risk at a time when people are suspicious of sentimental poetry. But I think that is what I need to do as a poet" (DBI). What is unique about Kooser is that, in a time when so many writers are trained-up in workshops to avoid "fault rather than achieve virtue" (Allen 172), he aims to achieve virtue—the virtue of stimulating the emotions of his readers (see Gioia ARP 90).

An issue for researchers to grapple with, then, is how Kooser manages to avoid lapsing into sentimentality in his poems of deep emotion. There have been several suggestions (see Kooser MSI 104; Link 309; Low SM 397; Manzione; Welch 435). Understatement and reporter-like distance are two devices he will use to avoid tipping: "I am moved by poems in which strong feelings are present, but are held or controlled by language which is slightly detached and restrained" (MSI 104; see Low SM 397; Manzione). By describing highly emotional phenomena in a tone of detachment and/or with some form of understatement, the idea is that the result will be a balance between mawkishness and stingy-heartedness. Kooser employs another strategy as well, I think: mixing moments of sentimentality and moments of humor (humor often bordering on the dark and stingy-hearted) such that the overall effect is somewhere in between. Take the poem "Father" (from *Delights & Shadows*). "Today you would be ninety-seven / if you had lived, and we would all be / miserable, you and your children, / driving from clinic to clinic, / an ancient fearful hypochondriac / and his fretful son and daughter, / asking directions, trying to read / the complicated, fading map of cures. / But with your dignity intact / you have been gone for twenty years, / and I am glad for all of us, although / I miss you every day—the heartbeat / under your necktie, the hand cupped / on the back of my neck, Old Spice / in the air, your voice delighted with stories. / On this day each year you loved to relate / that the moment of your birth / your mother glanced out the window / and saw lilacs in bloom. Well, today / lilacs are blooming in side yards / all over Iowa, still welcoming you." You will not find understatement or detachment here. Kooser throws us right into the sad and the emotional (lines 1-2) only to yoke us away—with a masterful line-break between "be" and "miserable"—into extended (purposively extra-detailed) dark humor (lines 3-8). Next he reverses course, priming us for sadness (lines 9-10), only to yoke us back into dark humor for a stint (line 11). Finally, he gives in to the seriousness of the emotion (lines 12-17), and yet prevents crumbling by putting a positive twist at the end (lines 18-20). The whipping back and forth is truth to life. When talking about a lost loved one, surely you have at least once used humor to avoid sending yourself, and those listening to you, into tears. That is an all-to-human move.

Humor in Kooser's works is itself an excellent research topic (see Challender 352; Evans 358; Mason MRW 191), and such research would, I imagine, bring up the influence of Shapiro and Frost. What I find interesting is that Kooser often pokes fun at himself. There is, of course, the famous "Selecting a Reader," a poem about how Kooser's ideal reader is a woman who, after thumbing through his poems at a bookstore, decides to use the money to get her jacket cleaned instead (see Contoski WR). Or consider Kooser's playful self-reproach in the "Domestics" (from *Twenty Poems*): "You take care of the house work / and leave the poetry writing to me. / Just leave the poems to me / and keep up with the house work. / I don't want to find any of your poems / lying around the house, / particularly when somebody comes to the house / to look at my poems. / And one other thing, and don't you forget it: / I'm the poet around here, / and you are the mistress of the poet. / If you think you can be the poet, forget it. / For as long as you live here, / You are the girl. I get to be the poet."

A related area in need of analysis is surrealism in Kooser's works (see Challender 353; Gioia GRS 617). Take, for instance, "They Had Torn Off My Face At the Office" (from *Sure Signs*): "The night that I finally noticed / that it was not growing back, I decided / to slit my wrists. Nothing ran out; / I was empty. Both of my hands fell off / shortly thereafter. Now at my job / they allow me to type with the stumps. / It pleases them to have helped me, / and I gain in speed and confidence." Or consider "Grating a Brain" (from *Local Habitation*), a how-to for grating a brain that involves images of a liverwurst-like mass being scraped down the sidewalk until—like well-used sidewalk chalk—only a nub remains at the terminus of the long trail. This is not the Kooser many readers first hear about! Now, reviewers sometimes say that Kooser's poems lack mystery, that they just unfold themselves completely—and that this is in fact one reason critics tend to be dismissive (Gioia ARP 89). Allen even says that Kooser writes the same poem over and over again, consistent as he is in tone and theme (175). There is truth to these positions, as I have indicated above in stressing Kooser's accessibility and that his poems form a rather coherent grouping. Nevertheless, when we start gathering all the surreal poems into a pile, the truth of the matter becomes a bit more complex. "The old woman, asleep on her back, / pulls up her knees and gives birth / to an empty house." What exactly is going on here at the start of this poem, "The Old Woman" (from *Sure Signs*)?

One under-researched topic is Kooser's interest in painting. Except perhaps for Steven Schneider (and of course Stillwell's superb essay in this special issue of *Midwestern Miscellany* on Kooser's use of chiaroscuro in both painting and writing), no one has really focused on Kooser and the visual arts: photography, drawing, painting, and so on. Not only is Kooser an avid fan of painting (particularly the American realist painter Edward Hopper), he has studied the basic techniques of drawing and watercoloring at Iowa State University and is himself a lifelong painter— mostly of 5x7 miniatures (Kooser DBI). Painting is, in fact, Kooser's most important form of artistic expression after poetry (MQI 338 and 342). Included in his small 1971 poetry collection *Grass County* are his own illustrations (see Gioia ARP 94). He has also written odes to painters. "A Box of Pastels" (from *Delights & Shadows*), for instance, is a celebration of Mary Cassatt. Kooser engages in ekphrasic poetry too. *Delights & Shadows*, a book full of museum visits, contains a tantalizing series of four poems on Civil War paintings by Winslow Homer (Gundy 938; see Challender 440). There we also get the poem "At the County Museum," which patiently describes a painting of a "lacquered horse-drawn hearse" (see 440; Manzione). *Weather Central* contains an ekphrasic poem as well: "The Gilbert Stuart Portrait of Washington" (see Low SM 397). Moreover, Kooser wrote a poem for George Ault's painting, *August Night at Russell's Corners*, which is on the cover of *Delights & Shadows* (see Kooser JMI 12-13). It is important to note that Kooser has written poems about, and painted acrylics of, Guttenberg—a town in Iowa where his maternal grandparents lived and where he wants his ashes sprinkled. An interesting research project would be to compare not only these poems and the paintings, but the poems and the paintings to the long essay, "Lights on a Ground of Darkness," which involves Kooser's remembrances of boyhood visits to Guttenberg (14). Another interesting topic would be how Kooser understands the relation between painting and poetry. He does think that there is a big difference between the two, and that some topics that might work with poetry cannot work with painting. Painting, Kooser says, cannot really depict processes (such as recovery) the way that poetry, which can be narrative, can; painting is better suited for static phenomena (such as sickness and death) (23). How Kooser's own work as a painter affects his poetry would be another worthwhile project—especially in light of the fact that both his paintings and poems are often miniatures (DBI).

Because Kooser is in many respects a formalist, there needs to be a thorough application of formalist and neo-formalist criticism to his work. One issue concerning Kooser's formalism is how the structures of his poems inform and are informed by their thematic content. Explaining just that in her study of *Winter Morning Walks*, Stillwell is one of the path-blazers in this area (as she is in so many others).

> Rarely more than twelve lines, frequently eight, of relatively the same length, Kooser's poems maintain a . . . restless and sometimes agitated, tetrameter that echoes his physical state as he recovers from surgery and radiation. Or perhaps it is more accurate to say that nearly every tetrameter line resists scansion, seeming to vary with each reading, just as impossible to read as the poet's future health. . . [T]he poetic foot, like the poet's footing, too, varies, giving way to spondee and dactyl, avoiding the more regular and predictable iambic foot and pentameter length as he contemplates his uncertain future. (WWP 409)

Stillwell, building on the work of Hansen, executes a similar structural analysis of "Etude" and other poems in *Weather Central*: "The metaphoric form that Kooser employs in 'Etude' can be found in a number of poems. . . Tom Hansen . . . describes it as the 'three-stanza or tripartite poem which loosely parallels the ABA sonata form.' Heron . . . becomes lover becomes heron" (IB 98-99). This precedent set by Stillwell and Hansen should be carried out with other works (which Stillwell in fact does in her essay here in this issue of *Midwestern Miscellany*). Moreover, since Kooser notes that his collections have common themes, this sort of work needs to be done at the larger scale; researchers need to figure out, that is, how the organizations of his books inform and are informed by the thematic contents. This a particularly pressing issue in light of complaints that Kooser's collections often provide, as Gioia puts it, "no clue to the principle of organization" (GRS 619). There have been brief discussions of other aspects of Kooser's formalism (see Kooser DBI; Contoski WR 86; RNC 205-206; Dacey 355-356; Gioia ARP 95), such as why he always begins his lines at the left margin (Low SM 398). But many others are in need of consideration.[10]

It would be interesting to examine diverging versions of Kooser's works. Seeing what he has omitted from, added to, and shifted within a poem throughout the course of its publication history allows us to see his poetical principles in action. There have been numerous cases where Kooser has revised his published poems and then published the revisions. There have been changes in title, for instance. The poem that Kooser published in the 1963 anthology *Lyrics of Love* called "Spinster" he changed to "Aunt Johanna, Spinster" in *Official Entry Blank* (1969). The poem that he published in *Rapport* 2.1 (1973) called "Utah" he changed to "Highway 30" in *Local Habitation* (1974). There have also been changes within poems themselves. "Splitting an Order" as published in *Prairie Schooner* 67.3 (1993) reads "keeping his shaky arms steady / by placing his forearms firm on the edge of the table." Kooser replaces the term "arms" here with "hands" in the version that appears in his book *Valentines* (2008). "Barn Owl" as published in *Weather Central* (1994) reads: "Behind those eyes is / a boudoir of intimate darkness . . ." Kooser replaces the "is" here with "lies" in the version that appears in *Valentines*. More drastic changes often happen. Consider the appearance of "Five Finger Exercise" in *Prairie Schooner* (1986) compared with its appearance in *Weather Central*. The 1994 version adds in an extra line: "of cracked corn, of millet and linnet seed." Consider the appearance of "The Giant Slide" in *Greenfield Review* (1978) compared with its appearance in *One World at a Time* (1985). The 1978 version reads: "Beside the highway, the Giant Slide / with its rusty undulations lifts / from the weeds. A chain link fence keeps out / the children and drunks, and the ticket booth / tilts to that side where the nickels shifted / over the years. Blue morning glories / climb halfway up the stairs, bright clusters / of laughter. Call it a passing fancy, / this slide that nobody slides down now, / bumpety-bump . . . ." The 1985 version is much different. "Beside the highway, the Giant Slide / with its rusty undulations lifts / out of the weeds. It hasn't been used / for a generation. The ticket booth / tilts to that side where the nickels shifted / over the years. A chain link fence keeps out / the children and drunks. Blue morning glories / climb half-way up the stairs, bright clusters / of laughter. Call it a passing fancy, / this slide that nobody slides down now. . ."[11]

Since Kooser revises extensively prior to publishing and yearly deposits his meticulously kept notes at Love Library, there are also numerous drafts in existence that differ considerably from published versions.[12] Here is a good example. The first two lines of a draft of "The Possible Lives" read: "There were once so many I might choose among, / a warehouse of coats and shoes, and all my size." In the version appearing in the *Hudson Review* 56.4 (2004), Kooser changed the metaphor present in the earlier version into a simile: "There were once so many I might choose among, / like a warehouse of coats and shoes, and all my size." Kooser comments that the change was needed to prevent the reader from thinking that the subject of the first line (namely, that of which there are so many) is coats and shoes (PHR). There are many more of these revelatory sorts of changes that have not been discussed.[13]

I have touched on several key areas of research: Kooser's proclivity for association, his influences, the place of abstraction in his work, didacticism and mystery in his work, his poetics, the effect of thirty years of business on his writing, his drive to chronicle and elegize, the political and moral issues in his work, the threat of sentiment in his work, humor and surrealism in his work, his interest in painting, his formalism, and the comparison of differing versions of his writings. There are other key topics that I have left out due to space considerations. I will close with a smattering of these to get researchers on their way.

(1) Kooser's gift for narrative poetry (see "The Beaded Purse" from *Delights & Shadows*) gets overlooked in the talk about him as a regional lyricist. For more on his narrative poetry, see Contoski RLH 112; Logan GAD 73; Mason ITK 13; Stillwell WWP 399. (2) A study of Kooser's found poems and how he massages them into poetic form is due. Of particular interest are Kooser's postcard poems: in *Local Habitation* alone there are fifteen. What draws him to this format? For more on his found poetry, particularly the postcard pieces, see Kooser JMI 13 and 22-23; Contoski RLH 112-113; Kloefkorn, 369; Stillwell WWP 401. (3) Kooser has written poetry about poetry, and this would be interesting to study alongside his ekphrasic work (see Dacey 355; Manzione; Kooser DBI).

(4) Kooser's confessional poetry has gone largely overlooked. He himself never mentions his confessional book *Old Marriage and New*. Many think that he is at his weakest in these sorts of poems, but this may need reconsideration. For more on Kooser's confessional poetry, see Brummels 348; Gioia ARP 98; Link 308; see Kooser LMP. (5) Kooser repeatedly reveals himself to be a fabulist, providing accounts of phenomena much in the spirit of folktales about how tigers got their stripes and how ravens became black (see "The Celery Heart," "Carp," and Kooser's discussion of the "weight of the weather" in Sanders MC 71). To be sure, Low is interested in what is magical and mythic in Kooser (see NT) and Contoski talks a bit about Kooser and fables (Contoski WR 85), but few others are involved in this matter. (6) Uncertainty about human knowledge and achievement (see Bunge 50), loneliness and isolation (see Stitt 663), silence (see Challender 352; Contoski WR 86), and also violence, old age, and death (see Barillas 214; Bunge 51; Mason MRW 188; Kooser JMI 18; MQI; Kloefkorn 369; Logan GAD 73; Sanders MC 69) are big themes in Kooser's works in need of examination. (7) A study of time is also needed. Stillwell has spoken about mythic and temporal time in Kooser's works (IB 103) and Low is interested in how time in his work tends to slip around and is often cyclical (see NT). (8) Hands make a frequent appearance in Kooser's works (see Kooser DBI). See, for example, "Old Soldier's Home," "A Washing of Hands," "Praying Hands," "Gifted Hands," "Father," "Mourners," "Pegboard," "Splitting an Order," "A Good-bye Handshake," "February 21," "Gyroscope," "They Had Torn Off My Face At the Office," and so on. (9) Worthy of attention is Kooser's skill at efficiently and satisfyingly closing his poems (see Baker TB 347; Gundy 937; Low SM 400; Manzione). (10) There needs to be an analysis especially of Kooser's use of irony (see Challender 352; Contoski WR 85), rhyme (see WR 87; Dacey 354-355; Logan VDM 66; McDougal 412), and pun (see Stillwell IB 101). (11) It would be nice to see work on Kooser's philosophical commitments (see Barillas 213; Stillwell IB): animism (see Link 308), pantheism (see Kooser MQI 336), fatalism (see Bunge 49; Stillwell WWP), stoicism (see Bunge 49), denial of immortality (see Kooser JMI; MQI 336), denial of a personal God (see MQI 336), pragmatism (see PHR), and so on. (12) Little attention is given to Kooser's prose works of both fiction and nonfiction. This is unfortunate since Kooser does not think of himself as merely a poet (see MSI 105).

(13) Eventually there needs to be a complete works of Kooser, together with a thorough biography and concordance.

ACKNOWLEDGMENTS: For their help on this project, special thanks are due to Gilbert Allen, David Baker, William Barillas, Matthew Brennan, Craig Challender, David Evans, Twyla Hansen, Jeffrey Hotz, Alesha Istvan, Ted Kooser, Denise Low, David Mason, Jo McDougall, Mark Sanders, Steven Schneider, Mark Vinz, Jeanne Murray Walker, and Warren Woessner.

NOTES:

1. For discussion of the important issue of Kooser and abstraction, see Allen 175; Gioia 90; Gundy 937; Low SM; Welch 434.

2. Of course, when comparing these two, it behooves the researcher to look at Kooser's poem "For Shapiro, Having Gone Back to the Sonnet" (from *Official Entry Blank*), as well as at his essay "Karl Shapiro in the Early Sixties."

3. For more on the important issue of Kooser and didacticism, see Kooser JMI 12-13; Dacey 355; Contoski RLH 113.

4. For more on Kooser and mystery, see McDougall 412; compare Gioia ARP 89.

5. Kooser's poetics is itself a book-length topic, and one that researchers should prepare for by consulting the *Poetry Home Repair Manual*, *Writing Brave and Free*, "Some Things I Think About When Working on a Poem," and especially Kooser's many reviews of other poets.

6. For more on the important issue of how thirty years of business life affected Kooser's writing, see Kooser DBI and *Journey to a Place of Work*.

7. Talk of the Tranströmer-Kooser relation naturally invites talk of the Bly-Kooser relation, which has received some attention (see Gundy 941; Low SM 399; Stitt 663). Not only does Kooser read Tranströmer through Bly's translation, but also worthy of notice is the affinity between his *Winter Morning Walks* and Bly's *Morning Poems* (see Mason MRW 188).

8. There are several other figures that the scholar is going to want to consider in order to adequately place Kooser in literary history: William Stafford (see Stitt 663); Louise Glück, who Kooser says he strongly admires (MSI 104); Denise Levertov (see Manzione); Nazim Hikmet (see Manzione); Carl Sandburg, whose poems are filled with humor like Kooser's (see Evans 358); Edward Thomas, whose poems are short and deal with quotidian subjects behind which nightmare lurks (see Greening RFN 26; RWC 508); Walter John de la Mare, whose children's works especially inspire Kooser (see PHR 9-12; DBI; Kuzma 373; Logan GAD 72); Chekov (see Holden); Aldo Leopold, who believed—in line with Kooser—that everything is connected, that humans are not radically different in kind from everything else, and that things can have intrinsic value independent of their relation to humans (see Barillas 215, 217, and 239; Bunge 50; Evans 356; Low SM 400); Robert Dana (Gundy 937); Jim Harrison, Kooser's close friend and co-author in *Braided Creek*; James Wright, to whom Kooser's poem "That Was I" is perhaps a tribute; Leonard Nathan; Steven Osterlund; Greg Kuzma; William Kloefkorn; Victor Contoski; Harley Elliott; Patricia Traxler; Lucien Stryk; Warren Woessner; Jared Carter; and so on. Several commentators have even started drawing connections between

Kooser and Asian poets such as Li Bai, Du Fu, and especially Basho and Issa (see Barillas 216; Evans 357; Gundy 938).

9. Barillas nicely captures the political nature of "Abandoned Farmhouse" (from *Sure Signs*), a poem filled with signs of quick desertion of farmhouse in question—signs indicating that "something went wrong." "Kooser does not attribute that failure to the family that once lived in the house. . . Whatever 'went wrong' may have had as much to do with government agricultural policy and, more broadly, attitudes about the land, as with the abilities of the farming couple. Something went wrong with pastoral ideology; the failure here is not merely personal but also cultural and political" (212).

10. When considering the formal aspects of Kooser's work, it may be helpful to keep in mind that some materials have been set to music. See *A Heartland Portrait: Five Songs for Baritone and Piano*; *Voyages through the Inland Sea: For Soprano and Clarinet*; *The Blizzard Voices: An Oratorio for Soloists*.

11. For rare manuscripts, the researcher should go to the Don L. Love library at the University of Nebraska-Lincoln. To fill in any holes, one should also consult the Jane Geske Heritage Room of Nebraska Authors at the Bennett Martin Public Library and the University of Iowa Libraries. Perhaps the following could be of help as well: the Manuscript, Archives, and Rare Book Library at Emory University; SUNY at Buffalo libraries; Library of Congress; Kenneth Spencer Research Library; Harry Ransom Humanities Research Center at the University of Texas at Austin; Criss Library at the University of Nebraska Omaha; and Brown University Library.

12. Also, and especially in the case of the poems for *Winter Morning Walks*, Kooser mailed off drafts to his friends (Kooser JMI 10). Studying the workshop correspondences between Leonard Nathan and Kooser (and perhaps Steven Osterlund and Kooser) would be extremely helpful into seeing how he revises (11).

13. Engagement in the sort of study that I have been mentioning will require access to diaries, workbooks, correspondences, personal books, and so on. In this case, the researcher might want to consult not only Love Library, which has pretty much all of such Kooser materials, but the following as well: (1) the Jane Geske Heritage Room of Nebraska Authors at the Bennett Martin Public Library; (2) Pentagram Press Archives at the University of Delaware; (3) the "Sallie Nixon Papers Relating to Ted Kooser, 1975-2005" at Wilson Library (University of North Carolina at Chapel Hill); (4) the "Patricia Wilcox Papers, 1974-2002" at the Manuscript, Archives, and Rare Book Library (Emory University); (5) the "Carol Bly papers, 1936-2003" at the Elmer L. Andersen Library (University of Minnesota).

REFERENCES:

Allen, Gilbert. "Measuring the Mainstream." Rev. of *More Trouble with the Obvious*, by Michael Van Walleghen; *Sure Signs: New and Selected Poems*, by Ted Kooser; and *Northern Lights* by Susan Ludvigson. *Southern Humanities Review* 17.2 (1983): 171-78. Print.

A Tribute to Ted Kooser. Ed. Stephen Meats. Spec. issue of *Midwest Quarterly* 46.4 (2005): 331-443. Print.

Baker, David. "On Restraint [**OR**]." Rev. of *Weather Central*, by Ted Kooser; *A Wedding in Hell*, by Charles Simic; *Imperfect Thirst*, by Galway Kinnell; *Song*, by Brigit Pegeen; and *Chickamauga*, by Charles Wright. *Poetry* 168.1 (1996): 33-47. Print.

---. "Ted's Box [**TB**]." *Midwest Quarterly* 46.4 (2005): 343-47. Print.

Barbieri, Richard. "Rhymes." *Independent School* 65.3 (2006): 102-04. *EBSCO*. Web. 11 Oct.2010.

Barillas, William. "Chapter 7: Further Views." *The Midwestern Pastoral: Place and Landscape in Literature of the American Heartland*. By Barillas. Athens: Ohio UP, 2006. 206-25. Print.

Brummels, J. V. "To Ted, from Two Cow." *Midwest Quarterly* 46.4 (2005): 347-49. Print.

Budy, Andrea Hollander. "The Things Themselves." *Midwest Quarterly* 46.4 (2005): 349-51. Print.

Bunge, Nancy. "Influencing each Other through the Mail: William Stafford's and Marvin Bell's *Segues*, and Jim Harrison's and Ted Kooser's *Braided Creek*." *Midwestern Miscellany* 33 (2005): 48-56. Print.

Challender, Craig. "A Sure Sign." Rev. of *Sure Signs: New and Selected Poems*, by Ted Kooser. *Midwest Quarterly* 46.4 (2005): 352-54. Print.

Cole, William. "Trade Winds." *Saturday Review* (November 2nd 1974): 44-50.

---. "Trade Winds." *Saturday Review* (January 24th 1976): 38-39.

---. "Trade Winds." *Saturday Review* (May 29th 1976): 40.

---. "Trade Winds." *Saturday Review* (December 11th 1976): 76.

---. "Trade Winds." *Saturday Review* (August 1985): 67.

Contoski, Victor. Rev. of *A Local Habitation and a Name*, by Ted Kooser [**RLH**]. *Great Lakes Review* 2.1 (1975): 112-14. Print.

---. Rev. of *Not Coming to Be Barked At*, by Ted Kooser **[RNC]**. *Prairie Schooner* 51.2 (1977): 204-206. Print.

---. "Words and Raincoats: Verbal and Nonverbal Communication **[WR]**." *On Common Ground: The Poetry of William Kloefkorn, Ted Kooser, Greg Kuzma, and Don Welch*, ed. M. Sanders and J. V. Brummels. Ord, NB: Sandhills, 1983. 85-88. Print.

Cryer, Dan. "Ted Kooser's Poetry of the People." *Unitarian Universalist World* (Winter 2005). <http://www.uuworld.org/life/articles/2326.shtml>. Web.

Dacey, Philip. "The School of Ted." *Midwest Quarterly* 46.4 (2005): 355-56. Print.

De Grave, Kathleen. Rev. of *The Poetry Home Repair Manual: Practical Advice for Beginning Poets*, by Ted Kooser. *Midwest Quarterly* 46.4 (2005): 441-43. Print.

Dictionary of Midwestern Literature. Ed. Philip A. Greasley. 3 vols. Bloomington: Indiana UP, 2001– . Print.

Evans, David Allan. "Ted Kooser: An Appreciation." *Midwest Quarterly* 46.4 (2005): 356-59. Print.

Galbraith, Jeffrey. Rev. of *Local Wonders: Seasons in the Bohemian Alps* and *Delights & Shadows*, by Ted Kooser. *Harvard Review* 28 (2005): 183-84. *ProQuest*. Web. 3 Oct. 2010.

Gioia, Dana. Rev. of *A Part of Speech*, by Joseph Brodsky; *Moortown*, by Ted Hughes; *Collected Poems 1944-1979*, by Kinsley Amis; *Seeing the World*, by Dick Davis; *Sure Signs: New and Selected Poems*, by Ted Kooser; *Denizens*, by Ronald Perry; *The Glass Houses*, by John N. Morris; *Goldilocks in Later Life*, by R. M. Ryan; *Wheat Among Bones*, by Mary Baron; *Nervous Horses*, by Vickie Hearne; *The Various Light*, by Alfred Corn; *Complete Poems*, by Li Ch'ing-chao; and *Pilgrim of the Clouds*, by Yüan Hung-tao **[GRS]**. *Hudson Review* 33.4 (1981): 611-27. Print.

---. "The Anonymity of the Regional Poet [ARP]." *Can Poetry Matter? Essays on Poetry and American Culture*. By Gioia. St. Paul: Graywolf, 1992. 93-112. Print. Rpt. of "Explaining Ted Kooser." *On Common Ground: The Poetry of William Kloefkorn, Ted Kooser, Greg Kuzma, and Don Welch*. Ed. M. Sanders and J. V. Brummels. Ord, NB: Sandhills, 1983. 88-99. Print. **[*Citations are to "Explaining Ted Kooser."]**

Greening, John. Rev. of *Flying at Night: Poems 1965-1985*, by Ted Kooser **[RFN]**. *TLS* 17 June 2005: 26. *EBSCO*. Web. 4 Oct. 2010.

---. Rev. *Weather Central*, by Ted Kooser; *The Simple Truth*, by Philip Levine; *5°
and Other Poems*, by Nicholas Christopher; *Music Appreciation*, by Floyd
Skloot; *Off-Season at the Edge of the World*, by Deborah Greger; and *Complete
Poems*, by Basil Bunting [**RWC**]. *Hudson Review* 48.3 (1995): 508-16. Print.

Gundy, Jeff. "Among the Erratics." Rev. of *Delights & Shadows*, by Ted Koos-
er; *The Morning of the Red Admirals*, by Robert Dana; *From the Meadow:
Selected and New Poems*, by Peter Everwine; *Tristimania*, by Mary Ruefle; *The
Orchard*, by Bridget Pegeen Kelly; *Desire Lines: New and Selected Poems*, by
Lola Haskins; *Invisible Bride*, by Tony Tost; and *Goldbeater's Skin*, by G. C.
Waldrep. *Georgia Review* 58.4 (2004): 936-53. Print.

Gustafson, R. Rev. of *Not Coming to Be Barked At*, by Ted Kooser. *Poet & Critic*
10.1 (1977): 45. Print.

Gwynn, R. S. "Plainsongs." Rev. of *Delights & Shadows*, by Ted Kooser; *Keeping
My Name*, by Catherine Tufariello; *Anatomical Venus*, by Meg Schoerke;
Tender Hooks, by Beth Anne Fennelly; and *Not Till We Are Lost*, by William
Wenthe. *Hudson Review* 57.4 (2005): 683-92. Print.

Hansen, Tom. Rev. of *Etudes*, by Ted Kooser. *North Dakota Quarterly* 61.3
(1993): 224-25. Print.

Harvey, Steven. Rev. of *Local Wonders: Seasons in the Bohemian Alps*. *Fourth Genre:
Explorations in Nonfiction* 6.2 (2004): 135-36. Print.

Holden, Jonathan. "Ted Kooser: The Chekov of American Poetry." *The Old
Formalism: Character in Contemporary American Poetry*. By Holden. Fayette-
ville: U of Arkansas P, 1999. 89-94. Print.

Jones, R. Rev. of *Sure Signs: New and Selected Poems*, by Ted Kooser. *Southern
Humanities Review* 16.3 (1982): 280. Print.

Kloefkorn, William. "Inhalations." *Midwest Quarterly* 46.4 (2005): 366-72. Print.

Kooser, Ted. *A Book of Things*. Lincoln: Lyra, 1995. Print.

---. "A Conversation with Ted Kooser [**DBI**]." Interview by David Baker and
Tim Hofmeister. *Kenyon Review Online* Jan. 2008: n. pag. Web. 2 Nov. 2010.

---. *A Heartland Portrait: Five Songs for Baritone and Piano*. With Stephen Paulus St.
Paul: Paulus, 2006. Print.

---. *A Local Habitation and a Name*. San Luis Obispo: Solo, 1974. Print.

---. "An Interview with Ted Kooser [**MSI**]." Interview by Mark Sanders. *On Com-
mon Ground: The Poetry of William Kloefkorn, Ted Kooser, Greg Kuzma, and Don
Welch*. Ed. Sanders and J. V. Brummels. Ord: Sandhills, 1983. 99-105. Print.

324

---. "An Interview with Ted Kooser [**MQI**]." *Midwest Quarterly* 46.4 (2005): 335-43. Print.

---. *Braided Creek: A Conversation in Poetry*. With Jim Harrison. Port Townsend: Copper Canyon, 2003. Print.

---. "Chapman Hood Frazier Talks with Ted Kooser [**CHI**]." Interview by Frazier. *Shenandoah* (2012). <http://shenandoahliterary.org/blog/2012/01/a-conversation-with-ted-kooser/>. Web.

---. *Delights & Shadows*. Port Townsend: Copper Canyon, 2004. Print.

---. "Dues-Paying Poet Laureate Depends on Us, Too [**DPP**]." Interview by Ed Darling. *Council Chronicle* (March 2005). <http://www.ncte.org/magazine/archives/119864>. Web.

---. *Grass County*. Lincoln, NB: Windflower Press, 1971. Print.

---. *Journey to a Place of Work: a poet in the World of Business*. Fargo: Institute for Regional Studies, 1990.

---. "Karl Shapiro in the Early Sixties." *Seriously Meeting Karl Shapiro*. Mobile: *Negative Capability*, 1993. Print.

---. *Lights on a Ground of Darkness*. Lincoln: University of Nebraska Press, 2005. Print.

---. *Local Wonders: Seasons in the Bohemian Alps*. Lincoln: U of Nebraska P, 2002. Print.

---. "Lying for the Sake of Making Poems [**LMP**]." *Prairie Schooner* 72.1 (1998): 5-8.

---. *Not Coming to Be Barked At*. Milwaukee: Pentagram Press, 1976. Print.

---. *Official Entry Blank: Poems*. Lincoln: U of Nebraska P, 1969. Print.

---. *Old Marriage and New: Poems*. Austin: Cold Mountain, 1978. Print.

---. *One World at a Time*. Pittsburgh: U of Pittsburgh P, 1985. Print.

---. "Some Things I Think About When Working on a Poem [**WOP**]." *Midwest Quarterly* 40.4 (Summer 1999).

---. *Sure Signs: New and Selected Poems*. Pittsburgh: U of Pittsburgh P, 1980. Print.

---. *The Blizzard Voices: An Oratorio for Soloists, SATB Chorus and Orchestra*. With Paul Moravec. Verona: Subito Music, 2008. Print.

---. *The Poetry Home Repair Manual: Practical Advice for Beginning Poets* [**PHR**]. Lincoln: U of Nebraska P, 2005. Print.

---. *Twenty Poems*. Crete: Best Cellar, 1973. Print.

---. *Valentines*. Lincoln: U of Nebraska P, 2008. Print.

---. *Voyages through the Inland Sea: For Soprano and Clarinet*. With Randall Snyder. Lincoln: Miltmore, 2006. Print.

---. *Weather Central*. Pittsburgh: U of Pittsburgh P, 1994. Print.

---. *Winter Morning Walks: 100 Postcards to Jim Harrison*. Pittsburgh: Carnegie-Mellon UP, 2000. Print.

---. "*Winter Morning Walks*: A Conversation with Ted Kooser **[JMI]**." Interview by Jay Meek. *North Dakota Quarterly* 68.1 (2001), 9-24. Print.

---. *Writing Brave and Free*. With Steve Cox. Lincoln: U of Nebraska P, 2006. Print.

Kuzma, Greg. "Ted." *Midwest Quarterly* 46.4 (2005): 372-78. Print.

Link, F. M. "An Unmistakable Voice." Rev. of *Sure Signs: New and Selected Poems*, by Ted Kooser, and *The Windflower Home Almanac of Poetry*, ed. Kooser. *Prairie Schooner* 55.1/2 (1981): 307-309. Print.

Logan, William. "The Great American Desert **[GAD]**." Rev. of *Where Shall I Wander*, by John Ashbery; *Elegy on Troy Piano*, by Dean Young; *Overlord*, by Jorie Graham; *Black Maria*, by Kevin Young; *Delights and Shadows*, by Ted Kooser; *Flying at Night: Poems 1965-1985*, by Kooser; *The Poetry Home Repair Manual: Practical Advice for Beginning Poets*, by Kooser; and *Collected Poems, 1943-2004*, by Richard Wilbur. *New Criterion* 23.10 (2005): 66-73. *EBSCO*. Web. 19 Nov. 2010.

---. "Valentine's Day Massacre **[VDM]**." Rev. of *Valentines*, by Ted Kooser; *Fifty-Two*, by Melissa Green; *The Wave-Maker*, by Elizabeth Spires; *Seven Notebooks*, by Campbell McGrath; *The Kingdom of Ordinary Time*, by Marie Howe; and *Sea Change*, by Jorie Graham. *New Criterion* 26.10 (2008): 66-73. *EBSCO*. Web. 11 Oct. 2010.

Low, Denise. *Natural Theologies: Essays About Literature of the New Middle West* **[NT]**. Omaha: Backwaters Press, 2011. Print.

---. "Sight in Motion: The Poetry of Ted Kooser **[SM]**." *Midwest Quarterly* 46.4 (2005): 396-401. Print.

Manzione, Gianmarc. "More Than Meets the Eye." Rev. of *Delights & Shadows*, by Ted Kooser. *January Magazine* March 2005: n. pag. Web. 13 Oct. 2010.

Mason, David. "Introducing Ted Kooser **[ITK]**." *Dark Horse* (Summer 2005): 10-15. Web.

---. Rev. of *Winter Morning Walks: 100 Postcards to Jim Harrison*, by Ted Kooser **[MRW]**. *Prairie Schooner* 76.3 (2002): 187-192. Print.

---. "Ted Kooser at Home [**TKH**]." *Midwest Quarterly* 46.4 (2005): 401-07. Print.

McDougall, Jo. "Of Time, Place, and Eternity: Ted Kooser at the Crossroads." *Midwest Quarterly* 46.4 (2005): 410-13. Print.

Nathan, Leonard, and Carol Nathan. "'A Glimpse of the Eternal.'" *Midwest Quarterly* 46.4 (2005): 413-15. Print.

Richardson, Mark. *The Ordeal of Robert Frost: The Poet and His Poetics.* Urbana: University of Illinois Press, 1997. Print.

Sanders, Mark. "Measurements of Compatibility in Contemporary Nebraska Poetry: The Verse of William Kloefkorn, Ted Kooser, and Don Welch [**MC**]." *Concerning Poetry* 13.2 (1980): 65-72. Print.

---. "Portraits of Kooser [**PK**]." *Midwest Quarterly* 46.4 (2005): 415-20. Print.

Schneider, Steven P. "Ted Kooser." *American Writers: A Collection of Literary Biographies, Supplement 19.* Ed. Jay Parini. Detroit: Scribner's, 2010. *Literature Resource Center.* Web. 10 Oct. 2010.

Singer, Marc. "Poetry Slam." *I Am not the Beastmaster.* TypePad, 12 Mar. 2007. Web. 13 Oct. 2010.

Stillwell, Mary K. "The 'In Between': Landscapes of Transformation in Ted Kooser's *Weather Central* [**IB**]." *Great Plains Quarterly* 19.2 (1999): 97-106. Print.

---. "When a Walk is a Poem: *Winter Morning Walks,* a Chronicle of Survival, by Ted Kooser [**WWP**]." *Midwest Quarterly* 45.4 (2004): 399-414. Print.

Stitt, Peter. "The World at Hand." Rev. of *Sure Signs: New and Selected Poems,* by Ted Kooser; *This Tree Will Be Here for a Thousand Years,* by Robert Bly; *Any Body's Song,* by Joseph Langland; and *The Everlastings,* by Norman Dubie. *Georgia Review* 34.3 (1980): 661-70. Print.

Von Glahn, George. Essay in *Late Harvest: Plains and Prairie Poets.* Ed. Robert Killoren Kansas City: Bk Mk Press, 1977. Print.

Welch, Don. "The Love of the Well-Made." *Midwest Quarterly* 46.4 (2005): 431-32. Print.

Woessner, Warren. "The Sound of One Hand Clapping." Rev. of *Braided Creek: A Conversation in Poetry,* by Ted Kooser and Jim Harrison. *American Book Review* 25.3 (2004): 20+. Print.

Index

Contributors

DAVID BAKER is the author of more than fifteen books of poetry and criticism, including *Talk Poetry: Poems and Interviews with Nine American Poets, Radiant Lyre: Essays on Lyric Poetry, Heresy and the Ideal, Never-Ending Birds, Treatise on Touch: Selected Poems, Midwest Eclogue, The Truth About Small Towns,* and *Sweet Home, Saturday Night.* He holds the Thomas B. Fordham Chair at Denison University, is a faculty member in the Warren Wilson College MFA program, and is the poetry editor of the Kenyon Review.

WILLIAM BARILLAS is the author of *The Midwestern Pastoral: Place and Landscape in Literature of the American Heartland;* his scholarship on American literature has appeared in many journals. He teaches English at the University of Wisconsin-La Crosse.

J.V. BRUMMELS recently retired from his professorship at Wayne State College in Nebraska. He is the editor of Logan House Press and Wayne State College Press; his books of poetry include *Book of Grass, City at War, Cheyenne Line, 614 Pearl,* and, most recently, *frontpew@paradise* from Stephen F. Austin State University Press.

VICTOR CONTOSKI taught at the University of Kansas until his retirement. He is the author of a number of books of poems, including *Names, A Kansas Sequence, Homecoming,* and *Broken Treaties.*

CHAPMAN HOOD FRAZIER is a professor at James Madison University and was poetry editor for the *Dos Passos Review.* He has won several awards for both his poetry and prose. He is currently working on a collection of interviews with contemporary poets from the United States and Northern Ireland.

DANA GIOIA is an award-winning poet and critic. He has published five collections of poetry—*Daily Horoscope, The Gods of Winter, Interrogations at Noon, Pity the Beautiful,* and, most recently, *99 Poems: New & Selected.* Among his critical works are *Can Poetry Matter,* which was a finalist for the National Book Critics Circle Award, and *Disappearing Ink: Poetry at the End of Print Culture.* He is currently the Judge Widney Professor of Poetry and Public Culture at the University of Southern California.

TWYLA HANSEN was appointed Nebraska State Poet in 2013. Her books include *How to Live in the Heartland, Sanctuary Near Salt Creek, Potato Soup,* and, most recently, *Rock · Tree · Bird.* Hansen collaborated with rancher and writer Linda Hasselstrom on the collection *Dirt Songs: A Plains Duet;* the book won the Nebraska Book Award in poetry and was a finalist for the Willa Literary Award and the High Plains Book Award.

ARNOLD HATCHER conducted his interview with Ted Kooser in 1976; it is the first published interview with the poet.

TIM HOFMEISTER joined the faculty at Denison University in 1986. Hofmeister's research centers on Homer and epic poetry, and he has written on ancient Greek comedy as well. He has also published essays on the relation between ancient and modern poetry, especially how that relation figures in the works of the St. Lucian poet and Nobel Prize-winner, Derek Walcott.

JONATHAN HOLDEN taught at Kansas State University until his retirement. He is the author of numerous books of poems and criticism, notably *Leverage, Falling from Stardom, The Names of the Rapids, The Fate of American Poetry, The Old Formalism,* and *Knowing: New and Selected Poems.* Holden also served as Poet Laureate of Kansas and once was on the review board for the Pulitzer Prize for Poetry.

MICHAEL A. ISTVAN, Jr. teaches Philosophy at Texas State University. His scholarship focuses primarily on contemporary continental philosophy and on topics in early modern philosophy (especially those concerning Spinoza) and contemporary analytic metaphysics (especially those concerning properties). He has completed extensive bibliographic work, yet unpublished, on Ted Kooser.

WILLIAM KLOEFKORN was Nebraska State Poet up to the time of his death in 2011. A long-time professor of English at Nebraska Wesleyan University, Kloefkorn authored many books of poems, notably *Alvin Turner as Farmer, Uncertain the Final Run to Winter, ludi jr., Not Such a Bad Place to Be, Houses and Beyond, A Life Like Mine,* and *Swallowing the Soap.*

GREG KUZMA, retired from the Department of English at the University of Nebraska-Lincoln, is a widely published poet and the former editor of The Best Cellar Press, which published Kooser's *Twenty Poems* in 1973. Among Kuzma's books are *Good News, Mountains of the Moon, The Buffalo Shoot, Adirondacks,* and, most recently, *Hose and Iron: Selected Poems* from Stephen F. Austin State University Press.

SHAWN LEARY left Nebraska many years ago to attend New York University of Law. She is currently a lawyer in Massachusetts. Her introduction of Kooser in 1979's *Omaha* magazine came at the head of the so-called literary Renaissance underway in Nebraska and featured other notable poets of the day: Kloefkorn, Kuzma, Welch, Nancy Westerfield, Gail Tremblay, and Patrick Worth Gray.

GLENNA LUSCHEI has published the poetry magazines *Café Solo*, *Solo*, and *Solo Café* for fifty years. Among her many honors are an NEA Fellowship, a D. H. Lawrence Fellowship, an honorary doctorate from St. Andrew's Presbyterian College, and a Master of Life Award from the University of Nebraska. She was also Poet Laureate of San Luis Obispo City and County. Among her recent books are *Zen Duende*, co-authored with Eric Greinke, and *Singing and Dying*.

PAUL McCALLUM is a professor of English at Pittsburg State University in Kansas, where he has twice been honored with the Robert K. Ratzlaff Outstanding Faculty Award for excellence in instruction and service to students on campus.

DAVID MASON teaches at Colorado College. His collections of poetry include *The Buried Houses, The Country I Remember, Arrivals,* and the verse novel *Ludlow* (awarded the Colorado Book Award for Poetry and named best book of poetry in 2007 by the Contemporary Poetry Review and the National Cowboy and Western Heritage Museum). His prose includes a collection of essays, *The Poetry of Life and the Life of Poetry*, and he co-edited the anthologies *Rebel Angels: 25 Poets of the New Formalism* and *Western Wind: An Introduction to Poetry*. He was appointed the Colorado poet laureate in 2010.

STEPHEN MEATS recently retired as Chair and Professor of English at Pittsburg State University, where he was the long-time poetry editor of *The Midwest Quarterly*. His books include *Looking for the Pale Eagle* and *Dark Dove Descending and Other Parables*. Since retirement, he has moved to the warmer climate of Florida.

LEX RUNCIMAN holds graduate degrees from the writing programs at the University of Montana and the University of Utah. Runciman taught for eleven years at Oregon State University and is now Professor of English at Linfield College, where he received the Edith Green Award in teaching in 1997. His newest collection of poems is *One Hour that Morning* (Salmon Poetry, Ireland, 2014).

STEVEN P. SCHNEIDER is professor of Creative Writing and Literatures and Cultural Studies at the University of Texas Rio Grande Valley. He is the author of several books of poetry, including *Unexpected Guests, The Magic of Mariachi*, and *Borderlines: Drawing Border Lives* as well as the chapbook *Prairie Air Show*. His scholarly books on contemporary American poetry include *A.R. Ammons and the Poetics of Widening Scope* and two edited collections of essays entitled *The Contemporary Narrative Poem: Critical Crosscurrents* and *Complexities of Motion: The Long Poems of A.R. Ammons*.

KARL SHAPIRO died in 2000. Among his many books are *V-Letter and Other Poems, Poems of a Jew, The Old Horsefly, In Defense of Ignorance, A Prosody Handbook, The Younger Son, Reports of My Death* (which includes a photograph of a very young Ted Kooser), and *Person, Place, and Thing*. Shapiro received numerous awards for poetry during his lifetime, including the Pulitzer Prize. Shapiro was instrumental in guiding Kooser to the publication of his first two collections of poetry.

MARY K. STILLWELL is the author of *The Life & Poetry of Ted Kooser*, as well as the poetry collections *Moving to Malibu* and *Maps & Destinations* (from Stephen F. Austin State University Press). She and Greg Kosmicki co-edited *Nebraska Presence: An Anthology of Poetry*.

GEORGE von GLAHN was born in 1941 in Brooklyn, New York, and died suddenly on September 16, 2002 in Hayward, California. A lifelong learner, he earned his BA from the University of Pacific, Stockton, Ph.D. from the University of North Carolina, Masters of Divinity from Yale University, and an MBA from St. Mary's College Moraga, California. His first love was books. He was the owner and purveyor of books at Gray Wold books in San Leandro at the time of his death where he loved to talk to customers about literature. He has two daughters, Maureen Powers and Kathryn von Glahn as well as a stepson, Benjamin Holland. His essay is the first long criticism of Kooser's poetry, published in Robert Killoren's *Late Harvest* in 1977.

DON WELCH taught for many years at the University of Nebraska at Kearney, as Reynolds Poetry Chair, as an English professor, and as a philosophy professor. His books of poems include *Dead Horse Table, When Memory Gives Dust a Face, Inklings: Poems Old and New, Gnomes* (from Stephen F. Austin State University Press), and *Homing: The Collected Poems*. He died in 2016.

About the Editor

MARK SANDERS is a Great Plains native—born, raised, and educated in Nebraska. His poems, stories, critical essays, and creative essays have appeared in publications in the United States, Canada, Great Britain, and Australia, including *Glimmer Train, Prairie Schooner, Ninth Letter, Western American Literature, River Teeth, Shenandoah,* and numerous others. Stephen King included Sanders's short story, "Why Guineas Fly," as one of the 100 outstanding short stories for 2007 in *Best American Short Stories;* his essay, "Homecoming Parade," was selected as one of the outstanding works of the year in the 2016 edition of *Best American Essays.* His writing has been nominated for Pushcart Prizes more than a dozen times and been listed among the notable works of several years. His work is also featured in *American Life in Poetry,* a syndicated series published by former U.S. Poet Laureate Ted Kooser, and on the *Poetry* Foundation website.

Among his books of poetry are *The Suicide* (1988), *Before We Lost Our Ways* (1996), *Here in the Big Empty* (2006), *Conditions of Grace: New and Selected Poems* (2011), and *Landscapes, with Horses* (2012; expanded version 2017). Other volumes include: *On Common Ground: The Poetry of William Kloefkorn, Ted Kooser, Greg Kuzma, and Don Welch* (with J. V. Brummels, 1983); *Jumping Pond: Poems and Stories from the Ozarks* (with Michael Burns, 1983); *Three Generations of Nebraska Poets* (with Stephen Meats, 2011); *Riddled with Light: Metaphor in the Poetry of W. B. Yeats* (2014); and, *A Sandhills Reader: 30 Years of Great Writing from the Great Plains* (2015), which won the Nebraska Book Award in 2016.

Sanders is the long-time editor of Sandhills Press, a small, independent press which he started in Ord, Nebraska, in 1979. For his work in promoting the poetry of emerging and established Nebraska writers, he received the Mildred Bennett Award from the Nebraska Center for the Book in 2007 for fostering Nebraska's literary heritage.

Sanders received his B.A. and M.A. in English at Kearney State College (now the University of Nebraska at Kearney). He later took his Ph.D. from the University of Nebraska-Lincoln, specializing in Modern Poetry, and a second Ph.D. in Higher Education Leadership at the University of Idaho. He is currently Chair and Professor of English and Creative Writing at Stephen F. Austin State University in Nacogdoches, Texas, where he and his wife Kimberly Verhines operate a small farm.

CPSIA information can be obtained
at www.ICGtesting.com
Printed in the USA
LVHW111735011019
632855LV00003B/519/P

9 781622 880300